Dukor
A Memoir

Author: Daniel Charney

JewishGen
מרכז עולמי לגנאלוגיה יהודית
The Global Home for Jewish Genealogy

A Publication of JewishGen, INC
Edmond J. Safra Plaza, 36 Battery Place, New York, NY 10280
646.494.5972 | info@JewishGen.org | www.jewishgen.org

MUSEUM OF
JEWISH HERITAGE
A LIVING MEMORIAL
TO THE HOLOCAUST

DUKOR

Author: Daniel Charney
Translated by: Michael Skakun
Name Indexing: Jonathan Wind
Cover Design: Jan R. Fine

Printed in the United States of America by Lightning Source, Inc.

Library of Congress Control Number (LCCN): 2022941584

ISBN: 978-1-954176-52-2 (hard cover: 272 pages, alk. paper)

About JewishGen.org

JewishGen, an affiliate of the Museum of Jewish Heritage - A Living Memorial to the Holocaust, serves as the global home for Jewish genealogy.

Featuring unparalleled access to 30+ million records, it offers unique search tools, along with opportunities for researchers to connect with others who share similar interests. Award winning resources such as the Family Finder, Discussion Groups, and ViewMate, are relied upon by thousands each day.

In addition, JewishGen's extensive informational, educational and historical offerings, such as the Jewish Communities Database, Yizkor Book translations, InfoFiles, Family Tree of the Jewish People, and KehilaLinks, provide critical insights, first-hand accounts, and context about Jewish communal and familial life throughout the world.

Offered as a free resource, JewishGen.org has facilitated thousands of family connections and success stories, and is currently engaged in an intensive expansion effort that will bring many more records, tools, and resources to its collections.

Please visit https://www.jewishgen.org/ to learn more.

Executive Director: Avraham Groll

About JewishGen Press

JewishGen Press (formerly the Yizkor Books-in-Print Project) is the publishing division of JewishGen.org, and provides a venue for the publication of non-fiction books pertaining to Jewish genealogy, history, culture, and heritage.

In addition to the Yizkor Book category, publications in the Other Non-Fiction category include Shoah memoirs and research, genealogical research, collections of genealogical and historical materials, biographies, diaries and letters, studies of Jewish experience and cultural life in the past, academic theses, and other books of interest to the Jewish community.

Please visit https://www.jewishgen.org/Yizkor/ybip.html to learn more.

Director of JewishGen Press: Joel Alpert
Managing Editor - Jessica Feinstein
Publications Manager - Susan Rosin

DUKOR

A Memoir

Daniel Charney

Front cover:
Daniel Charney, 1929
Courtesy of Rosalind Charney Kaye

Back cover:
Daniel Charney, Workmen's Circle Sanatorium, Liberty NY 1950
Courtesy of Rosalind Charney Kaye

Contents

Foreword.. ix
An Explanation of Words Describing Distance................. x
A Note on Spelling and Pronunciation......................... x
Map of Belarus and Surroundings (contemporary).............. xi
Map of Dukor and Surroundings (about 1900)................. xii
The Worth of a Ruble.. xiii
Introduction... 1
1 Things are Great, I am an Orphan...................... 6
2 My First Boat Ride.................................... 11
3 Between Wolves and Snakes............................ 16
4 A River Without Bridges.............................. 21
5 Why is Sea Water Salty?.............................. 25
6 Iron Cotton Balls (Steel Wool)....................... 30
7 I Became Commander of the Shtetl..................... 35
8 The Big Robbery...................................... 40
9 I am Drowning.. 45
10 My Uncle Feitel the Angel............................ 50
11 Masha the Lunatic.................................... 55
12 Mother's Tasty Meals................................. 60
13 Ascend, Rav Zev Wolf, Son of Yoel.................... 65
14 My Brothers and Sister............................... 70
15 My Uncles and Aunts.................................. 74
16 The Rabbi's House.................................... 79
17 Dukor's Times Square................................. 84
18 The Town's Intellectuals............................. 89
19 I Become a Bird...................................... 94
20 A Story about Pistachios............................. 100
21 My Sister's Wedding.................................. 106
22 I am Drawn to Berezin................................ 111
23 Matchmaking.. 115
24 Flies.. 120

25 The First Kiss...125
26 A Chapter of Russian Grammar.........................130
27 Zusha the Sexton..133
28 I am Drawn to Minsk.......................................138
29 A Tiny Heap of Earth......................................143
30 Tisha B'av was the Happiest Children's Holiday........148
31 On the Threshold of the Twentieth Century............153
32 My Second Operation.......................................158
33 A Story of a Wig Peg.......................................163
34 Two Sisters Schmooze......................................168
35 Dukor Goes by Foot to Lubavitch......................172
36 Dukor Jews..176
37 A Pesach-like Sukkus.......................................181
38 With My Brothers in Minsk................................186
    Photographs...189
39 Idealism and Philanthropy...............................199
40 Every Circle Has its Quadrant..........................204
41 The City Lunatic..209
42 I Study a Page of Talmud with My Polish Doctor.......214
43 A Small Letter to Mother.................................219
44 I Want to Remain a Boy...................................223
45 A Tale about Vilna...224
46 Between Minsk and Vilna..................................229
47 A Full Cellar with Summer Freckles....................234
48 Vilna Urchins...239
    Epilogue...245
    Glossary...248
    Name Index..254

Foreword

Daniel Charney (1888-1959) published this memoir in Yiddish in January 1951. It covers his life and that of his mother, Brocha Hurvitz Charney, his sister, Mirl, and his brothers Mendel, Zalke (Charles), Shmuel (Charney) Niger and Boruch Charney Vladeck until 1903. During those years family members lived in Dukor, Russia (now Belarus), with about 100 Jewish families, and Minsk, and in 1903 Daniel arrived in Vilna, Lithuania, for medical treatment.

Daniel Charney was a Yiddish poet, writer and journalist. His brother Shmuel Charney Niger was a Yiddish writer and literary critic. Daniel's brother Boruch (Baruch) Charney Vladeck was a labor leader, general manager of the Jewish Daily Forward, and a member of the New York City Board of Aldermen and City Council.

This translation into English was completed by Michael Skakun in 2022, except for one chapter. That chapter, "With My Brothers in Minsk," was translated earlier by Judy Montel, and a portion appears courtesy of the JewishGen Yizkor Book Project. The material translated by Michael Skakun is the property of relatives of Daniel Charney.

Contact is DukorBookProject@gmail.com.

An Explanation of Words Describing Distance

In the chapter "My First Boat Ride" the author wrote that Berezin was 12 miles (84 viorsts) from Dukor. The author was referring to Russian miles. A Russian mile was 7.4676 kilometers = 4.64 US miles. The Russian mile was divided into seven viorsts, each of which was 1.0668 kilometers. One US mile equals about 1.61 kilometers or about 1.51 viorsts. So the distance from Dukor to Berezin was about 56 US miles.

A Note on Spelling and Pronunciation

This translation tries to capture the way the Jews of Dukor, like other Yiddish-speaking Jews of Eastern Europe, spoke and pronounced things. For example, they would have pronounced the word for a blessing (which is also a woman's name) Brocha whereas the Israeli pronunciation is Bracha. They would have called Daniel's brother Boruch as opposed to Baruch. So also they would have called the Sabbath shabbes whereas the Israeli pronunciation is shabbat.

Contemporary Map of Belarus and Surrounding Countries

The contemporary names for Dukor, Kiev, and Vilna are Dukora, Kyiv, and Vilnius

Map of Dukor and Surrounding Towns, Railroads, and Rivers (about 1900)

Approximate distances from Dukor (US miles)

Berezin........................56 miles/ 90 km
Borisov.......................70 miles/ 112 km
Materova.....................7 miles/ 10 km
Minsk.........................23 miles/ 37 km
Rudensk train station...........7 miles/ 10 km
Smilovitch.................... 7 miles/10 km
Zembin ....67 miles/ 108 km
Kiev (Ukraine)............328 miles/ 528 km
Lubavitch (Russia)..........183 miles/ 294 km
Vilna (Lithuania)...........140 miles/224 km

The villages of Svislovitch and Loyev are located as described in the book, but we have not found a map confirming those locations.

The Worth of a Ruble

The book gives a sense of what a ruble (100 kopecks) was worth in Belarus at the turn of the last century:

The "cheap kitchen" for indigent Jews in Minsk charged three kopecks for a thick lentil soup with a pound of thick bread, and five kopeks if there was also a piece of meat in the soup.

A train ticket from Dukor to Minsk (23 US miles) cost nine kopecks for a minor, 36 for an adult.

A barrel of cherries cost less than a ruble.

Two of Daniel's brothers "hoped to save the first hundred rubles in order to leave for America."

The Charneys' supply of leather goods, sold from their house, was worth about 50 rubles.

The house itself rented for 20 rubles per year.

A Jewish draft dodger was fined 300 rubles by the Russian government.

Introduction

The winter of 1919-1920 was extremely cold and hunger-stricken. The October Revolution's tumultuous red capital was beleaguered by camps of forlorn children and so-called refugees from every corner of the land.

Even the renowned Russian writer Constanty Belmont, attired in his black Pushkin fur cape, would wander about as a "refugee" on the snowbound streets of Tverskoi Boulevard and walk towards the magisterial Pushkin monument. In one of his cape's pockets he stashed the frozen twigs struck down by snow-lashed winds.

And Sergei Esenin, the newly emerging village poet, drunk on too much schnapps and headed to colorful night spots, hired a buxom maiden to warm his bed until he returned home at 3 a.m.

And Yehezkiel Bleicher, the Jewish writer, who had made his name with the Yiddish translation of Byron's "Childe Harolde," came to me every evening with two nearly frozen potatoes, which he received daily at the war commissariat where he worked. We baked the two potatoes on my lead oven, the size of a fire pot which stood at the foot of my writing table, where I always found kindling at hand. (I was then the unofficial editor of the monthly journal "The Communist" and didn't lack for manuscripts.)

As the potatoes baked, we discussed the engulfing fire of the world revolution on the cusp of setting the entirety of Europe aflame. We would speak as well about emerging American Yiddish literature, as well as discussing our destiny, our "immortality" in Soviet-Jewish literature.

But later, only when my potato partner had left, when my stove had cooled, and I retreated half undressed under the frozen quilt, did I realize I was not entirely certain of my "immortality" in

Yiddish literature. At that time not even one of my poetry books had seen the light of day, and Zalmen Rayzen's "Lexicon" did not yet exist where future literary historians might find a trace of my biography.

In that cold and hungry Moscow winter of 1919-1920 the bright idea dawned on me to write my own autobiography, be that as it may.

First off, at least some trace will remain of me, and secondly, in penning my own biography I would not permit the ink to freeze in my inkwell.

When writing about the old home, about my mother, my brothers and my romantic childhood years, the inkwell must always be heated. Cold ink may be used to write history but not the budding story of one's own life.

I was then a mere 32 years old, perhaps the youngest memoir writer ever. I worried if my memoirs would ever reach my elder brothers in America.

Soviet Russia was blockaded on all sides. No ties were to be had abroad. The civil war continued to burgeon in every corner of the country. In Moscow itself the internal enemy—typhus—proliferated. There weren't enough hospitals or medical doctors to combat this anti-Bolshevik plague. To die in Moscow then was so easy!

I feared that after my death a strange figure would empty my room, my writing table, my little stove in the midst of a frosty winter night, and use my "Family Chronicle" for kindling, the stuff to bake a few potatoes, just as I had done with the manuscripts of others.

I decided to hide all the written pages of my "Family Chronicle" in the Jewish Commissariat's great wooden writing table, where I then worked. There I had stashed the new Ukraine and White Russia pogrom documents which the Jewish commissariat had begun to collect, and amid these pages I would hide the pogrom-smeared story of my life amid our mad century.

Understandably, I entrusted this secret of my direct loss with the Jewish commissar. I told him the truth; I feared to keep the manuscript, in which I had enclosed my entire life, in case anything should happen to me.

Shimon Dimonstein was the first and only Jewish commissar, a position designated by Lenin to serve as the general governor of

INTRODUCTION

the Jewish people in all of Russia, and, as representative of Stalin, the folks commissar of all national minorities in Soviet Russia. This very quiet, optimistic Dimonstein, who already in 1905 had gone and joined the Bolsheviks, despite the rabbinic ordination he had received from the Yeshivas of Telz, Slobodka and Lubavitch, understood exactly why I feared to keep the manuscript at home.

The Jewish commissar trusted me deeply, notwithstanding my insistent refusal to become a member of the Communist Party.

He also inquired as to why I began writing my memoirs at such a relatively young age. I declared that I feared if I waited it would be too late. I showed him my left hand, the healthy one, and asked if he saw the ring I wore on my pinkie.

Comrade Dimonstein gazed at the left pinkie and conceded that the ring was too tight-fitting; one could see it sunk in my swollen flesh.

I explained that the pinkie ring had formerly been worn on my middle finger, but when I noticed in winter that it had become too tight I switched it to my pinkie. But now all my fingers had become so swollen from cold and hunger that the ring had eaten into flesh. Under no circumstance could I pull it off.

Now you understand Comrade Dimonstein that such a "hero" as me can easily fall prey to typhus or lung infection and be done for, and went on to explain myself thus:

I began to write my memoirs early on precisely because one wishes to leave a memorial trace of oneself in Yiddish literature.

The Jewish Commissar insisted on knowing why I was so eager to hide my work, although he had earlier allowed me to keep my manuscripts at the Jewish Commissariat.

I declared, "You know, Comrade Dimonstein, I do not belong to the party and because I occupy such a lofty position the 'Cheka' might take an interest in the content of my domestic drawers. If the 'Cheka' snatched my 'Family Chronicle,' it may very well be that I would never see it again - so I would be much more relaxed if my papers were kept in your domain.

Comrade Dimonstein appreciated my answer and asked me to recite at least the first few pages of my "Family Chronicle."

Obviously, I didn't need to be asked twice. I read just the short introduction in order that the commissar should have an idea of it.

DUKOR

With a scratchy voice (I then had a cold), I read to him the following two paragraphs:

"Death's hand brushed me with its black wing while I still lay in the crib. My father's dying sighs ate into the birth pangs of my mother and my voice is until this very day an echo of these two screams of woe.

"My mother, with her embittered widow's milk, tried with all her strength to drive away my father's grim inheritance, the only one he left me."

Comrade Dimonstein's approbative head nods led me to believe that the "Family Chronicle" impressed him, but as I was then very hoarse I promised to read the memoir a second time, once the frost broke.

"The introduction is very good, Comrade Charney. Continue writing and we will later be able to issue it as a book," he announced happily.

That was the first sign of approval I received for my work from the highest representative in the Soviet—from the Jewish Commissar himself.

But fate had it otherwise: when I completed the first section of the "Family Chronicle" Comrade Dimonstein was no longer the Jewish Commissar and I—his co-worker—had already left for Berlin.

Only first in Berlin did my memoir receive its proper reception when it appeared in the journal "In Shpan," which David Bergelson, Alexander Khashin and I edited in Berlin in 1926.

A bit later (in 1927) it appeared in the Vilna publishing house of B.A. Klatzkin, but now, a quarter century since I have become a memoirist, I realize that my past work was written too hastily. I'd have to first fill it out with fresh content, remembrances and experience, which now at the age of 64 I begin to recall.

Now I will rewrite my childhood and youth on a different tack, allowing my dedicated readers, who long ago became partners of my entire life story, to experience not only the trajectory of my life but also the whole gallery of soulful Yiddish folk types of the old home in whose merit we continue to live until a hundred and twenty!

4

INTRODUCTION

Following my lead, the first and last Jewish Commissar, S. Dimonstein, began to write his own memoir, but wrote only one chapter, which he bequeathed to the public, come what may.

S. Dimonstein's "Autobiography" will be included in my forthcoming book of memoir.

1

Things are Great, I am an Orphan

I was my mother's eighth child only because two boys had hightailed it to heaven, leaving only six; an eldest daughter and five sons, like five fingers, one smaller than the next.

I say my mother and not my parents because father died at the age of 38, when I wasn't even a year old. Until today, I still don't know what carried him off.

In those days—that's to say sixty years ago—in the shtetl Dukor (Minsk region) there wasn't even a nurse apprentice to be had, so no one could know for sure what was the cause of death.

But I heard from mother that my father was a big cougher, so I understand now that he died from tuberculosis (which by us was called "the der.")

My father provided me for life with three pedigrees—first, an orphan, who when he recites the kaddish the entire congregation responds with amen, although the mourner is hardly even bar-mitzvahed (an orphan doesn't have to leave the sanctuary for the reciting of Yizkor as is customary for other children.)

Second—the "plague." At the age of two I had already become a "pliage" (a plague) (it stems from the word "plog.")

It appears that mother's widow-milk could not drive away the entire "the der" inheritance of my father, and when I was still nursed in the crib I was already covered with wounds, which only gypsies and Tatars know words for, but for which there is no cure. True, in the shtetl Smilovitch, ten viorsts from Dukor, a doctor could be found, although a Christian. My mother would have had to leave the other children and her store unsupervised to take me on such a difficult journey.

Yes, I forgot to mention that my mother had inherited from father a shop of leather goods. I say a "shop," but it was a hovel in which one could cut out pieces of leather to make a pair of boots. There was also a hard pelt from which one could cut out a pair of tight soles and heels. Mother stored the pelts and leather in a locker because they gave off a strong odor, and kept small nails, belts and bundles of thread in our home drawer.

I believe that her whole business amounted to fifty rubles, but every day at least one of five cobblers, who was in urgent need of a pair of boots to mend, would appear; or perhaps a peasant from a nearby village who spent hours bargaining for a pair of soles, in order to better steal a second pair.

As a result, mother never found the time to take her "pliage" to the Smilovitch doctor. And even if she had had the time, she would have lacked the rubles for the driver and the doctor.

My mother cured me with her widow's tears and many blessings (as it happens her name was Brocha) [brocha means blessing].

My mother, who knew many blessings and biblical passages, even served as a prayer leader and translator in the women's section on the Sabbath. She enjoyed reading interesting and often curious stories for the children, and parables from the "Tzena Rena" for the adult women.

It stands to reason that, as her youngest, I hovered near mother, because in addition to a wise passage or parable she would also give me a "nash" (a snack) but the older children were never jealous, although they were orphans too.

Mirl, my only sister, older than me by 12-13 years, helped mother at home. Every Friday she washed the heads of my brothers, but only mother could manage my own.

I was angered when the shtetl wives called me "idol," meaning that mother pampered me too much.

I had already become habituated to the nickname "pliage," but "idol" really bothered me. Only non-Jews had idols, not Jews.

Once I caught an exchange between our neighbor Malka and her husband, Lipa the tailor. Malka told Lipa: "I think if he died on her, it would be good for the 'idol' and for Brocha."

Our neighbor obviously didn't notice that I overheard what she said to her husband, but I did not inform my mother because it would have wounded her to know that I was belittled in such a manner.

Later on, God himself punished our neighbor for her malevolent speech. She gave birth to a child and when she took it to bed to nurse she suffocated it while asleep even before it could have a bris. Lipa shouted very loudly at Malka and she wept a flood of tears.

In a contrarian fit, Malka did not want to die. Now I realize that contrarianism is the best bet for longevity; it enhances the will to live.

Other than my neighbor I had no one to spite and vilify. I loved my mother and my siblings very much, and I even loved Matruna, the water carrier who spoke to me in good Yiddish, although she was not Jewish.

If I had been in cheder I would have surely found enough people to spite, but at the age of five I was not such a "pliage" that could be sent to school.

Mother hired an old man, Moshe Hirsch, who constantly took a whiff of tobacco, which sent me into a paroxysm of sneezes; nevertheless, he taught me the Hebrew alphabet, as well as nighttime prayers such as "kriyas shma." And who knows what else old Moshe Hirsch, with his snuffbox and discolored whiskers, might have taught me if he hadn't suddenly died and thus acquired new posthumous powers. He became nominally my doctor.

Fate would see to it that the dead Moshe Hirsch would cure all my illnesses, if only he would embrace me once he was cleansed and purified of this world.

So mother took me to Blotze Street, at the edge of town, where in a hovel without floors Reb Moshe Hirsch lay on the naked ground with a stone for a pillow and clothed in new shrouds. One of the Jews of the burial society led me to my dead rabbi, lifted his two cold hands and with his stick-like finger caressed my head, throat and entire living body.

From then on I felt the angel of death riding on my shoulders, and until now my head is bent to the ground, as if I carry a heavy weight.

But my mother was not satisfied with just this tactic. She had me sold (so to speak) to a lucky Jew, Elya Karabvetcher. His luck consisted in never having served in the army and his little house in the village having never burnt down even during the great conflagration.

Once mother took me to Elya Karabvetcher and pleaded with him to purchase me, pure and simple, at least until my bar-mitzvah, if I lived so long. Once bar-mitzvahed I could live on my own merit, or so my mother thought.

Elya Karabvetcher looked me up and down and quite seriously asked my mother how much she wanted. Mother answered quite businesslike that she wanted five groshen, that's to say one groshen per year [until age 13].

Elya answered that perhaps I was worth such a sum, but he couldn't offer more than three groshen.

Seeing that she had no choice, mother sold me for a total of three groshen, which she dropped in the alms box of Rabbi Meir Bal Haness [a rabbi in Roman times who was said to have miraculous power].

In such a manner did Elya Karabvetcher become my second father. I wasn't angry at mother for having sold me to a strange Jew; after all, she did take me back home. What irked me was that my new father was impoverished and worked at cutting the skins of dead horses and cows. [The "sale" was evidently another tactic by Daniel's mother to prolong his life by fooling the Angel of Death. Elya's good luck was supposed to rub off on Daniel. Also, a father was responsible for his son's sins until the son became 13 years old. As Daniel's father was not alive to carry that responsibility, Daniel's "second father" would bear that responsibility. Therefore, the Angel of Death could not take Daniel for his sins before age 13.]

Elya had a very fine son-in-law, Osher the Teacher, my real father's best friend. My elder brothers had already studied in his cheder. And Reb Osher never forgot to declare to my mother that she would take much pride in her children.

Thus had mother on every side provided me with the promise of longevity: on one side the late Reb Moshe Hirsch and on the other, the lucky Elya Karabvetcher. Obviously, my own father was also serving as a good intercessor in the world to come.

Mother finally came up with a plan to take me along to Smilovitch, where she had to travel periodically to deal in leather goods. In the end, a doctor would not hurt, God willing, mother answered our neighbors.

However, the Smilovitcher doctor was a known anti-Semite. He terrified her that I wouldn't live all that long—so why waste money on doctors or remedies. Mother couldn't stop crying all the way home, swallowing and strangling her tears. She was certain that I had understood what the angry, evil doctor had told her in Russian.

But I had already stumbled on the idea that the doctor had forsaken my life. So I decided to console my mother in this manner:

"Be calm, dear mother, as long as I'm not in Berezin and not married I will not die. The doctor should sooner die!"

But by then mother had fallen into such loud weeping that Kusha, the cart driver, could barely quiet her.

2

My First Boat Ride

In the previous chapter I promised my mother that I wouldn't die before I'd visited Berezin and before I married.

I was then no more than seven or eight but mother already understood what drew me to Berezin and why I already spoke of marriage.

My late father was born in the shtetl Berezin, which is twelve miles (84 viorst) from my tiny shtetl Dukor. [The text is referring to 12 Russian miles, which were equivalent to about 56 US miles/90 km from Dukor.]

True, my father died very young, but two of his brothers lived in Berezin—my two uncles, one of whom, Munia, was still single.

I knew that Uncle Munia wanted to wed my only orphaned sister. But I also knew that my mother, the widow, couldn't offer my uncle, her brother-in-law, a dowry. She hardly had enough to keep body and soul together for her six orphans.

True, Uncle Munia wasn't looking for a dowry. My sister was such a "beauty" that anyone would take her for no money at all. But it isn't nice to marry off a daughter without a dowry, mother answered our neighbors.

I got the bright idea that I myself would offer my uncle a respectable dowry! My calculation was very simple: both my uncles in Berezin lived in a house they had inherited from their father, my grandfather [Yoel]. A third of this inheritance belonged to my father. But as my father had died, his inheritance passed on to his five sons, of whom I was the youngest. So it stood to reason that I came into a fifth of a third.

This piece of inheritance belonged to me personally. I was willing to offer it to my uncle so he shouldn't think that he was taking my sister for nothing!

This in fact is what drew me to Berezin, where I could appraise the house—how many panes lined the windows, how many shingles comprised the roof. Only then would I know how much to give uncle, even before he weds my sister.

Now it is clear why marriage and Berezin were linked in my mind.

I was also drawn to Berezin on account of my two brothers, Mendel and Zalke, whom mother had sent off such a distance to Reb Itche, the rosh yeshiva, where he would provide bed and board.

How one learned Torah was evident in Dukor, but how one received bed and board I had yet to see with my own eyes.

I once asked mother to explain how "essen teg" worked in Berezin. I imagined that the yeshiva boys spent all day eating, and I quietly envied them because I too would have liked to eat all the day long, if only mother had what to give.

My mother soon stumbled across my profane thought, and she soothed me that I had nothing to envy my elder brothers.

"One eats, thanks heaven at the sideboards of strangers, and one chokes on the side dishes."

(Mother used to enjoy responding with a rhyme when possible so it should resemble a biblical verse).

I was soon fated to eat at strangers' tables, and I realized it wasn't so bad!

Mother had conjured up a long trip to Kiev, where our distant but rich relative with the name of Shick resided.

Mother was convinced that this very same rich relative would help her with the dowry for her only orphaned daughter, who was ready to marry her uncle Munia from Berezin. (My mother was in the dark about my secret plan to surrender part of my inheritance of my late father's house.)

Of course, Mother decided to take her "fool" (plague) to Kiev, where a prominent professor, who knew of wonders and miracles, might be found.

In such a manner her trip would achieve two objectives: one for her only daughter, the wedding bride-to-be, and the other for me, her youngest.

My sister was thrilled to learn that mother would travel such a distance because then she herself would remain the boss of the house and store. This would serve her well in becoming a good balabusta when she would, God willing, marry her uncle in Berezin.

My two elder brothers — Mulya and Bonya — (who became S. Niger and B. Vladeck) — were overjoyed that mother and I were traveling so far. They would then be able to handle the Dukor cobblers and even cut the soles out themselves, if only their sister would allow it.

Other than that the elder brothers cast an envious eye on the eggs the hen had laid every week. They longed for an omelet, but mother hid the eggs for me, because I was the weakest!

When it came to saying goodbye to mother and me, my elder brothers and even my bride sister burst into tears. Looking at them, I too began to cry, even though mother had taken along many goodies for the road.

She had baked a whole sack of long and short breads, covered on both sides with sugar and cinnamon, which I loved. She also took along a dozen hard-boiled eggs and a half dozen dried meats.

Mother announced that all these items would be of use on the vessel that would take us from Bobruisk straight to Kiev.

She also took a few pillows and quilts, which she managed to squeeze into a sack. Between the pillow cases she shoved in the volumes "Tzena Rena" and "Korben Mincha."

When Kusha, the horse-and-buggy driver, who took us to the station in Rudensk, saw the pile of bundles and packs we had, he shouted across the entire marketplace so everyone could hear:

"Jews, see Brocha is traveling with her fool all the way to America; she should have taken the samovar as well!"

Mother ignored Kusha's outburst. Everyone knew Kusha the driver was a happy-go-lucky lug and he enjoyed playing pranks. Yet in the end she replied, "Kusha, you think Kiev is much closer than America? Water is water!"

"Brocha, I should be blessed with what I wish for you and your 'idol,'" Kusha quickly retorted, thinking God forbid he had insulted mother.

Several days later I realized that mother was indeed right in having taken along so many things. Our trip from Dukor to Kiev lasted two weeks, as if we were really traveling to America!

13

As long as one travels on dry land one senses where one stands in the world. When one travels by horse and buggy one knows the location of all the inns to stop at. By train one knows every station where the locomotive stops. But the moment one gets on a boat and takes to water one takes one's life into one's hands and no longer knows where in the world one is.

Not for nothing was our boat named "Sutbo," destiny in Yiddish.

Traveling on the "Sutbo" was fateful indeed. The boat could not load more than 50-60 people. but when it arrived in Bobruisk, where we waited for a long time, it was brimming with people from Borisov and Berezin. Each passenger was loaded with sacks of mushrooms and dried apples because the Ukraine lacks forests or orchards, and therefore mushrooms and dried apples are worth their weight in gold.

Also, there's no succor to be had in the Ukraine. Therefore, the entire Berezina River was overflowing with refugees, and our boat could barely make its way. Our captain maneuvered with agility in order to avoid a collision with refugees who swam in the current. Yet all that to-and-fro resulted in the sacks of mushrooms and dried apples opening up and encumbering the passengers who slept nearby.

Shklovsky, the owner of the vessel, quieted us by saying that after Svislovitch (where later the famous Dr. Shmaryahu Levin would be born) [a Jewish Zionist and orator] the boat would proceed more quickly because the "Bereoza" (a shortened term of the Berezina River) became wider and deeper. I was indeed happy to learn that we would soon have easier passage.

I was peeved that the sacks of apples opened up and their contents rolled out, and I could only savor their smell and not chew on them.

Nothing was left of the eggs and dried meats which mother had taken along. A miracle to behold: at a sort of boat buffet one could purchase for a mere two kopecks a porcelain kettle with boiled water, as well as a tiny tea kettle. Bread and herring were for sale. Very rich Jews, who traveled first or second class, could acquire most anything at the buffet, but mother, looking askance, said that the prepared foods didn't seem to her entirely kosher.

So we would eat properly in Kiev at our rich relative's home, yet the road to Kiev remained difficult and fraught, as we shall soon see.

3

Between Wolves and Snakes

My mother was in fact correct when she said to Kusha, the cart driver, that water by nature spells great danger.

Nevertheless, she risked traveling with me as far as Kiev by water rather than by land because the steam vessels were cheaper than the railroads.

Later it became evident that waterborne travel cost mother far more dearly than the rails. Instead of swimming with our steam vessel, "Sutbo," for more than two days, as we had been promised in Bobruisk, we drifted two weeks from Bobruisk to Kiev.

At fault were the skimpy sailboats occupying the length of the Berezina River. Our steam boat kept constantly whistling to the mariners to drive the blocking vessels ever closer to the bank so that we could forge a path midstream. The "Sutbo" needed deep water to navigate because she was encumbered by masses of people and bundles. In comparison to our very own modest Dukor River, the Svislovitch, the Berezina River was in fact deeper though not always wide enough to allow for the peaceful passage for all the boats of various make and design.

One dawn our "Sutbo" met with a great catastrophe. Another vessel suddenly pecked a hole in our steamboat through which water began streaming into the first and second-class quarters, reserved for the wealthy and the well-born.

The captain ordered the passengers to be woken immediately. We were lined up at the edge of the vessel, where the rudder is found. Four mariners rapidly tossed sacks filled with dried and dainty mushrooms and apples to the other edge. The captain's calculations were simple: when the passengers with all their sacks and bundles will find their way to the other end of the steam vessel,

16

that is to say, to the front edge, the hollowed out nose will rise up like a rearing horse. Thus, no more water would be able to seep in.

Then the captain and his sailors filled up the hole in the vessel's nose, and we arrived at the bank after great effort, where the boat listed for an indefinite time until the hollowed-out nose could be mended.

A miracle — our maritime misfortune occurred only a short distance from the shtetl Svislovitch. The town, quickly alerted to our great misfortune, gave a warm response; everyone approached us with help and consolation. It happened to be Sabbath and entire platefuls of challah, brimming pots of gefilte fish, cheese, boiled eggs and even sweets for the children were arrayed in front of us.

Only then did I perceive how deeply heartfelt Jews are as a people, a blessing on them!

Total strangers offered help and consolation. We were proffered bed and board in Svislovitch because our "Sutbo" would be grounded several days until the shipbuilders succeeded in patching her nose.

The richer Jews in fact went to Svislovitch for Shabbes, but the women and children were left on the steamboat.

As soon as a plethora of provisions arrived, why drag ourselves all the way to Svislovitch, we reasoned? Mother's only request was that candles be brought for the Shabbes lighting.

Hearing mother's pleas, the other women made similar requests. A few hours thereafter a sprinty go-getter brought kilos of candles which come twenty to a pound. But our captain was a shrewd and evil man and an even bigger drunk. He categorically refused to allow candles on the steamboat itself. A fire might break out and then, he insisted, he would truly be "at sea."

So everyone had to forage in the forests, with the result that broad branches of a hacked tree were brought forth. Mother also scavenged for a broad stem (she knew what to look for; after all, she hails from clergy) and she smelt all of her Sabbath candles on it, one for herself and the six others for her six children, they should be well.

It happened to be a quiet Friday evening; no wind blew, the setting sun dappled over the tops of the quite tall pine trees. It appeared as if the sun itself lit the candles on the kindled treetops. Perhaps I just invented the setting sun image now. Some fifty years on, I think even a memoir writer has to be imaginative when looking back into the remote past. Therefore, I am now more than certain that the sun kindled the candles in unison with my mother, may her memory be for a blessing.

In any event, I remember quite well that even the birds in their nests repeated in their peculiar avian language mother's Sabbath candle blessings.

"In honor of God, our faith and in honor of our holy Sabbath, which God vouchsafed us, may we have the privilege of fulfilling all the 613 commandments, Amen, So be his will!" mother recited.

I couldn't repeat the other Sabbath prayers because mother whispered them out of her prayer book, but when it came to "Go and Ye Shall See," mother lifted her voice and I heard how she addressed the seven lights on the sawed-off branch:

"Lchu Neranenoh — we will chant to God, we will cleave to our all-powerful helper, we will strive to come to him because God is the strong and omnipotent king over all the angels and his hand covers all — the heights of the mountains and the depths of the seas which he created and the dry land which his hand created as well...."

When my mother had finally reached the dry land of "Lchu Neranenoh" I was overjoyed precisely by this portion of the earth God had seen fit to create; for if not for the dry land, God forbid, our steamboat would have sunk and my four brothers and my sole sister would have been left total orphans, and who knows if my Uncle Munia of Berezin would then want to marry such a round orphan, may the Compassionate one spare us.

And if there was no dry land, as it says in Lchu Neranenoh, the Svislovitcher Jews would not have been able to provide us with such a delicious Sabbath meal, after which my heart pined.

I could scarcely wait until the few minyan Jews ended their evening prayers in the forest.

Then we all boarded our steamboat, where the sailors had set up a table around the extinguished smoke stack.

One big-bearded Jew who resembled Patriarch Abraham made kiddush over the Svislovitcher challah. His wife, who resembled Matriarch Sarah with an ample stomach in her elder years, began to distribute pieces of gefilte fish and sweet carrots with kishka and plum compote, in which it was very heaven to dunk soft challah, as well as cooked chickpeas which one consumed right after dinner out of simple, unadulterated joy.

I must admit that I have never eaten such a joyous Sabbath meal in all my life (I was then eight) as we had following the boat disaster.

Soon after dinner a comedian, who claimed to be a cantor, insisted we all become his musical abettors. Only thus, he said, would he teach us to sing "Lcha Dodi" in a new key.

The comedian clambered unto a chair as if he were the conductor of a choir and began to command.

—If I say "Lcha Dodi" you should respond "Tschiribom;" if I utter "l'kras kala," you should answer "tschiri-biri-bom."

So then fellows—

"Dodi."

"Tshiribom!"

"Lekras Kala."

"Tschiri-biri-bom"

"Dodi lekras kallah" - "Tschiri-biri-bom!"

I sang along and my mother was bursting with pride as I was finally showing myself to be a bit of a mentsch.

After finishing with "Dodi," we returned again to dry land and watched the Sabbath lights burning on the hacked off branches. The small flames of lights attracted many butterflies and various other kinds of winged creatures from every quarter of the forest, which circled around the lights, offering a real oneg-Shabbes.

The guys and gals went deeper into the forest to welcome the Sabbath bride, as it says in "Dodi," but mother prevented me from venturing forth alone because night had already fallen and she was terrified by stories of preying wolves and snakes.

Mother made our bed not far from the extinguished roof and she told me quite sternly not to forget to say "krias shma" because we were in a dangerous place.

But I was so distracted from all that I had experienced, all in the passage of one day, that when it came to reciting "kriyas shma" and the phrase "Blessed be his name and kingdom forever," I confusedly added the "tschiri-biri-bom." Thereafter I couldn't fall asleep at all.

The guys and gals were to blame in all this; they carried on (sang that is) in the dark forest, as if their song could drive off the wolves and the snakes, which had me terrified.

But what terrified me above all else was the iron belt that stretched along the walls of the boat, from the captain's wheel to the rudder. When the steamboat sails, the iron rod squirms like a headless and tailless snake.

I feared that if I fell fully asleep the iron snake would begin to squirm of its own accord, and we would then all be lost and done for. The steamboat would then slip from its moorings into the water, and it would be all over with "tshiri-biri-bommmm...."

4

A River Without Bridges

In the old days, preceding World War I, one would say that the sun never set on the British Empire, which ruled the seas.

Wherever there's a sea—English ships were said to be present.

But on rivers, the British Empire did not reign.

In any case, not on the rivers of our region—Byelorussia and the Ukraine.

Antiquity reigned over the Berezina and the Dnieper, a kind of ancient Jewish empire even though the Jews did not have a state of their own.

All the steamboats of every size, shape and variety which bobbed on the current of these two rivers belonged largely to Jews.

Summertime the Jews of White Russia and the Ukraine lived nearer to water than to dry land. Even the bridges belonged to the Jews.

A "parom" is a kind of suspension bridge extending from one bank to the other. Bridges could not be constructed across the Berezina because they would impede the passage of the steamboats with their tall chimneys, and even the smaller vessels needed free passageway.

When the bridge controller spotted a steamboat approaching, he would lower the drawbridge deep into the water and the steamboat would pass by peacefully.

Years ago it wasn't yet known that one could construct tall suspension bridges without pylons, as for example, the Brooklyn Bridge or the magnificent George Washington Bridge across New York's Hudson River.

One says that Napoleon met with wholesale disaster at the Berezina because his soldiers had no bridges on which to withdraw in a timely fashion from Russia to France. Now, it appears to me that Shklovsky, the owner of our steamboat "Sutbo," had a bigger downfall than Napoleon's.

In the end Napoleon, notwithstanding all his disasters, appears in the pages of world history as one of the greatest of warriors, while Shklovsky and his unfortunate "Sutbo" would have been completely forgotten had I not memorialized them in my chronicle.

I still remember very well how this pitiful Jew, a "nebekh," wrung his hands when a boat holed through the nose of his "Sutbo," and he had to make a forced landing on the verdant shore a few miles behind Svislovitch.

The other boat was the "Aunt Fania," which constantly competed with the "Sutbo." Every spring when navigation on the Berezina began in earnest, "Aunt Fania" announced that she would charge passengers a quarter ruble less than the "Sutbo," which, ever competitive, announced that she would take on passengers for a quarter of a ruble less than than the "Aunt Fania" already lowered charge. Price warfare between the two steamboats reached such a frenzied point that "Aunt Fania" declared that it would ferry passengers from Borisov to Bobruisk for free, and would throw in a white roll with each passenger's cup of tea. So the "Sutbo" had no choice but to take on passengers for no money at all and also for each passenger to receive a free roll with his tea.

Things proceeded this way for the first few weeks, until "Aunt Fania" and the "Sutbo" had finally a tariff placed on each. When "Aunt Fania" saw how our "Sutbo" dragged itself along with a patched nose from Svislovitch to Loyev, where the Berezina flows into the Dnieper, a loud hurrah of joy broke out among the passengers with the captain in the lead.

People, alas, possess such a rotten nature — when someone slips and falls laughter replaces help and compassion. I thought so then and I still do now even when the whole world lies on its face with a bloodied nose.

The owner of our steamboat cursed awfully at "Aunt Fania" and told it off so rudely that one cannot quote it on paper.

One of the curses of our "Sutbo" owners came soon to pass.

"Aunt Fania," which had loaded far more passengers and cargo than it could manage, suddenly found itself stuck in the middle of the night on a sandbar, barely covered by water.

"Aunt Fania" vainly slapped the waters with its oars and shovels—nothing helped. She dug into the shallows of the Berezina, even where the smaller boats dare not go.

"Aunt Fania's" captain ordered that with the coming of dawn the ship's passengers should be divided in two. One party would be lowered on a tiny boat on the right bank and the second party on the left bank. Then a long chain would be drawn through the nose of "Aunt Fania." Thus passengers on both sides of the river would in effect be harnessed, allowing the steamboat to be dragged off the sandbar.

Our "Sutbo" arrived just as the captain of "Aunt Fania" was shouting orders from his perch as to how the harnessed passengers were to proceed—left or right.

Our captain was delighted with the disaster that had befallen "Aunt Fania," and he began to sound his siren for "Aunt Fania's" captain to let our boat pass. But the enraged captain began to sound his siren to similar effect, implying he doesn't give a hoot about us.

It appears that ship sirens possess a flexible language in which whistles can be read as friendship greetings or angry hoots.

The captains cursed each other at length via the ship sirens until they finally reconciled, and our steamboat, "Sutbo," harnessed itself onto "Aunt Fania" and dragged her off the small sandbar.

Only then did the owner of "Aunt Fania" offer whiskey for the captain and sailors of both ships and free tea and fresh Svislovitcher rolls for the passengers who had endured such travail.

Thus did we shlep ourselves with great wearied effort to Loyev, where the Berezina empties into the Dnieper, whose waters are twice the former's breadth and depth.

I became very curious to see how one river empties into another. Watching this sight, I remembered the story told of the Minsk Jewish drunk named Morgenstern.

When Morgenstern became wasted, he would explain to the Jews of Minsk that he now understood the prayer verse: "Come to Zion in joy."

When one is dead drunk, one falls into the gutter. The Minsk gutter banks into Svislovitch which passes into Berezina which empties into Dnieper which drains into the Black Sea which finally brings Morgenstern straight to Zion. That's why the prayer declares "Come to Zion in joy."

My mother didn't much care for such stories mocking the prayer book. She therefore kept me away from the grownups and, as a result, I couldn't see and hear everything that transpired during my first big trip from Dukor to Kiev.

The journey lasted a full two weeks as a result of the compounded catastrophes that befell us instead of the three-to-four-day voyage my mother had allotted. Travel by train would have cost us less.

From the outset I wasn't put off that we went by boat, because had we taken the train my mother would have hidden me under the seat to save the cost of the quarter ticket, and I would now not be able to recall with any kind of accuracy my experience on the waters of the Svislovitch, the Berezina and the Dnieper.

5

Why is the Sea Water Salty?

When I was a cheder boy I knew the geography of Israel and the neighboring Levantine [Middle Eastern] countries better than my own native region.

So, for example, the Red Sea, the Jordan and even the rivers Pras and Khidekel were far more familiar to me than the "Svissla" (Svislovitch), "Bereioze" (Berezina) and the Dnieper.

Some fifty years ago I had no idea that our native river, the Svisle, drains into the Berezina, that the Dnieper empties into the Black Sea, which in the end brings us to Eretz Yisrael (the Land of Israel). But during my first water journey from Bobruisk to Kiev I saw in crystal-clear terms how one river falls into another and then both drain into a third, etc., until all the rivers empty into the big sea.

This reminded me powerfully of mother's books, where one story segues into another until it becomes a skein of wonder tales which children savor. But one thing I couldn't understand: why is sea water salty, in view of the fact that it absorbs all the rivers of the world? Rivers, themselves, are not salty!

Even mother couldn't figure it out, but the jokester of our steamboat, who had taught us to chime "Dodi" with a tchiri-biri-bom accompaniment, answered my query: the herring swimming in the sea makes the water salty.

I longed for a piece of herring, but the steamboat buffet charged five kopecks for a herring and mother could not afford it.

Mother strongly complained that our water trip to Kiev was as arduous as "crossing the Red Sea." It was already a week since we had left home, and we had only reached Loyev.

25

I rather liked Loyev. Near this shtetl the Berezina falls into Dnieper and on the banks of the river one finds a constant fair. All the steamboats halt at Loyev in order to load provender as well as wood for the steamboat ovens, which burn day and night, like hell itself.

No sooner did our steamboat "Sutbo" (with a soft D) arrive in Loyev to load stuff for our further voyage than a halt was put to it. The professionals had carefully examined the patched nose of our boat and decided that it would be dangerous to proceed into the turbulent Dnieper.

We disembarked in Loyev to wait for another steamboat, vainly pleading with the owner of "Aunt Fania" that he allow us on his boat, which we had just recently with utmost care and effort dragged off the sandbar near Svislovitch. But "Aunt Fania" could not take us along to Kiev because she was packed to the rafters with travelers and sacks from Borisov, Berezin and Bobruisk.

I began to plead with mother that we should transfer to a smaller, festive-looking boat. Each of these vessels possessed a small booth where I might easily hide from the rain, as well a small mound of sand on which a fire could be kindled to bake potatoes or fry them in oil.

Mother informed me that Jews don't voyage on these smaller boats because the non-Jews who sail them eat "sala" (pig-fat) and speak uncouthly. Far better to wait in Loyev for another steamboat; as a consolation prize she offered me an overflowing glass of sunflower seeds.

On the bank of the river in Loyev everyone cracks "seeds." The entire riverfront is strewn with its shells, black on the outside and white on the inside.

In our sectors of White Russia sunflower seeds don't grow as readily as in the Ukraine. To make up for it, mother bought me a flowing bag of "seeds" and I soon got busy.

You have to know how to crack sunflower seeds, something of an art. The more agile the cracking, the greater is the pleasure. The first glass of seeds took very long because I didn't know how to spit out the shells. I achieved greater mastery with the second glass, but it never came to a third glass, which would have sunk mother. Each glass cost a kopeck, and it appears mother hadn't taken along many kopecks.

She had to leave the kopecks for the children at home, something with which to sustain them while we were at sea.

Mother began to dissuade me from the seeds in this manner:

"Take a look, my child, at the appearance of those people who consistently crack the shells open. They look as if they've crossed themselves. This is work for 'Shgotzim' (non-Jewish ruffians)."

Actually, when I began to watch from afar the seed crackers of Loyev they indeed looked like people crossing themselves, heaven save us!

My desire for the seeds quickly dissipated. Now, residing in America, I realize that cracking sunflower seeds is a more productive activity than chewing gum. The mouth alone is involved in chewing gum, which gives one the look of a repulsive cow, while the art of cracking sunflower seeds involves the deftness of the hand, which affords the body nourishment; after all, sunflowers produce a fine, health-inducing oil.

But better let me return to our ongoing trip to Kiev, with its new trials and experiences.

Even the new steamboat, larger than the previous "Sutbo," had to return in midcourse because of the blockage of the smaller boats, gathered in a spot where the Dnieper turns. The small boats had gotten entangled in one spot, preventing easy passage.

Who knows how many days and nights we would have lost waiting by this watery barricade if another boat had not appeared, journeying from Kiev to Loyev.

Both captains of the steamboats went on to exchange passengers and goods so that the Kiev steamboat could return to Kiev and ours to Loyev.

The transfer from one boat to the other smelled of imminent danger because it had to occur across small boats, which constantly flitted over the agitated waters of the Dnieper.

The steamboat couldn't reach the banks because of what appeared to be two roofless stone walls of a tower. Until this very day I find it hard to understand how the Dnieper could sluice through such tall structures!

Lucky that the peasants of the small boats showed us how to cross the barricade so that we would not fall into the water.

When we boarded safely on the new steamboat, which turned its nose back to Kiev, mother took out her prayer book and benched "goymel" (said a benediction after great danger).

After such a terrifying "Egyptian" journey on the Dnieper my mother would surely have bought me another glass of sunflower seeds for a kopeck, but no such purchases were to be had on the Kiev steamboat.

I softly attached myself to mother, who crouched over her thick prayer book, soon sensing her tears.

"Mother dear, why are you crying? May you only know of health," I asked and mother answered very quietly:

"I don't know, my child, it's a pity on the children."

It appears that mother suddenly pined after the children she left behind without supervision, and she was incensed at an interminable journey already entering its second week.

Who even knew if the rich relative in Kiev would help with a gift for her only daughter or if the Kiev professor would manage to find a cure for her youngest—my plague-ridden self. Mother's pain pierced her through and through.

I turned very warm and soon blood seeped out of my nose. In those years I frequently had nosebleeds, for which no cure could be found. Several drops of blood dripped on mother's prayer book, which lay on her lap.

At least her Sabbath dress, which she donned in anticipation of arrival in Kiev, was not spotted with blood.

But at the banks of the river in Kiev she soon discovered dismayingly that a Jew has to have habitation rights to be in the metropolis. Only big-time Jewish merchants and skilled workers could obtain such rights in Kiev.

Mother had no documents on her other than the blood-stained prayer book and the Tzena Rena, on the covers of which were written the memorial days of her parents and of my father a"h (olov hasholem—peace be unto him).

Good people advised us that we should remain on the riverbank until our relative would come to meet us.

One of these good people, a big Jewish timber merchant, promised to inform our relative that we were waiting for him at the riverbank. We sat on our pillows and coverlets waiting for our relative to take us from the Dnieper. Mother took out her prayer book again and I heard how she whispered teary-eyed:

"On the banks of the Babylon, ye we sat and wept..."

How far is Kiev, after all, from Babylon?

6

Iron Cotton Balls (Steel Wool)

I still don't know how much money mother was able to get from
our rich relative in Kiev for her only daughter—the bride-to-
be— but for me, her plague-ridden one, she obtained such a
wonderful remedy that it was already worth enduring such a long
and difficult trip, which we had scarcely survived.

Our rich relative, who owned a big sugar store on the largest
thoroughfare in Kiev, on "Kreshtchatik," did indeed pick us up at
the steamboat, but instead of taking us home he conducted us to
the other side of the Dnieper to a shtetl called "Slobtoka," because
in Kiev itself, our relative explained, we didn't have dwelling rights.

For the life of me I still couldn't understand why the Russian
Czar should care one way or the other if a poor Jewish widow and
her eight-year-old youngest son would sleep through a few nights
in Kiev until we finished with our business.

I also couldn't fathom why individual Jews could live in Kiev
and the others were strictly forbidden to do so.

After all, we all stem from one source: Abraham, Isaac and
Jacob. So the question arises why our relative can dwell in Kiev and
my mother, a descendant of the holy man, the "Sheloh," is not
allowed in.

When I asked mother the reasoning behind the Czar's
position, she answered that Jews are in exile and thus persecuted.

So I was astounded as to why Jews strive to go to Kiev in the
first place, where they are unwanted and even assaulted, rather than
remaining in their own midst, such as Dukor, Smilovitich, or even
in Minsk, where there is no exile whatsoever.

As far as I remember the goyim were in exile but not, God forbid, the Jews. The Jews were well shod in boots, while the goyim wore battered shoes. Jews drank tea with sugar, while the goyim drank tea with saccharin. The Jews ate challah, fish and kugel each Sabbath while the goyim wolfed down black bread with cabbage dipped in pig fat. Jewish children would go to cheder to learn Torah, while the shgotzim (loutish young non-Jews) and shikses (non-Jewish women and girls) of our town would put pigs to pasture or buy up geese on "Sasazentz" (The Meadow).

So who, in fact, was exiled or who exiled whom?

Even Matruna, the water-carrier, who spoke a lush Yiddish laced with holy tongue expressions, would heat our Sabbath oven, milk the cows and take the candelabrum off the table. To this very day I still don't understand why Jews abandoned the shtetlekh for Kiev or Moscow, where they were shamed and assaulted, only to be forced to return home.

When I asked our rich relative why Jews were permitted to reside on one bank of the Dnieper but not on the other, he answered that Slobtoka belonged to another region, to Chernigov, and thus Jews may reside there.

The answer didn't satisfy me because I could see no difference between one region and the next. Both the Kiev riverbanks and those of Chernigov's Dnieper had the same trees and even the same people.

True, I spotted some very strange types in Slobtoka, who resided by day in the Kiev region and in Chernigov at night. It appears these people didn't have dwelling rights in Kiev and so came to sleep in our Slobtoka inn.

Every night the very crowded inn came fully alive. Two slept to a bed and ten to a room. I was deeply angered that the owners of the inn didn't consider me as an adult and put me in the women's room together with mother in one bed.

The other women, like mother, were widows, and they probably came to visit rich relatives in Kiev for donations for yet-to-be married daughters, or possibly even for themselves.

Some of the women were still quite young and kept constantly gabbing about making "assaults" on potential grooms.

Why assaults were to be made on grooms I couldn't then understand. My mother warned that I had better not listen to women's talk because it made no sense.

Sleep in the inn could not be had. All the bedbugs of the Chernigov region came after us and we spent all night "assaulting" them. I started to plead with mother that we should return home.

Truth be told, bedbugs thrived by us as well, but they were domesticated, rather homey creatures, and they didn't bite as mightily as those of Chernigov.

We could hardly wait for the dawn, when our relative took us to Kiev to visit a famous professor who might find some kind of cure for all my ills.

Our relative brought me several boxes of various candies, the likes of which were not to be found in our neck of the woods.

We traveled to the professor in a peculiar conveyance, neither buggy nor train.

Had it been what is known as a "kontka," two horses would have driven it, or had it been a train it would be driven by a locomotive. Our relative explained that it in fact was a tramway operating on electricity. But mother even didn't know or grasp the meaning of electricity.

We were lucky that the tramway had big, clear windows and I could see all of Kiev as we rode by, a city of imposing cathedrals and shops.

I'll be damned if I know why a city such as Kiev needed quite so many stores and an imposing church, to boot, if Jews were not allowed to reside there.

Churches are, in fact, good for Jews inasmuch as they serve as a marketplace established every Sunday, allowing Jews to derive their living from the peasants. But if no Jews are present to begin with then who would serve as middlemen in such places, and who would run the shops?

I was very eager to ask our relative how such a big city as Kiev gets by without Jews, but my relative was deeply engaged in a conversation with my mother and I didn't wish to interrupt them.

I understood that my mother was unburdening her widow's soul concerning my elder sister, who was trying to marry her uncle from Berezin.

But her main plea was for her youngest, who all the doctors had given up on. Her only hope now lay with the Kiev professor, who, it was said, worked wonders.

We finally arrived at the famous professor, who it happens was a Jew with a long gray beard much like Abraham the Patriarch, but who spoke Russian.

The Russian Abrahamic patriarch ordered my mother to undress me entirely, as if I were Isaac being led to the sacrifice. A great fear befell me. I wanted to cry but I was embarrassed to do so in front of the professor. My blood raced into my head, and my nose began to bleed.

The professor approached a small drawer filled with many small bottles, tubes of medicine and cotton balls. He drew out yellow swabs of cotton gauze from one bottle and stuck a piece in my nose.

Wonder of wonders! The nosebleed soon stopped.

Mother asked the professor where one could obtain such wondrous cotton. He answered that every pharmacy carries it. It's called iron gauze (have you ever heard that gauze can be made of steel?).

And what of his other ailments, mother asked?

As for the other ailments, the only cure to be found was to place me for a year's time in a dermatology clinic, where I would be healed with electricity.

Mother suddenly burst into tears.

"Why are you crying, my good woman?" the professor asked puzzlingly.

"How should I not cry, Herr Professor! He is the apple of my eye, my plague-ridden one. I cannot separate from him even for a minute. Why if I should have to give him up for a year in a clinic, I'd die of longing. And where can I, a poor widow, obtain so much money to maintain him in a hospital? In our shtetl there isn't even a medic to offer a cure," mother broke out in sobs. Had I not feared the professor, I would have cried along with mother.

The good professor soon appreciated mother's outburst, though she cried in Yiddish, a language beyond his ken. He gave her a bottle of anti-fainting drops, which one sniffs on Yom Kippur just before the final prayer, neilah. [By late afternoon on Yom

Kippur, after fasting almost 24 hours, many people feel faint and need to sniff something to revive them.]

When mother calmed down a bit, he asked her to dress me and put on my shoes which, in fact, were not mine. They were the clothes and shoes of my elder brother, Bonya (B. Vladeck a"h), who had the habit of constantly outgrowing his clothes and shoes.

But mother had promised that if she would obtain a substantial gift for my sister from our rich Kiev relative, she would then weave me a special suit and personally make me a pair of shoes for the festive occasion.

It appears that my rich relative's donation was not big enough to provide me with both a suit and shoes, but sufficient to purchase a whole pound of iron-like gauze. When I returned from the long and difficult trip with mother I, in turn, became a veritable professor of medicine in Dukor.

As soon as someone in town would cut his hand or foot, they'd come running to me for a piece of iron gauze.

I even once tried to stick a piece of iron gauze in the nose of our samovar, which kept on constantly dripping, but to no avail.

7

I BECAME COMMANDER OF THE SHTETL

After my first round-the-world journey from Dukor to Kiev I came alive in cheder.

My mother fairly burst with stories about my experience on the River Berezina and the Dnieper, as well as about the Kiev tramway, which travels in the middle of the street on the power of electricity, without even the hint of horses.

Even Shmuel the melamed, our own Rabbi, who beat the Talmud tract "Beytza" into our heads, would put aside his whip and say to me very slowly:

"Nu, Donya, tell us how your mother lit candles in the middle of the forest."

The children pleaded with the rabbi that I should recount how "Aunt Fania" was pulled off the sandbar by the nose.

Other boys much preferred that I sing "Lcha Dodi" with the tchiribiribom accompaniment, which I had learned on the steamboat.

A terrible tumult broke out until the Rabbi negotiated a compromise in which I would tell how a tramway without the benefit of horses travels in Kiev.

"A vehicle without horses is called a tramway in Kiev," I would correct my Rabbi, "and a tramway goes on rails, not unlike a train but without a locomotive."

"And how does this train run? You traveled already on one?" the children would pull at my tongue.

"A train goes on steam, like a steamboat; that is why the locomotive is called 'paravoz'" [steam engine], I'd answer like a cosmopolitan, who knows of such things.

"And where does a steamboat go? After all, Donya, you've had trouble on steamboats." The Rabbi encouraged me to tell more about all the wonders on my long journey.

"A steamboat, Rabbi, travels quite simply, much like the yeshiva's water mill. When the sluices are opened, the water rolls on the 'lopatkes' [shoulders] of each big wheel and the wheel begins to turn of its own accord. A steamboat, Rabbi, has two wheel rods, instead of one, and the oars of the wheel begin to splash the water, thus guiding it into the middle of the river."

"Take heed of how the fellow masters everything," Shmuel, the Melamed, would say with great astonishment to his wife, and caress my head with loving admiration.

The children sat thunderstruck and awaited my further storytelling.

But the Rabbi suddenly remembered that we still had to finish a page of the Talmud and grabbed hold of his whip.

"Na, children, let's start from the beginning."

"An egg born on a holiday, Beit Shamai says, may be eaten and Beit Hillel says it is forbidden."

"And what happens when an egg is born on the Sabbath, is it allowed to be eaten?" I asked the Rabbi.

"The Sabbath is greater than the holidays, my child," the Rabbi answered. "The world is held together by the Sabbath!"

"But why do you ask?" the Rabbi suddenly asked me, knowing beforehand that if I inquired I was already in the know.

"I'm asking in view that this past Sabbath our hen laid an egg. I wanted to drink it while it was still warm because the Kiev professor had told us that I must consume the eggs laid by a hen. But my elder brother, Mulya, told mother that the egg could, heaven forbid, hurt me because Beit Hillel opposes the eating of eggs laid either on Sabbath or holidays."

"So, my child, as the egg is your cure, you are allowed to eat it even on the Sabbath because 'saving a life supersedes the Sabbath,'" Rabbi Shmuel declared decisively.

I felt as if I were in seventh heaven, for the Rabbi had taken my side and not that of my older brother, Mulya, who had learned many signs from Rabbi Osher, the melamed, and probably knew by heart the entire tractate of "Kedushin" and "Gitin," though he was yet to be bar-mitzvahed.

The cheder boys also were greatly pleased that the Rabbi decided in my favor, and they agreed to select me for their "commander."

Every cheder in our shtetl had to have a commander, so that we could properly conduct wars among ourselves.

The commander himself didn't go into battle. He needed only to make his decision. Therefore the children were greatly pleased when I shouted "Right," "Left," just as the captain of the steamship "Aunt Fania" had done when we dragged it off the sandbar.

I was chosen as commander because I possessed such wondrous gauze (the so-called "iron cloth" of Kiev), which stops all bleeding. And as soon as a soldier in my army fell wounded in the battle against the enemy hordes of other schools I sutured his wound and, in effect, cured him on the spot with the yellow swabs of cotton, constantly stashed in my pocket.

Aside from these merits, which allowed Shmuel the Melamed to crown me as commander, I also knew the following secret: how to make artillery, which the other commanders could not provide.

My artillery had terrified the other schools more than the atomic bomb would come to strike fear in the nations of the world, which as of yet they did not possess.

The trick of how to make one's own artillery was taught by a go-getter who traveled on our steamboat from Svislovitch to Kiev to "eat days" at the home of rich relatives. He carried a key and a pack of matches with a thick wad of cotton. He would squeeze four or five matchsticks in the keyhole and then would fill it up with gauze.

Now, the go-getter told me the artillery was ready. One only needed to place a fire beneath it.

He struck a match and began to warm the key with the "ammunition." It didn't take very long when the key shot out of the gauze, as if it were a real bullet.

All the women took fright at this unanticipated noise on the steamship, and my mother began to scream, "Donya, Donya, where are you?"

I calmed my mother, telling her it was nothing; just a game which the Svislovicher yeshiva boy was playing with me.

A bit later I asked the boy the reason for such an awful game. He replied that as he is to travel to a new yeshiva "to eat days," he had to bring along a new trick; otherwise the school gang would not include him in its ranks and instead cover him with slaps.

And so it was I learned the great trick of making artillery, and it served me well when I became commander of Shmuel Melamed's school.

I armed all my soldiers with the key artillery, and as soon as our enemies at Aryeh Leib's school heard the booming of our heated weapons they scattered to their hideout, and the commander of Aryeh Leib's school surrendered on the spot.

He promised me five buttons and five pens for my artillery secret, but I had sworn an oath with my entire army that the secret of our new weaponry would not be disclosed.

It happens that in times past spies and provocateurs sold secrets to foreign powers, and wouldn't you know it, several days later Aryeh Leib's school began to shoot with artillery keys.

In one week, all the keys in Dukor's bookcases disappeared as did the matchsticks.

In the Dukor school there were 40-50 students and each wanted his own piece of artillery. Trade in artillery burgeoned because not all the boys were able to steal their mothers' keys.

The shtetl was seized by chaos. The women complained they couldn't open their drawers, teachers insisted that we, God forbid, might start a fire in the shtetl. We children were chastised until all the four commanders met at an assembly (now called a conference) and we decided to disarm our forces (would this were the case at the United Nations) and nearly all the keys returned to their drawers and cases. Only the commanders held on to their artillery because a "commander" without weapons hardly merits the title.

But I warned the other three that if anyone did not keep our pact I would stuff my key artillery not with gauze, but with my famous "iron cotton" from Kiev, and then my artillery would shoot like real iron!

So it was that I remained the strongest commander in all of Dukor, feared by all.

I BECOME COMMANDER

A disaster occurred once and mother took the commander to the cleaners.

It appears the Kiev professor had warned my mother that she needed from time to time to wash me all over, in order for the scrofula not to spread.

And where can a poor widow take her small orphan if not into the women's bathhouse?

One Friday, when all the Dukor wives and girls were at the bath, my mother dragged me along, and from then I was done as a commander.

Friday at mincha prayer all the boys in the synagogue knew I had been to the women's bathhouse and soon the nicknames began flying: "Donya the Jewess", "Donya with the women!..."

All my life I will never forget that black Friday. Among the boys I was finished as both commander and as a man.

My oath that I had seen nothing in the women's bathhouse counted for nothing. First, the steam was so thick that it cloaked everything and second, mother told me to keep my eyes shut because the green soap would blind me.

Now I can admit that I swore falsely then (what doesn't a commander/king do to save his throne?) I deliberately saw all that transpired in the women's bathhouse, although the green soap bit into my eager eyes.

I saw, namely, that even the girls of Dukor, as all women, have two breasts, which look like yeasty challahs with raisins in the middle.

From that time on I asked mother to bake two small challahs with raisins in the middle and I would make kiddush over them, much like an adult.

What only a child in distress and disarray can think up!

8

THE BIG ROBBERY

The thieves in our neighborhood had sniffed out that my mother had traveled as far as Kiev to visit a rich relative; surely she must have brought back a full container of goods. Now was the time to strike.

The first to observe the robbery was the herdsman of our shtetl. Positioned smack in the middle of the marketplace, he began to blow into his lead trumpet indicating that the women should milk the cows more quickly because he needs to drive the animals into the field.

As soon as mother heard his trumpet call, she would quickly do "negel wasser" (ritually wash her fingers) and would run with her pail into the barn to milk the cows.

No matter how many times I begged mother to wake me when the herdsman sounded his horn—I wanted at least once to see the sun rise from that side of the forest—she never did.

One summer dawn mother emitted such a cry that all the children jumped out of their beds to see what had happened.

Mother stood in the middle of the house with a pail in hand, shrieking that we had been robbed from head to toe.

It happened that both house doors were shut from the outside with locks so that they could not be opened from within.

The cow herd, the first to notice the locks on our doors, started to blow his horn in front of our windows, forewarning mother to see what was going on in our "storage space."

When mother looked there everything turned black in front of her eyes and she began shrieking as if a fire had broken out.

With great effort, the cowherd pulled out the locks from the external handles and only then were we able to notice how the thieves had gotten into our "storage space."

We realized that the thieves had burrowed out a big stone, which weighed at least a hundred pounds, and through the hole they entered the antechamber where our "storage space" was found brimming with leatherwork.

Mother's piercing scream soon brought the women running with their milk pails. As if in unison, the half-naked women began wailing, as if these choruses of heart-rending outbursts could help my unfortunate mother!

Mother's outcry brought forth a lot of the men of the shtetl running in various states of undress, and the atmosphere around our home became quite animated.

In the meantime, I had the good opportunity to see for the first time in my life how the sun rises on the other side of the forest and how the pre-dawn market brims with animal life.

I had no idea that our village streets possessed so many sheep and pigs that pasture together with our cattle. I was strongly drawn to the marketplace, where the cows mooed, the sheep bleated and the pigs squealed, each waiting for the cowherd. But I could not cleave away from mother, who was still standing with the empty pail in hand by the stone of our very own "western wall" and bewailing our bitter luck.

The Jews who surrounded us from all sides kept constantly consoling mother, that the robbery would surely be solved and the thieves, once caught and brought to trial, forever banished to Siberia.

We had to immediately awaken the "policeman" to track down the robbers as long as it wasn't too late, insisted one fringe-clad Jew.

Another Jew, who ran out of his house in his bare underpants, told mother that it must have been the thieves themselves who cast such a deep spell of sleep on us that we would hear nothing.

They have such a potent potion, the underpants-clad Jew continued, that when scattered over the windows under which one sleeps it's a wonder that one ever awakens. Indeed, we would be advised to first bentsch goymel (a blessing after surviving great peril) that we even came to.

But Yoel the cobbler, who was our great good friend and even greater sleuth, was the first to look for the robbers' traces. He noticed on the sand the traces of the thieves' footsteps and immediately pronounced that Yaacov the blacksmith, a big drunk, had a hand in the theft.

Only Yacubka the smithy has such big boots as these would indicate, he pointed out the footsteps etched in sand. He'd be the first that we'd go after, he coughed heatedly.

Meanwhile the policeman was awakened by the cowherd himself, who informed him of the great robbery in the shtetl.

The constable had already arrived in full uniform. The Jews moved to the side and allowed him to take good note of the burrowed stone in the big hole. Then the policeman went to investigate the emptied storage space and he closely examined the broken lock. The Jews and their wives tried to follow in his footsteps but he screamed that they not disturb him. So they all returned home. Only then did he enter our house and begin writing his report.

I sat myself down just opposite him to get the best view of how he goes about writing his report. I thought that should he need the commander of Shmuel Melamed's cheder, I would show quite accurately how to write a protocol report.

I was more than certain that once the policeman completed the protocol report mother would be helped. The robbery would be solved and the thieves would be deported to Siberia forever.

But in the beginning, to my utter dismay, the policeman didn't show any haste in writing his protocol.

He wrote a line or two while smoking a cigarette, and once again asked mother to enumerate precisely how many soles she had missing and how many items had gone wanting.

Teary-eyed, mother answered all his questions, but when she had to answer how much money the robbery cost she was too confused to calculate it in her head. She was used to making her calculations with a piece of chalk on a blackened tablet.

Mother rummaged through the drawers for the chalk, but if I wasn't scared of the policeman I would have told her that the night before, when she went off to milk the cow, I ate the piece of chalk.

So the policeman took a rough guess that the robbery came to 50 rubles, but mother insisted that fifty rubles would not cover the loss.

"Fine," he responded. "Let it be a hundred," he conceded while pulling a cigarette from his tobacco pouch.

Only then did I notice that the policeman's two long, sharp whiskers framed his proud face much as if a clock had two pointers indicating 2:45 p.m. even though the one on our wall indicated it wasn't even eight in the morning.

When mother heard that the policeman had evaluated our loss at a mere hundred rubles she again burst into tears. Looking at her frightened children, she began to ask the Lord, Creator of the World, that if the robbers were not found, she would have to leap from the bridge into the water.

"What will I do with you now, my orphans? Who will worry about your welfare?" Mother said, wringing her hands, but neither the children nor the policeman replied.

The cow's sudden mooing gave indication that she too intuitively understood our big misfortune.

The cow had been left unmilked all day and I so yearned for the half glass of warm liquid mother gave me after the milking.

Only by the afternoon did the policeman finish the protocol, which he would then send off to the authorities in Smilovitch, and only then would the search for the robbers begin in earnest in the surrounding villages.

As soon as the policeman left our house, people streamed in. Everyone brought something to eat: a herring, a pair of stuffed cabbage — like after a funeral, when everyone is sitting shiva.

Our house became quite merry. The children took to the food, and I kept boasting that I helped the policeman write the protocol.

If not for my new pen, which I had bartered in cheder for three buttons, the policeman would never have finished his protocol. His own leaked constantly, ruining three whole pages, a fact I kept reminding the people in the house.

Mother went to the other room to commiserate with her two older sisters, who had arrived to solace her.

My two aunts—Aunt Itka and Aunt Toybe—talked my mother into going the very next morning to Smilovitch to buy goods, some of which could be had on charity. When mother would return, if it pleased heaven, the robber would already have been caught.

Also other munificent people in Dukor brought mother offerings without charging any interest—at least thus she could continue to support her orphans.

I felt very proud that everybody in the shtetl proved so nice to us that even the Rabbi himself, the Rabbi Moshe Charney z"l, my grand uncle, came to console us.

"Don't lose hope, Brocha, you'll still live to see pride from your children. God is a father!" So said the Rabbi to my mother and she cried for joy, as everyone was proving to be so nice to her.

I too have the nature to cry for joy when I'm treated well, an inheritance from my late mother.

The next day after the big robbery the carriage driver took mother to buy goods in Smilovitch with the money that had been lent to us. I followed the wagon until Smilovitcher St. and reminded mother that she must, in the name of heaven, not forget to buy chalk in Smilovitch, because I had eaten the last piece.

My little mother said nothing. It appears she started crying while sitting on the wagon.

Did you ever see the heaving back of a crying mother?

9

I AM DROWNING

After the huge robbery at our home mother had to send her other two boys (Mulya and Bonya) to Berezin to "eat days" (take meals in the homes of strangers).

True, Osher the Melamed argued that mother should better send her two other sons to Minsk, where there was a bigger yeshiva than in Berezin. The teacher insisted that mother would have, God-willing, a great deal of pride from her two sons.

How Osher the Schoolteacher could have foreseen fifty years ago that my two elder brothers would become famous Jews is still today a riddle to me, but mother answered Reb Osher that in Berezin her children will have better "eating days" than in Minsk.

After all, father's brother lives in Berezin, my Uncle Munia, who is preparing to marry my sister, and he will see to it that his nephews and future brothers-in-law will have the best "eating days" in Berezin.

My two eldest brothers, Mendel and Zalke, were already in Berezin, and when they came home for Pesach they couldn't praise enough the good "eating days" they found there.

I too was in favor that my other brothers, Mulya and Bonya, should go to Berezin. My calculation was simple:

Insofar as mother will have her only daughter, Mirl, and her husband, Uncle Munia, as well as her four healthy sons in Berezin, she would then also move to Berezin with her "plague" of a son - that is to say, me.

I held Berezin to be far superior to Minsk, the latter lying in the small and shallow river, Svislovitch, much like Dukor, while

Berezin is on the big river Berezina, which empties into the Dnieper.

Ever since my water journey from Bobruisk to Kiev our hometown river, the "Svisle," had lost much of its appeal for me. Hardly worth the name of a river, with no steamboats and other vessels floating on it!

Summertime one could cross our native river practically by foot from one edge to another. The Svisle, in fact, had only a few deep spots, where the big boys, good swimmers all, could bathe.

My sick hand prevented me from swimming, and so I had to hug the shore and watch the others.

My elder brothers, Mulya and Bonya, were good swimmers. I remember Mulya enjoyed submerging himself into the deep recesses and grabbing a chunk of sand from the bottom, while Bonya swam far away.

Gazing at my brothers I would long to swim even if only for a little bit. I would enter the river up to my belly button and, using my elbows, created such frothy waves by stirring the waters that I could imagine I was actually swimming.

One time I actually took a swim, which nearly cost me my life. Aunt Chaya was at fault, the wife of my Uncle Feitel, the "Angel." If Aunt Chaya had not married Uncle Feitel, who was my mother's real brother, she wouldn't be my aunt.

I never liked Aunt Chaya the way I did my other aunts, who were my mother's direct sisters.

Until such time as my Uncle Feitel suddenly became a hermit in his own home, that's to say, to renounce this world and separate himself in a tiny room where he became an "angel," as he was known in our shtetl, Aunt Chaya succeeded in having three children, a son and two daughters, one named Frada and the other, the youngest, Masha.

God saw to it that Frada grew up to be wise and beautiful and Masha became an idiot or, plainly speaking, mad as all hell.

Because Masha was crazy, Aunt Chaya had a harder time marrying off Frada, her eldest daughter. Not all grooms were willing to be connected with a crazy sister-in-law.

But as soon as Aunt Chaya heard that my sister, Mirl, who was a bit younger than Frada, had already become a bride, she couldn't rest until her own gifted daughter would become as lucky.

I AM DROWNING

The groom was Bentsche from Smilovitch, a tall, healthy fellow, who one Friday arrived in Dukor to visit his bride.

He came to Dukor in a princely cart with a big wheel, an aristocratic looking horse, the kind that only Yona the Priest had kept in the stables of Dukor, the first-rank horses that are driven by top doctors and other muck-a-mucks.

The groom's horse made such a strong impression on me that I immediately agreed to the match. As Bentsche was to marry my cousin Frada, his horse became, as well, a kind of relative, and as a result I had a hold on the animal, including his tail.

Among us cheder boys it was a custom right before the coming of the Sabbath, when the Dukor cart drivers would bathe their horses, to grab hold of the animals' tails and swim along for the ride.

I did the same with Bentsche's horse, which had practically become my cousin, my next-of-kin. As soon as Bentsche drove his horse deeper into the river, I grabbed hold of the beast's tail with my healthy left hand and let myself swim off.

The groom didn't notice how I was swimming after him because he hopped on the horse's back, as befits a groom who wants to make a name for himself in town by employing big tricks. But as the horse was not from Dukor but rather from Smilovitch, it couldn't know the depth of our river, which required that animals swim for their life. He suddenly kicked me in the stomach, forcing me to let go of the tail and I began drowning.

While drowning, I could not stop thinking about my unfortunate mother. Woe upon woe, when she would find out that her "plague" of a child had drowned. How could she possibly endure it?! She would, heaven forbid, jump off the bridge into the water, just as she had told the policeman after the big robbery.

"Mother, save me. I won't bear it without you in the world to come! Oh, my poor mother!!" In such a manner did I shriek in the water as I submerged and then surfaced again and again.

A miracle that Leyb, Aunt Toybe's husband, who knew very well that I could not swim, would just in the nick of time see me drowning amid the turbulent waters and grab me safely to shore.

I was rolled in sheets, placed upside down, with my feet in the air and my head on the ground. They blew air into my nostrils and I was carried bareback, feeling as if I were tumbling off an unsaddled horse. I heard shouts and shrieks until a crying plea emerged from my lips:

"Dear mother, save me, save..."

All the naked people around me jumped for joy that I was actually speaking. Even Bentsche, the groom, jumped around on one foot as if he were trying to dry out his ear. He was happy that his horse had not killed me altogether. If the horse had struck me in the stomach with his backside and not with his forward hoofs I would have been a goner, by drowning. So did Kusha, the cart driver, a big family friend, declare authoritatively.

I still wonder how quickly mother found out about the gathering misfortune. She was standing over her Friday oven and hastened to get the cholent ready for the morrow. My two elder brothers were outside because they were preparing to go to Berezin. My one and only sister was off in a village street looking for some yellow sand to cover the swept floors. But mother somehow sensed while at the oven, as if through the medium of the holy spirit, that something was happening to her "plague." She ran out of the courtyard. "Donya, where are you?!" She then ran off to the marketplace, whereupon she saw all the people in the shtetl running to the river's edge. She asked everyone why they were running but no one answered her. So she herself sped off to the river's edge and screamed:

"Donya, where are you?"

But from the shtetl to the river was quite a distance! First you had to cross the entire length of River St. and then you have to traverse a field full of wild grass and only then do you come to the big bridge, where the men bathe.

The men soon heard my mother's screams across the length of the entire field. Several boys from my cheder ran towards her with the good news that I was still alive!

Mother fell into a faint. Both of us were scarcely alive at that point.

What a disturbed Sabbath it was! Mother kept constantly crying and said prayers over me:

"God of Abraham, God of Isaac and God of Jacob, take pity over my unfortunate orphan and put him back on his feet. Guard him and defend him from all misfortunes, he should grow up with Torah, marriage and good deeds and on and on...Amen!"

As it appears, mother's prayer was personal for she had recited it by heart.

On that Sabbath night the marriage between Bentsche and Frada took place in Aunt Chaya's house. Neither my mother nor I could be there, but while I couldn't be there I wouldn't have minded if the match had come apart.

Later I found out that Masha the Lunatic was opposed to the match of her elder sister. But about Masha I will have more to say in the following chapters.

10

MY UNCLE FEITEL THE ANGEL

In the previous chapter I already recounted that Aunt Chaya became my aunt only through marriage to Uncle Feitel, the "Angel." He was my mother's older brother, her only one residing in Dukor, but somehow she never managed to see him.

Only I had the fortune to see Uncle Feitel every day because he needed secret errands done for him, which I complied with.

Earlier, when my elder brothers were still in Dukor, they would serve him, but after the big robbery, with them having been sent off to Berezin and Minsk to "eat days," I remember I was the sole one to serve Uncle Feitel, the "Angel."

According to the nickname, which the shtetl had bestowed on him, my uncle, as you understand yourselves, was a holy man.

He had enough reason to become an "angel" because he was the twelfth generation of the Sheloh Hakodesh, who was named Rabbi Yeshaya Hurvitz. Uncle Feitel's family, like my mother's, was named Hurvitz.

So it was that mother's children were the thirteenth generation, the bar-mitzvah one of the Sheloh Hakodesh [a great rabbi born in 1558], and now it is clear to me why my two older brothers (S. Niger and B. Vladeck) became Yiddish writers and communal activists, as did I.

But fifty years ago I wasn't aware of our great pedigree. Therefore, I kept wondering why the shtetl had fixed my uncle with the sobriquet "Feitel the Angel."

I know that angels, who do not eat or drink, live in heaven, whereas Uncle Feitel, the angel, ate, drank and was firmly planted on earth.

My wonder became all the more intense when Uncle Feitel allowed the construction of what appeared to be a small sukkah without windows.

Besides his carpentry workshop, Uncle Feitel possessed a tailor, as well as a cobbler, workshop, where he would patch or sew his curious slippers and shoes.

His pants looked like a broad sack with a big hole on top and two smaller ones below, and his big leather shoes were a sight to behold.

When Uncle Feitel had to measure a pair of feet in order for the cobbler to make shoes, he would make the customer stand on a hard piece of carton and leave a stamp of his swollen feet which he would then very carefully cut out from the carton. Only then did I take the cut-out to the cobbler so he could match it with the right sole.

All the difficult jobs Uncle Feitel left for the afternoon. Between morning and afternoon, prayer took priority. Until noon he would be swathed in his prayer shawl and phylacteries [tefillin, worn on the arm during prayer] and take part only in sacred work. He peered into his holy books, of which he had written one himself.

His book was entitled "Sefer Hapolze" (with a soft "l"), that is to say, a book of great utility to the wider world.

His great great grandfather wrote a book entitled "The Two Stone Tablets" and as a result became the "Sheloh Hakodesh," and why should not the great great grandson, my Uncle Feitel, write such a book that would also benefit the whole world?

I never had the merit to peek into my Uncle Feitel's "Sefer Hapolze," and even if I had I wouldn't have understood a thing, but I heard later that Uncle Feitel had a genial idea how to study languages drawn from Rashi's "vernacular." [Rashi wrote a commentary on the Bible and Jewish law.]

Since Jews travel the wide world and need familiarity in various languages, one could set up an entire dictionary from Rashi's "vernacular," which would serve as a key to all the world's languages.

51

Uncle Feitel, himself, knew no more than two languages: the holy tongue [Hebrew] and jargon (at that time, the lowly name for Yiddish). But he didn't even need these two tongues, because he was a silent man.

Even as his servant I heard him emit only a few discrete words, and made out the rest by intuition.

In general, he was aureoled by an extraordinary stillness, such an eerie quiet that can throw you into a panic.

His old clothes, his books, papers and his body, which he scarcely ever bathed, had all absorbed the stale odors of the house, which itself was several centuries old.

In this very house Aunt Chaya had her store, and as soon as the door was opened a host of mingled odors were emitted which caused me to sneeze and cough. In one corner stood a large lead cover lit with a gas fire, and in another corner an open barrel of herring, and in yet a third, boxes of tobacco and snuff. On the shelves stood open cases with various kinds of spices, such as pepper, cinnamon, plants and saffron. On the other shelves were creams of various kinds, cordage and various manufactured goods which tickled the nose with their various odors.

All these odors found their way into Uncle Feitel's closed rooms, where the window was never opened, and as soon as I approached him I would explode in coughs and sneezes.

Uncle Feitel understood that he needed to give me his cigarettes.

Yes, I forgot to mention that Uncle Feitel was a big smoker. He would roll cigarettes from tobacco, shaped broad at the top and small at the bottom, which in the end would fit into the black hole of his burned-out wooden cigarette holder.

He would pay me for my yeoman labor with just these kinds of cigarettes, which I would later divvy up among my friends in cheder. Thus it was that at the age of ten I came to savor smoking.

My most difficult task came on the eve of Yom Kippur when I had to lead him to the mikveh (ritual bath). Everyone in the shtetl knew that once a year Uncle Feitel would appear in the street. It was clear that everyone, no matter their age or position, wanted to take a peek at Uncle Feitel, the Angel.

This very festive walk to the mikveh was, however, replete with dangers for Uncle Feitel, the biggest peril being a woman crossing his path and rendering him entirely impure.

The path to the bathhouse was quite a distance. First you had to cross the entire marketplace, then the length of the river road, and only then would you reach the bathhouse, where the only mikveh in all of Dukor could be found.

But on Yom Kippur eve there was great motion, especially on the riverbank street where the Rav, my great grand uncle, Reb Moshe Charney z"l (may his memory be for a blessing), could be found.

Many wives and girls would run to him brimming with questions about all manner of sacrifices; others would rush to purchase Yom Kippur memorial lights and yet others would come to pay their debt for the candles, all of which seemed to keep the rabbi afloat.

My duty was to run ahead of Uncle Feitel and warn all the women and girls to clear the way for him as he heads to the mikveh.

Understandably, I took great pride in my task. I derived great pleasure that all the females of Dukor listened to me and hid out in the courtyards, so that Feitel the Angel, heaven forfend, not become impure.

I would notice, however, that the women and girls would stare out from all the windows. They winked and laughed that Uncle Feitel proceeded so slowly and cautiously with his thick, wooden-like feet, thick as those of an elephant.

I would return the wink, as if hinting that their behavior was out of line, after all, the very idea of mocking an angel on the eve of Yom Kippur as he heads to the mikveh on his annual ritual bath! Yet, at the very same time I would be impelled by the profane thought: what would become of my Uncle Feitel if he were suddenly accosted by a bevy of naked girls and women as I had seen them when my mother had taken me into the women's bathhouse?

Uncle Feitel would surely have lost his mind on the spot, just as his daughter Masha had turned mad from excessive piety.

Shtetl comedians would recount that years ago, before my Uncle Feitel became an "angel," a dog had bitten him—and the dog became rabid. From that point on my Uncle Feitel became a recluse, separated from his wife and children, and had begun to write the "Sefer Hapolze."

Aunt Chaya, it appears, did not care that her husband had put a distance between the two of them and had turned into an "angel." On the contrary, she was proud of her holy husband as she was proud of her youngest child, Masha, who had gone totally nuts.

I also took great interest in Uncle Feitel and Masha, both of whose talk sounded as if "God's speech tripped off their lips," in the words of Aunt Chaya.

As it appears, I had become a bit infected by the magpie insanity that prevailed in Aunt Chaya's house—otherwise how would I ever have become a writer among Jews?

What else to make of this?

11

MASHA THE LUNATIC

An urban lunatic once observed that the whole world is crazed, but as he cannot run after the whole world, better it run after him. I think a bit of the truth inheres in this cracked notion.

Did we not see not so long ago how the entire world followed an Austrian maniac until he turned the globe into a madhouse?

Pursuing a lunatic itself is a piece of madness!

Modern psychologists say that in our day everyone is at some point and at some place a bit cracked. But the psychologists themselves are after all just human beings and are subject to the same distemper.

I knew a psychoanalyst in Paris who at home was a real nutcase, beating his wife and cursing the Holy Mother despite going to church every Sunday. His name became known far and wide in part because he would have the temerity to charge no less than three hundred franks for a visit, as if he were Sigmund Freud himself.

It appears that one and the same person can at a certain point be a big thinker and researcher and at another crazy and brain-addled.

The real reason for madness has yet to be clarified. It is anecdotally recounted that in one madhouse two young people were confined in separate rooms, one having lost his mind over a woman who declined to marry him and the other precisely because he had wed her.

Also, in this anecdote inheres a bit of truth. One becomes crazy from too much loneliness and poverty, while the other from an excess of luxury and good fortune.

All these ideas and notions have come to the tip of my pen because I am about to describe my cousin Masha, the daughter of Uncle Feitel, the "Angel," whom I have described in the previous chapter. Then, some fifty years ago in Dukor, we had no idea of the "unconscious" or the "superconscious," and had no notion of the sex drive and other impulses which now vex the whole world.

We only knew that Dukor must possess its own lunatics—if only to enliven shtetl life. God had sent along Masha, turned mad because of her lack of a "superconscious" and the presence of a very ample "unconscious."

One dark Sabbath eve my Uncle Feitel, the "Angel," suddenly took ill. He had to be brought quickly from home to the town's non-Jewish medic. Masha was sent after the medic. A fearsome downpour fell outside and a mist enveloped the shtetl. In front of Kadar St. the white stone church stood with its three rounded cupolas reaching to the sky. A tile tore off one of the cupolas and the angry wind kicked it around in the dark night. Masha imagined that witches were dancing on the church's steeple. Somehow she wandered into the church but quickly exited, screaming at the top of her lungs, "Shema Yisrael" [Hear Israel, the Lord our God the Lord is one.]

As she ran from the witches, she slipped and fell into the mud in a faint. Passersby brought her home with foam flecked on her lips and eyes glassed over.

When Masha came to she invented a total lie about the non-Jewish medic: that he had raped her. Just near the church, right in the mud, he had violated her and the devils danced their wedding round on the church's steeple. From then the entire shtetl began to speak of "Masha the Lunatic."

Understandably, neither Uncle Feitel nor Aunt Chaya could bear such a nickname. The fanatical Aunt Chaya would instead insist that "God's speech trips off Masha's lips," that her daughter is sadly made a sacrifice to the shtetl's sins.

If not for Elke Aryeh Yitzhaks, the aristocrat who wanders around in a small forest behind Dukor with strange men, Masha, she insisted, would be as clear-headed as the other Jewish daughters of Dukor. And while looking at her mother, Masha the Lunatic would demonstrate to all who cared to watch how Elke Aryeh Yitzhaks sinned with the strangers in the small forest.

In truth, Elke Aryeh Yitzhaks was an honest, upstanding Jewish daughter like all the other women in Dukor whose husbands were foresters and would come home only for the major Jewish holidays —Pesach and Sukkus.

Aryeh Yitzhak himself, Elke's husband, was a nice, intelligent man, who read the paper "Hamelitz" and he didn't care at first if his wife meandered in the summer dusk with the teacher Zalman, who taught Russian to young cheder students and whose wife would invite guests during the winter nights to drink tea from the samovar.

Even I myself would often drop by with my mother to Aryeh Yitzhak's for a cup of tea, and mother would take a donation for the Duzhitzer market.

But Masha the Lunatic would stir up everybody by claiming that as a result of Elke Aryeh Yitzhak's misdeeds, young children were dying in the shtetl and thus her father, Feitel the "Angel," could summon the Messiah.

Itke Masha Zeligs, a neighbor of Aunt Chaya's, a huge impoverished woman who would come into Aunt Chaya's shop for a taste from the herring barrels, the likes of which are incomparable, once said to Aunt Chaya that according to her understanding of things Masha needed to be wed quickly; only then would sanity return to her distressed mind.

I happened then to be in Aunt Chaya's shop when Itke Masha Zeligs offered the following piece of advice: I should run off to my friends in cheder and bid that they help find a groom for Masha or else she would descend into total madness.

The entire cheder quickly realized that no sane person could possibly marry Masha. Therefore, it was up to us to find a maniac who would agree to this sort of match. We hit upon the idea that the best groom for Masha was in fact Moshe Zelig, the elder son of Itke Masha Zeligs.

The fellow would wander over the shtetl all day long empty-handed and hungry. He would do odds and ends, help widows carry water jugs or chop wood, for which he was paid with a snack. We conceived the idea that this very Moshe Zeligs would enjoy being wed to Masha. He would in fact fall into a vat of fat, consume a whole herring every day with a full pot of skinned potatoes to boot.

However, Moshe Zeligs absolutely would not consider such a match.

"What, am I so crazy as to wed a lunatic?" he would say, slipping through our fingers.

"Oy Moshe Zeligs, what do you care if you wed Masha?" we pleaded with him.

"You won't need to go house to house chopping wood and you both will be called 'Moshe-Masha,' the sound of which is music to the ears. You will be honored with maftir (the honored last reading of the weekly biblical chapter)."

But no matter how appealing our offer, he managed to slip away with a trick, declining ever to become part of "Moshe-Masha."

"Children, you know what? I will show you a trick: how iron floats on water," Moshe Zeligs tried convincing us.

"Get out of here, you nutcase; how can iron float on water?" all the cheder kids shouted in one hurrah.

"Just give me a glass of water, a piece of paper and a needle and you will immediately see how iron floats on water," Moshe Zeligs announced, standing his ground.

When we gave him all three, he very carefully placed the piece of paper into the glass of water and on the paper he placed the needle and shouted: "Aha, here you see how iron floats on water!"

We would shout derisively, "This you consider a trick—such a trick any of us can pull off!"

Then Moshe Zeligs tried distracting us with a ditty which he alone thought up.

"Just listen, children," he said as he began the melody of "Akdomos" by Elke Aryeh Yitzhaks/ "the pantry is locked/and Masha the Lunatic consumes everything/" By Elke Aryeh Yitzhaks "/the very roof shakes/And Masha the Lunatic/Imagines them ghosts."

I too would chime in, although Masha the Lunatic was my cousin. Now that I know all the modern theories about the "unconscious" and "superconscious" I realize that she was a victim of both complexes.

From her mother, Aunt Chaya, Masha got her "unconscious," which constantly foraged for sins in the shtetl, and from her father, my uncle Feitel the "Angel, she received her superconscious, which was always engaged with the divine.

Looking at her father, Masha turned madly pious. So, for example, every Sunday when the neighboring non-Jews would stream in from the surrounding villages to make their purchases, she twisted towels to cover her hands. Then she used this stratagem to better cover her mouth and nose up till her eyes in the belief that non-Jews shoot forth swinish elements, and she, for one, didn't want, God forbid, to become impure.

Following her father, Masha also began to smoke. She heard that it was a good antidote to dental pain, but she couldn't even roll a cigarette the way Uncle Feitel had been able to do. She would take a bronze pipe, fill it with tobacco, kindle it and draw on it as if from the fumes of a smokestack.

When her older sister, Frada the Bride, saw how Masha filled the entire house with smoke, she began screaming that she could, heaven forbid, start a fire.

By then Masha turned uncontrollably wild and screamed across the entire length of the marketplace that Frada would once again go into the back rooms and whisper to her groom.

Masha could be heard screeching amid columns of cigarette smoke. "As if Elke Aryeh Yizthaks hadn't suffered enough, she now has to have Frada whispering to a strange man," she ranted. I must admit that when Masha got infuriated and lost it she would appear prettier than usual—an oval rosy face with two hot flashing eyes and a high bosom, often unbuttoned.

For this reason alone I loved for Masha to speak her mind. No one held it against her for uttering the bare truth.

She even insulted her parents to the nth degree.

"Mother is mad and father is off his rocker," she often complained to me.

And she had a point!

How does our folk saying go: "Crazy geese, crazy goslings." If the parents are mad the children will follow suit.

12

MY MOTHER'S TASTY MEALS

I saw my elder brothers only twice a year: Sukkus and Pesach. All year long they "ate days" somewhere in Berezin or in Minsk, but on the major holidays they'd return home and quicken to mother's meals.

My mother was no ordinary cook and she could whip up finger-licking-good dishes.

Our main staple was, as always, potatoes, but mother made a different dish each day and we didn't feel as if we were just eating potatoes yet again.

For example, she'd prepare on Sunday a huge dish of unpeeled potatoes. This despite the fact that she was busy in the shop on Sunday on account of the peasants from the surrounding villages who blundered their way into her shop for a piece of leather or for some soles.

Mother forewarned us to keep an eye out for these characters because of their ugly habit of stealing.

When the sheriff himself arrived, mother warned us to watch him like a hawk because he had the ugly habit of lifting things with his tin box.

So, in general, on Sundays mother lacked the time to prepare special meals. So we made do eating unpeeled potatoes. We would pull the thin peels off and then dunk the spud into the "sauce," which I obtained from Aunt Chaya's herring barrel.

If one eats potatoes with herring sauce, it's almost like eating them with herring itself.

On Monday, mother would already peel the potatoes but before she placed the platter of spuds on the table, she would first pour out the water from the pot and put it closer to the fire so the potatoes would emerge bronzed with delicious roseate cheeks. What a pleasure it was to bite into them! These dried potatoes, each a creation unto itself, contained a lot of heat. Therefore, mother gave each of her children a scoop of sour cream; no greater treat can be had than to cool hot potatoes in cold sour cream.

Tuesday, mother would again cook a huge platter of peeled potatoes, but this time she mashed them and mixed in poppy seeds.

Have you ever eaten potato kasha with poppy seeds? Try it and you will thank me for it.

On Wednesday mother would cook a stew of fish and potatoes. Instead of fish she would throw into the pot a pair of "tarhanas," —ten to the pound. Each of us would get an entire plate of fish-potato stew and a tough sinewy piece which contained a remnant as hard as wood, even when cooked.

You see I do not recommend this dish for tasting because it needs an iron stomach and I dare say none of my readers possesses such anymore!

On Thursday mother had already purchased meat for Sabbath. She would then prepare a meat-potato stew. The meat she kept for the Sabbath feast, but Yasha the butcher gave her a heap of good marrow-filled bones which fattened the potatoes. Enough marrow remained in the bones, allowing my older brothers to suck them out into a spoon.

Other than the above-mentioned potato dishes, mother prepared other important meals, which melted into our limbs.

Did you hear, for example, of a dish called a "hen's head"?

Yes, in America you may well have heard of "kop hon" and maybe even had the occasion to eat it, but for mother kop hon from the start went with the hen or rooster.

Mother made it from the pieces of baked bread which she had gathered over the week. Once the container became full, she'd pour water into it and cooked the dried out rinds until they turned into a liquid brown mush.

The hen's head tasted a bit tangy but if one held a piece of sugar in one's teeth, one consumed a whole plate and would feel sated until dinner.

True, afterwards one's stomach was uproarious, as if ten hens were crowing at once, but by dinnertime the hubbub would still.

What such a dinner consists of during the week I still don't know to this very day. Sometimes supper would amount to a piece of bread with dried preserves, at times a piece of bread smeared with butter and yet it might even be a glass of milk with an "akraitshik."

When I approached mother and asked her to give us a real dinner, she would ask me:

"What would you like my child, heaven's plate or perhaps marzipans?"

By then I would be satisfied with a slice of bread with honey.

In summer, mother would cook another of her specialties which looked like "kop-hon" but to the former one did not need a sugar cube.

Every Rosh Chodesh mother would bake in oil flour-based blinis.

I would plead with God that Rosh Chodesh never fall on Friday or Saturday, when the house would already be brimming with foodstuffs.

Every Friday morning, when mother took out the challahs and rolls, she would dish out butter and sour cream and we dunked hot pieces of freshly-baked challah in the fat stew. The challah would slither unchewed into our stomachs. True, at times this led to stomach aches, but it was worth it!

On Friday nights the famous onion dish, "tzibulnitza," would be served up. This is a regional specialty, native to Byelorussia and Lithuania. I am more than sure that if Galitzianers would eat at minimum ten years without a stop every Friday our "tzibulnitza" they would become forevermore Litvaks.

I know that there are many Galitzianers among my readers. I will, therefore, narrate how "tzibulnitza" is made and they, once and for all, will free themselves of their Viennese pretensions (every Galitzianer insists he comes from Vienna!)

Take a moderately large container, fill it to the brim with several dozen onions of average size and then stick in a pound of fat meat (the fatter the better), put in an old honey cake left over from a circumcision or from a wedding, pour in a little pinch of salt and several pieces of sour salt, cover it with water, but not too much, and then put the pot deeper into the oven right after one has taken out the Sabbath challahs. Even better, surround the pot on all sides with "zhar," with glowing coals striped with ash. This source of heat never permits the "tzibulnitza" to overrun the rim, but quietly simmers until miraculously a very hot, fatty and brown liquid appears which looks like heated honey. The pleasure of dunking pieces of challah into this liquid gives us a quintessential pleasure of Shabbes.

I forgot to add that one needs to add a little bit of sugar, but not more than a pinch because an onion, no matter how bitter, has the nature to sweeten the longer it is cooked.

So it was that before the onset of Friday eve we would already have dunk pieces of challah which had been baked for the entirety of the Sabbath.

True, these dunkings led us boys to get stomach swellings and ulcers which would need removal, but in the end it was worth it! Even to this very day I would gladly eat mother's "tsibulnitza," risking even getting a new ulcer.

I want to add that mother kept hidden the piece of fat "tzibulnitza" meat until the morning of the big Sabbath meal. Just like the carrot-meat, it's best to cut it while cold into thin slices, spread it out on a big platter, edged with small heaps of pepper and raw onions. "Tzibulnitza" meat demands to be eaten with raw onions and pepper.

After this wonderful appetizer, mother served the cholent, the kugel and plum compote, which would be superfluous to describe as explanations abound in every Yiddish cookbook.

According to how much my elder brothers enjoyed mother's cooking, I surmised that eating days among strangers is not, in fact, such a big deal.

I would marvel how my diminutive mother could whip up all these scrumptious foodstuffs for all her six children and still be able to conduct her business. I do not recall that she ever hired a maid to wash the floors or to scrub the oven.

Only once a year, on the eve of Pesach, she did hire Catherine the Great (so she was named) to wash all the floors, tables, bed, chairs, as well as the wooden shelves in the kitchen. This Catherine was very tall and thickset and could be found knee-deep in river water, beating laundry with a stick.

It was said in our shtetl that when Catherine the Great froze her bare feet on the eve of Pesach she would get a sore throat by

Shavuos, so long did it take for the cold in her case to reach from bottom to top [52 days].

In a matter of two days, Catherine the Great would make our home kosher for Pesach. When she finished all her work she would fill the house with straw.

But just on the eve of Pesach the widow Chana Zoriger, the real balabusta of our house, would bring along her children — two daughters and her youngest, Moshe Arnike. She had inherited the property from her late husband, who died in middle age in the house where we were all born. Mother paid Chana Zoriger twenty rubles rent a year.

On all the major holidays, such as Rosh Hashana, Yom Kippur, Sukkus and Pesach, Chana Zoriger and her children descended on us in order to be together with Jews. Her youngest, Moshe Arnike, who grew up in the village, would hide out in a corner and I would not play with him.

Chana Zoriger would be very annoyed that her only son, an orphan, the supposed true heir of the house in her estimation, felt like a stranger in his own home.

Chana Zoriger placed her youngest smack in the middle of the house, unbuttoned his fly and urged him on "Pish, Pish, Moshe Arnike, it's after all your home!" And Moshe Arnike didn't have to be asked twice.

13

ASCEND, RAV ZEV WOLF, SON OF YOEL

Such was my late father's name. I personally don't remember him. He died, as you know, right after my birth. He was then about 38 years old.

Why did he pass away so young? Until today I still do not know the answer.

And what difference does it make what it is that buries a man. The essential thing is, be it a long or short life, that he accomplish some tangible thing by which he will be remembered!

I can say with great pride and pleasure that my father left a good name. He is remembered until today in a positive light. Among my readers in America are some shtetl natives who still remember him, and have written to me charming letters in which they describe my father's goodness and great spirit, for which I thank them.

I recently summoned a "conference" of my two older brothers Mendel (from Paterson NJ) and Shmuel (from Brooklyn) and inquired as to what they recalled about our father.

My brother Shmuel still remembers the tragic day of my father's death: Friday just before the lighting of the Sabbath candles, just ten days before Shavuos (39 days in the counting of the omer).

Shmuel was no more than five years old, but he remembers quite vividly being sent to the synagogue to inform the worshipers that his father had just died. The outcry and chaos in the synagogue were unforgettable.

My older brother, Mendel, who was then nine years old, remembered discrete details that left a lasting impression on him. For example, he informs me that our grandfather, Rav Yoel, commanded our mother to light the Sabbath candles, as was customary every Friday evening, but with one fewer candle. Generally, mother was accustomed to bless eight lights; two for her husband and herself and six for the children. But from that Friday on she blessed only seven, not eight.

Right after the kindling of the candles grandfather Rav Yoel went to the synagogue to bring in the Sabbath, and when he returned home after the prayer of Maariv he made kiddush on the two uncovered challahs. We ate the Sabbath meal as if nothing had happened.

My older brother is still amazed at mother's bravery: she followed her father-in-law every step of the way and did not disturb the holy Sabbath with a widow's cries and sobs.

The funeral took place after Sabbath. All of Dukor showed up at the cemetery, which was illuminated with burning brands.

My brother Mendel still remembers that father was a great Chabadnik on the Lubavitcher nusakh. For fifty rubles father added a part to the shul named a "Chabadnitza," where he prayed daily until after noon. He didn't have his own synagogue.

In this very "Chabadnitza" the Torah was read every Sabbath and on holidays. The best aliyas would go to the Jews sitting at the Western wall, i.e., artisans, drivers, indeed all manner of people.

As it appears, father was a folks person, and for that reason the common man loved him greatly.

As Father dealt in leather, he was especially tight with the cobblers in Dukor and often loaned them money. When one gives material on loan one typically gets collateral in return, which eventually is paid out.

Father firmly opposed the giving of security. But Yoel the cobbler, who every evening between the hours of mincha and maariv prayers heard a chapter of "Ein Yaacov," insisted that collateral must be taken from him.

"If one stops taking collateral, it's virtually the end of the world," Yoel the cobbler insisted.

Father finally had to give in and took security from Yoel; it consisted of Yoel's Sabbath gabardine, which had been sewn for his marriage ceremony, a worn, fifteen-year-old garment.

Father hung the cloth deep inside the closet, but every Friday after candle lighting Yoel the cobbler would come in his scruffy clothes, throw off his outer weekly garment with its patched elbows and slip into his long Sabbath gabardine, which covered his underwear, black and shiny as coal.

Father would then say, "Good Shabbes to you, Yoel."

Yoel would reply, "Good Shabbes, Good Year!" and the two would set forth in quiet, Sabbath-like footfalls to welcome the holy day.

Right after maariv, the nightly prayer at the conclusion of the Sabbath [on Saturday], Yoel would return to our house, meticulously disrobe the collateral and hang it back in the closet. When Father had concluded the havdalah, Yoel would sit down at the table and smoke one cigarette after another to cover the smoke deficit he had accrued over the entire length of the Sabbath [when smoking was prohibited]. Mother would serve tea and sweet things, which is fitting for a "melava malke" (a post-Sabbath feast). Yoel would always savor those evenings following the Sabbath.

When either an engagement, a marriage, or circumcision or just any old joyful occasion came around, Yoel would come in the middle of the week to father to claim his "security."

This went on for years. Father had to protect the "security" from mother. Every month he would have it dusted and every pre-Pesach he would air it out in the fresh sunlight and knock out the dust that had accumulated within its folds.

But when father began to weaken and take ill he once said to Yoel the cobbler: "You know what, why don't you take your 'security' home. You see I can barely stand on my feet. I simply don't have the strength to attend to your 'security.' Whatever might possibly happen, better it be with you."

This proposal greatly flustered Yoel.

"But, after all, Velvel, I owe you so much money. If I were to take away the 'security,' then it would, heaven forbid, be the end of the world." [Velvel was a nicknake for Daniel's father, deriving from his middle name, Wolf.]

67

Father consoled Yoel that he would not, God willing, renege on his debt.

"With 'security' or without one, you will have with what to pay out the debt; if God forbid you don't, we'll settle the score in the world to come…"

They bargained so long until Father convinced Yoel to make an exchange for the entire debt and be done with it.

Yoel's promissory note for one hundred rubles and some other monies were stashed away by mother in her usual hiding places kept from me, her plague-ridden one. This would be my only inheritance from my father.

When I once asked mother why she kept worthless scraps of IOUs she replied that she didn't want to mix into the Lord's calculations. She knew that Yoel's children had left for America and it might even happen they might well pay out the debt.

It actually came to pass in 1941 when I managed to escape occupied Paris for New York a delegation of the Dukor landsmanshaft offered me a grand gift, a very fine gold watch. Heading the delegation was its president, Nahum Rosen, the son of the late Yoel the cobbler.

When I proudly displayed the gold watch for the Rabbi of our shtetl, a relative of mine whose name is known and beloved in rabbinical circles far and wide arising from his penning a sacred book, Rabbi Nissan Telushkin told me: "You see, your mother was right in the end! Yoel's son remembered his father's debt of fifty years standing!"

In so doing the Rabbi told the above-mentioned story of Yoel the cobbler, which was very characteristic of my father, the Chabadnik.

But the Rabbi didn't know my father personally. When Rabbi Telushkin became the rabbi of our shtetl my father had already passed on a decade before, but Dukor Jews kept on telling the various stories and ideas of my late father.

Rabbi Telushkin, who assumed the rabbinic chair from my grand uncle, the late Dukor spiritual leader, Rabbi Moshe Charney, had imbibed all these many tales and legends of the Charney family in Dukor and brought them all the way to Brooklyn.

True, the Charney family does not spring from Dukor proper but from Berezin, and Bereziners have always had a good name over the world.

Bereziner lumber merchants, who knew how to unite scholarship and commerce and who were the crux of the trade for many centuries spanning the Black Sea, came to serve as central players in the commerce that linked the Black Sea to the Baltic Sea. Regarding the curious "Bereziner" system, much adequate information can be obtained in all Russian encyclopedias. I am proud to say that the Bereziner system greatly enriched the lumber trade in Russia, a fact permanently recorded in the annals of Russian history.

I am actually also very proud that my mother originates from Berezin, and draws her lineage from the "Sheloh Hakodesh." [Rabbi Isaiah Halevi Horowitz, a Jewish scholar born in Prague in 1558 who died in Israel in 1628].

Thanks to the matchmaking system between Berezin and Dukor my parents brought forth five sons, three of whom set sail across the broad and deep expanse of wisdom, knowledge and understanding.

The names of these sons: S. Niger, B. Vladeck and me, the humble Daniel Charney.

14

MY BROTHERS AND SISTER

Now that you know a bit about my parents I will introduce you to my elder four brothers and my sole sister, who was the eldest of us all.

My mother found it advantageous that her sole daughter was older than her five sons. When mother became a widow my sister, Mirl, was about twelve or thirteen, in a position to be of great domestic help.

At that time my sister proved to be well-learned, although I don't until this very day know when and how she found the time to write and read so well.

When she became an orphan at the age of thirteen she had to care for her five brothers, each smaller than the next, like five fingers of a hand.

When I turned about six or seven my sister became a bride. Although she wrote her own bridal letters to her prospective groom in Berezin—to our uncle—she found time to write letters for the other brides-to-be in Dukor.

I very much enjoyed listening in as my sister read out loud the bridal letters which she wrote to other grooms. The bride-to-be, who would listen to my sister's letter written in her name to her respective groom, would often break down in tears and then warmly thank my sister for having so finely and precisely laid out on paper her passionate feeling to her groom, may he be blessed.

Some typical lines: "If you are my sun, as you write to me in your letters, I am your sleepless, restless moon counting the days until we will be together, be united…"

Just so did my sister, Mirl, write to the unknown grooms of the Dukor brides-to-be, although I then did not quite comprehend how the sun and the moon "could be together."

My sister would never read out loud her own letters to her groom in Berezin, who was father's brother, and I still do not know what she wrote to him every other day.

I would only see the envelopes and their addresses, from which I discovered that my uncle was named Kazna Samuel Yevelovitch Charney, which is to say that he was Shmuel and that his father was named Yoel, although all of Berezin used to call him "Munia Genenders" (after our grandmother).

When I once asked my sister why she writes our grandfather's name on the envelope, considering that he passed on long ago, she explained that in Berezin there is yet another person with the name Shmuel Charney, and were she not to write "Yevelovitch" the letter carrier might deliver it to the other like-named Jew.

At that time I imagined how confused and frightened the other Shmuel Charney of Berezin would have been if he received a letter from my sister about the orbits of moon and stars of Dukor, awaiting their sun to arrive from distant Berezin.

Sadly, my sister never had enough time to spend with me because she had to pay attention to my older brothers, prepare meals, clean the house and mend clothes.

Mother would constantly run about the shtetl seeking out charity and conducting her business.

True, my elder brothers helped out in the store. Mother would buy out the felts, or "ososkei," as they were called by us, which needed to be dried.

My brothers would cut ears out of the "ososkoi" and stick pins in those spots where the felt would wrinkle (faldev-en).

I, too, would eagerly approach the bovine felts, but my older brothers would discourage me because I might, heaven forbid, injure my hand, and I only had one healthy one from the outset.

My older brothers, Mendel and Zalke, no longer lived at home but, rather, "ate days" in Berezin.

All of my brothers returned home for the major holidays. My mother didn't allow me to dally in the sukkah because my circumcision, which had originally taken place there, provoked a years-long cold. For me Sukkus became a disturbed holiday.

But on Pesach mother would preside at the Seder table together with all my brothers, and I even possessed my very own wine cup, which I still long for today.

My blue wine cup had a white crystal-like glass handle. I would kiss the cup as if it were a younger sister of mine who visits but once a year.

My older brother Mendel would lead the seder, and he would turn to me to ask the four questions, as if he were my father.

Three of the five sons resembled our father, namely the eldest, Mendel, and Boruch (Vladeck), the youngest of my older brothers. I too strongly resembled my father, while the middle two brothers —Zalke and Shmuel (Niger)—more closely resembled mother. Father was just slightly taller than average height, thin, with a somewhat longish face, whereas mother was short with a round face and two luminous "Tzena Rena" eyes.

The brothers who resembled father were more imaginative and extroverted and possessed grand ideas, while the brothers resembling mother were quieter and more introverted.

So, for example, my brother Boruch would sing by heart all manner of songs and was more nimble at playing nuts than the other brothers who resembled mother.

My brother Shmuel, for example, would always sit apart and peer into a book. He worried that at Pesach our small river might, heaven forbid, entirely dry out because during this festive holiday people drank a lot of tea drawn from samovars, which used river water.

But my brother Shmuel had a friend named Bentsche Moteh Berezhankers, a sort of philosopher, who calmed him by explaining that our river, the Svisle, could never dry out because in nature there was a law, "the eternal recurrence," that is to say that all the waters emitted by humans and animals were purified in the earth, refilled the underground caverns from which they then streamed forth to all the rivers.

How Bentsche Berezhankers discovered some fifty years ago some of nature's secrets remains a mystery. I only know that he became a philosopher because his house stood opposite an old Russian cemetery, nearly bereft of monuments, which not all the Dukorers had the courage to cross when night fell.

It once happened on a dark night, when Bentsche retired home, he suddenly saw a profusion of lights in the Russian school building which adjoined the cemetery. How macabre that the Russian dead conducted a midnight ball, and that one naked female with a cross on her neck had winked at Bentsche to enter the school and participate in a dance of death. From that point on Bentsche became a philosopher and a big pessimist, as he would be described down to our own day.

His past pessimism expressed itself in his blackening his galoshes bought him for Pesach in order that their sheen not pierce his eyes. He became the best friend of my brother Shmuel, and the two would philosophize hours long on lofty matters while we kept on warbling Pesach songs and playing with nuts.

One song especially appealed to me and I would sing along, although I didn't then understand all its curious words.

The first lines began this way: "In the land of the pyramids/An angry and evil king reigned/And all the Jews waited there/Pharaoh's servers, Pharaoh's slaves."

Mother gleaned much pride when she heard the choir of children's voices tinkling through the shtetl, whereas all the other Dukor women were bitten by jealousy of her and her fine, blessed children.

Only I, the youngest, was a bit cursed, but during the festive Pesach days I would mix with my older brothers and forget that I was plague-ridden and a schlimazel.

Mother's wondrous plum tzimmes with potatoes would quiet my pain. I would entreat God that Pesach last at least until Shavuos, when the world turns green and beautiful, when one is more outside than in.

Dukor's public spaces were lovely, especially when I had enough friends and cronies on practically every street with whom I could play, as if I were entirely healthy, with no cares.

15

MY UNCLES AND AUNTS

On the last day of Pesach our synagogue would recite "yizkor" for the dead. All the Dukor boys whose parents were alive exited the synagogue during this mournful prayer. Only I and my four older brothers would remain with the adult Jews in the building and say kaddish for our father, who had passed away early on in life.

I was proud that I was allowed to remain in the synagogue with all the older Jews, while all the school-aged children were made to wait, pitifully, in the courtyard until the conclusion of the kaddish.

I didn't feel like an orphan when I said yizkor. After all, I had never known my father. Mother, however, gazing down from the women's balcony and watching her five children reciting the prayer for the dead, would burst into tears, as if she had just found out that she was a widow.

I would follow my older brothers in saying, "May God remember the soul of my father and my teacher Zev-Wolf, son of Yoel." I was suffused with the feeling that my father now resided in paradise with all the patriarchs and matriarchs—Abraham, Isaac, Jacob, Sarah, Rebecca, Rachel and Leah—as it says in the Yizkor prayer, and would be served in the middle of an average celestial week such delicacies as the leviathan and the heavenly ox, swallowed by flagons of heavenly nectar.

My father, after all, now dwells in paradise and has it all fine and dandy, but on the last day of Pesach mother would descend teary-eyed from the women's balcony. Just looking at her deeply saddened me.

I knew that soon after Pesach all my older brothers would leave home for an entire semester and life at home would turn lonesome. I also knew that my only sister would marry my uncle in Berezin on the Sabbath after Shavuos and then mother would be left alone with me, her shlimazel!

Precisely because mother would turn very sad on the last day of Pesach we would spend the entire time visiting our aunts and uncles, who received us with open arms.

We had three uncles and three aunts in Dukor: Uncle Feitel was my mother's brother and was nicknamed by the shtetl "Feitel the Angel," of whom I've written in a previous chapter.

We didn't stay very long with this uncle, although Aunt Chaya offered us nice delicacies. First off, we took fright of their daughter, "Masha the Lunatic," who could blow her top and start screaming that we were wolfing down all their good food. I want to add parenthetically that we did not eat much at Aunt Chaya's because her Pesach treats smelled moldy, which filled their half-sunken house with an overripe odor. Also, Uncle Feitel emitted a moldy smell, as from a copper pot gone green. We were happy when mother took us to Aunt Toybe, her elder sister.

We were very joyous to arrive there. First, she had four fully grown sons, but, alas, one, Hillel, was a deaf-mute. Secondly, Aunt Toybe was our richest aunt in all of Dukor. Her husband, Chaim Krudompay, our uncle, only came home for the big holidays, i.e., Sukkus and Pesach. All year long he was on the road in Ukraine or in the woods of the big Minsk lumber merchants.

Resulting from his frequent contact with aristocrats and other worldly travelers, Uncle Chaim would constantly enfold his earlocks inside his hat, so that they not peep out. That is why the town nicknamed him "Chaim Krudompay."

He was by nature a silent Jew, but he didn't run away from people as did Uncle Feitel, the Angel. Uncle Chaim liked playing chess but there wasn't another worthy chess player in all of Dukor, so he taught Aunt Toybe how to play with him. But she never had sufficient time to occupy herself with such trifles.

The kitchen needed constant attention, and she had to look carefully after her dishes. She was a tireless, tip-top homemaker who baked goods which were meltingly delicious.

She herself preferred her own food, and could pack away a whole herring while quietly eating in the kitchen.

Because of her fondness for food she was thickset with a fine goiter. Mother was much prettier than Aunt Toybe.

They used to recount in Dukor that when suitors would come to take a look at Aunt Toybe, mother, who was a few years younger and far prettier, would be hidden in another room so as not to tempt the suitors.

I would quietly thrill to the fact that Uncle Chaim married Aunt Toybe and not my mother. Had he, heaven forbid, married my mother, I might have been born a deaf-mute like his own son Hillel. I think still until today that it is better to be an orphan than a deaf-mute!

Besides, I carried a heavy heart about Uncle Chaim because he once fooled me with black plums brought home for Pesach from Kiev or Ekaterinoslav. He told mother that these fruits would be very good for me because they possess a lot of fat. I once popped a small plum in my mouth but had to spit it out because it was very salty and smelled like cod liver oil. It appears they weren't real plums but olives, and until today I cannot bear the sight of them.

I liked only one thing about Uncle Chaim: his fine small bag of real Istanbul tobacco. Such a fine sample I had never yet seen in Dukor. The smell of Uncle Chaim's cigarettes was far superior to those of Uncle Feitel's, which were made from a cheaper tobacco.

One could surmise from just the small box of tobacco that Uncle Chaim was a very rich man. Therefore, Aunt Toybe could offer a seemingly endless array of baked delicacies for the Pesach nights.

Aunt Toybe's doughy matzah-farfel or her concoctions of matzah meal with honey would melt in one's mouth and, no matter how much we consumed while their guests, nevertheless a groaning table of offerings still remained, and on departing we found Aunt Toybe giving us little packages for the post-holiday period.

Besides being a top-notch cook and baker, she was also well-learned. When Uncle Chaim had departed she would have enough time to peer into the holy books. She had a full shelf of her sacred texts.

She brimmed with maxims and chapter and verse, the equal of a rabbi. So, for example, I once heard Aunt Toybe address

Chaim: "Don't be too sweet—they'll eat you up. Don't be too bitter, they'll spit you out."

It appears Uncle Chaim followed his wife's advice—he, in fact, was neither too sweet nor too bitter.

He was, simply put, a silent man, one of those types at a loss as to what to do with their hands. He would use a finger to curl his ear ringlets and with the other he'd play chess with himself, peering into some kind of book or other about chess instruction.

From Aunt Toybe we ventured forth to our third aunt — Aunt Itke—who was the oldest of the sisters. Here things were even merrier. It was a house brimming with children: three sons and four daughters, but the youngest, Rochelle, suffered from jaundice and was entirely green. More often than not she lay stretched out more than running about upright. I pitied her and gave her some of the things Aunt Toybe had distributed for us on Pesach.

Uncle Yehoshua, it appears, was a feeble wage earner, and Aunt Itke, consequently, would not serve as much as had Aunt Toybe or Aunt Chaya.

He was very talkative, in contradistinction to my mother and other two uncles, a man embroiled in matters political, especially the Dreyfus Affair, which then took place somewhere in distant Paris.

Uncle Yehoshua would declare to my older brothers that Jews should return to the Land of Israel and become the equal of other nations.

As I then didn't grasp the import of all this talk, I naturally gravitated to the white-serviette-covered Singer sewing machine, which stood upside down. I would press my foot on the wooden pedal; and as if of its own accord a small wheel would spin madly above, which created a big wind which would blow against the white napkins. The tumult in the house was such that even the older girls didn't notice how I was playing with the sewing machine. Only Rochelle with her green eyes and yellow, parchment-like face took notice of my play. She declared it as sinful to play thus on the Jewish holiday, but I riposted by saying that I'm not sewing, but only playing just for the heck of it, simply so I could go on playing with the sewing machine. To play it safe, I would give her another goodie from Aunt Toybe's gift package.

(Apropos "playing for the heck of it," it later on became the essence of my life, and until today I very much enjoy pressing each and every lower pedal as long as the upper wheel skirls madly).

When we returned safely home from all these visits Pesach was by then over and we could eat leavened bread. Mother would cook a full kettle of potatoes and my older brothers would help her pack away the Pesach dishes into a big wooden box filled with straw which would then be hoisted to the attic.

For the last time I kissed my very own kiddush cup with its narrow mouth, and wished it the best until I would see it the following Pesach. Soon, thereafter, mother would fold my small drinking cup deep into the straw and she, too, moist-eyed, uttered something to the cup.

I would then console mother that all my Dukor aunts had worse plagues on their hands than she did. Aunt Chaya had a daughter, God spare us, who was mad; Aunt Toybe had a son who, spare us again, was a deaf- mute; Aunt Itke had a daughter, God keep us, who is jaundiced—in view of all these misfortunes my mother should be lucky that my illnesses were external rather than internal.

True, I had three other aunts and uncles whose children, thank heavens, were healthy, but those relatives didn't live in Dukor, so I'll speak of them at another opportunity.

For the time being I have not yet finished telling the story of my family in Dukor itself. I've also not had occasion to describe the Rabbi's family, a most charming household with which down to this very day I continue to be tightly bound. Thus the Rabbi's family requires its own chapter.

16

THE RABBI'S HOUSE

I n comparison with New York, Dukor, my little town, was a lot smaller than even one street in Brooklyn.

I believe that the hundred Jewish families of Dukor could have squeezed into one large apartment house, where I now live, and a few rooms would still remain to rent.

But some fifty years ago, when I was still a schoolboy, I imagined that a more beautiful and roomy town than Dukor did not exist in all the world.

Truth be told, I can even now claim that my small town of Dukor in some sense remains in my own eyes nicer and grander than New York.

Now, for example, I have been living many years in Brooklyn in quite a large apartment building, but don't ask who my next-door neighbors are. Neither do I interest myself with them nor they with me.

I have many more friends and relatives in New York than in Dukor, but who has time in the metropolis for family sentiment and friendly meetings, savoring the simple joy of it?

It was entirely different in Dukor, where the hundred Jewish families were bound and tied to one another, as if they belonged to the same family. Even more, my little shtetl possessed some fifty years ago all the important Jewish self-help organizations which burgeon now in New York.

The Dukor "Joint," or more aptly put, the Dukor UJA, which provided for all the needy, ranging from "Maot Chitim" to R' Meir bal-Haness, didn't require "publicity" and such office machinery as adding machines to get its work done.

The Red Patchele, whereby a few important entrepreneurs collected funds as they promenaded from house to house, sufficed as acts of mercy for the most needy.

The Rav himself would see to the Pesach "Maot Chitim" campaign. Who, after all, knew better all the needs of our shtetl than our very own worthy Rabbi Moshe Charney z"l?

As you have gleaned from above, the Rav of our shtetl was my great uncle. Mother was very proud that the Rav began his "Maot Chitim" campaign with her.

She had reserved a whole silver ruble, a bit of currency worth more than a "tithing" of her pre-Pesach budget.

The Rav knew quite well that my mother could have made very good use of the silver ruble for the needs of her orphans, but he realized how abashed she would be if he did not begin his charity campaign with her.

Until today I am very grateful to our very esteemed Rabbi, who via this clever strategy hugely lifted mother's status.

Also, we children sensed the extraordinary love and benevolence on the part of the Rabbi to our entire family. As a result, he and his family are deeply enshrined in our hearts until now.

In general, we found it more cheerful to be at his home than in those of our other aunts and uncles.

The Rabbi and his wife had nine children: three boys and six girls. My mother had six children: one daughter and five sons (if mother had not become a widow at such a young age she would probably have had more children, like the rabbi's rebbetzin). [In the chapter "A Story About Pistachios" the author says that the Rabbi and his wife had ten children.]

The rebbetzin (aleha hashalom, peace be upon her), despite her thinness and smallness, always had the house brimming with tasty things and a big yellow-tinged samovar always sat boiling.

The Rabbi was elderly and weak, and simply did not have the strength to celebrate with us; yet he would manage to ask each of my older brothers what they had learned the past semester, and he would take pride that Velvel's orphans were walking in his footsteps.

The Rabbi never put me to the test because he understood that whatever I knew sufficed for me. The Rabbi's main worry was that I not be too great a spoiler.

As it appears, Zelda, his youngest, whom I befriended, told him that I climbed a tree in the garden with one hand while with the other pulled down a pear or apple.

He told me once that I should not do it again, because I could fall and injure myself and that the fruit of the trees, from which one cannot benefit, are ritually strictly forbidden.

Until today I still cannot comprehend the logic behind the rule that one is not allowed to derive any benefit for three successive years from a young fruit orchard. [This Jewish rule, known as Orlah, may have been considered good agricultural practice.]

So far as I remember the book of Genesis, God forbade Adam to eat from the tree of knowledge, but he was allowed to partake of the fruit of the other trees which were not three years old!

If the trees in the Rabbi's garden were trees of knowledge, I could understand the law forbidding my enjoying their fruit.

And what's more, the orchard and the entire house where the Rabbi resided didn't even belong to him.

The shtetl had rented a nobleman's house with stalls and a fruit orchard at the very edge of River Street for the Rabbi's use. The yard was large, and in summer proved a pleasure ground in which to play hide and seek.

As the Rabbi's house was so near to the river, the rebbetzin raised hens. I believe these were the only ones of their kind in Dukor, and I was proud that only I could play there when and how I wished and even lead the birds to the river.

It's very joyous to see ducks on the run. They tottle from one side to the other like limping Jewish women and therefore these birds have acquired the name "limpers."

The ducks would take their sweet revenge in the water, swim away very far and I, sadly, couldn't follow after them.

Thanks to the hens, the Rabbi always had chicken on the Sabbath. The Rabbi, like others in our region, was not a big earner, but he did have a lock on the candle and yeast markets. Erev Sukkus he'd make some money from the lulav and esrog trade, and Erev Pesach from the sale of unleavened bread. [Jews were not allowed to have leavened bread in their homes during Pesach. The Rabbi sold matzahs before the holiday began.]

Because of the tightness of income, one of the granddaughters of Rav Charney, Chaya z"l [may her memory be blessed], learned to make socks on a special machine.

I do not believe that the Rabbi's granddaughter sewed socks with the intention of selling them. Who in Dukor would buy socks, when every homemaker had her own thread and needles. But just to provide for his large family's footwear needs, it was already worth buying a special sock machine.

I used to love to watch how socks were machine-made. Looking down, it appears quite simple. One need only turn the handle of the machine back and forth and you're on a roll! But in truth a sock machine is full of caprices, as it brims with teeth and spindles! Suddenly a spindle with threads jumps out at you, refusing to cooperate with the others working in tandem. One had to struggle a long while until one succeeded in coaxing the recalcitrant needle back into the machine. (Also in story writing, it often happens that a word stubbornly refuses to participate in the rhythmic flow, resulting in the thread of the narrative being broken, forcing the writer, in effect, to create a knot).

How good it was to have learned while still a child to make knots, when the thread tears. It now serves me well when stringing the stories and legends of my own life.

I became a virtual dweller in the Rabbi's house not only because of these games. I also came for purely spiritual reasons. Thus, for example, the late Rabbi would learn Torah in his home every Sabbath or repeat a piece of Lubavitch-inspired wisdom.

Right after the third meal, several dozen Jews would arrive to hear what the Rabbi had to relate.

These were essentially folk people: artisans and wagon drivers. They surrounded the Rabbi's table on all sides and listened quietly to his holy speech.

In the adjoining room the women would take their seats, including my mother.

I knew that when my father was still alive he would come between mincha and maariv (afternoon and evening prayers) to hear Torah or hassidus recited by the Rabbi. I was even shown the small sofa where father would listen with great fervor and focus, seated in a half-supine position in the direction of the Rabbi, who was also his uncle.

I, too, would squeeze in among the Jews and listen to the Rabbi's sacred words.

True, I didn't understand a word because it was something from the "Tzemackh-Tzedek," or perhaps even the holy "Zohar" itself. But the sacred spirit that hovered over the Rabbi was for me far more important than his softly cadenced words.

Through the window I would see the Sabbath sun setting over the Rabbi's face. The house gradually darkened and the few dozen Jews stood as if frozen around the Rabbi's table, taking the shape of half-lit silhouettes. They reflected the light emanating from the Rabbi's head, which still carried the holiness of the Sabbath, although the sun itself had nearly fully set. [Jews did not light a match or candle until after dark, when Sabbath was over.]

The Rabbi wanted to conclude the Sabbath with a niggun and suddenly he burst forth in a Lubavitch-style chant. The silhouetted Jews picked up his melody and the more they sang the greater the intensity of their devotion.

I, too, would weave my small voice into the Rabbi's niggun and only then would I begin to feel my father's presence from above, as well as within me.

I knew that in just such an end to the Sabbath my father's spirit could be found in the Rabbi's house, but I wouldn't dare share this with mother for fear she would sob if I told her father was present but she hadn't seen him.

Perhaps my mother made out the voice of father streaming, as it were, from the world to come, weaving into the Rabbi's niggun, and then started weeping softly, "God of Abraham, God of Isaac and God of Jacob..."

Only when the sky was illuminated by stars did the Rabbi and his community of worshippers stand up to pray maariv and then make havdalah [prayer marking the end of the Sabbath].

I still yearn for those wondrous Sabbath evenings in the Rabbi's house, where I had both my mother and father near me.

May they be good intercessors for us all.

17

DUKOR'S TIMES SQUARE

Dukor's marketplace was understandably a huge bit smaller than New York's Times Square, but as a result one could promenade more calmly and securely than in Manhattan's Great White Way.

Even the two tall white chalked churches—one Russian Orthodox, the other Catholic—scared no one. Dukor Jews drew their livelihood from the peasants and the petty nobility who frequented these churches every Sunday and every holiday. Even Jewish goats and geese would pasture at ease in front of these houses of worship. The clerics never thought for a moment to drive them away.

Priest Shimanovski was well favored towards Jews. When it became necessary to chalk over the church, the cleric deliberately chose Jewish artisans from the neighboring town of Smilovitch, and all the Jews of Dukor eagerly watched how fellow Jews went about this task.

In those days, when Jewish artisans worked on the Russian Orthodox church we schoolboys would recite a biblical verse pleading that no Jewish worker fall off of the tall spires.

When the old nobleman, Artinka, who was favorably disposed to Jews as well, died, all of Jewish Dukor followed his bier. Even some of the schoolboys secretly glanced inside the Catholic cathedral, into which his bier was carried.

The schoolboys later recounted that there was nothing to see in the Catholic church interior; it was dark and the wax candles cast a terrible shadow, the kind which only gentiles can bear.

How does it even compare l'havdil (keeping the thousand-fold difference strictly in mind) to our lit and festive synagogues?

No matter how small Dukor was, it managed to possess two synagogues—one old and grand, the other small but ever joyous. The festivity of the new synagogue consisted in no small part to the cobbler, Chaim Osher, who had learned in Minsk the art of drawing animals and then had sketched our synagogue walls with biblical animals, as if fully alive.

When Chaim Osher finished drawing the lion, deer and eagle, we schoolboys begged him to draw the Leviathan and the "Shor Ha-bor" (the Leviathan's carnivore double), the biblical animals that one is to eat in paradise. But Chaim got out of it with the excuse that since he never found his way to Eden, he didn't know the lineaments of these paradisal beasts.

It was understandably a lame pretext because he also never had seen the lion, the deer or the eagle alive in Minsk. After all, Minsk didn't have a zoo then, and not even a circus where wild animals could be observed.

Yet, nevertheless, we upstanding children were always drawn to the new synagogue, although our parents, and my mother in particular, would pray in the old one.

We schoolboys were not only drawn to the new synagogue interior because of its painted walls but also because of the interesting Jews who came to pray there or just hang out between mincha and maariv (afternoon and evening prayers).

The synagogue possessed salt-of-the-earth type Jews, the artisans and cart drivers brimming with tales. Above all, they loved to laugh at Moteh, the money-hungry butcher, who served as the longstanding head sexton (shammes) of the old synagogue. Though the congregation was opposed to him, once the election took place he somehow emerged victorious. He insisted that he had made nearly all Dukor Jewish. As the mohel (circumciser) for forty years who had circumcised nearly all males, he assumed he should now lead them by the nose.

When Rabbi Moshe Charney, my great uncle, may he rest in peace, once declared that the congregation opposed him, Moteh, the butcher, told him off.

"What is the congregation and who is the congregation? Here you have all the Dukor!" he uttered as he pointed to Gershon the water carrier, who could be found dragging uphill from the river a pair of water pails.

"So this is your congregation!" snarled Moteh.

By then the old Rabbi had taken the butcher's real measure.

Gershon, the water carrier, was, in fact, as one says, an indigent seven times over, and on top of it not too sharp, because he charged the same for river water as for well water, even though the river was a shlep from the shtetl, whereas well water could be had at every Dukor street corner.

"Good heavens! Gershon. What could possibly be the reason you charge the same for river water as for well water? In an hour you could draw ten times as much water from the well as from the river," the jokers of Dukor would ask.

Gershon always gave the same answer: "The reason is quite simple: where I go to draw well water, I would need to carry the pail all the way to the houses, but when I carry pails from the river I can rest several times along the way—and that for me is the heart of it."

This idea of his, such as it was, did not leave an impression of a clever man; therefore, Moteh, the butcher, conveniently chose him as the laughing-stock symbol of the Dukor congregation.

I, however, regard the water carrier's seemingly feeble answer to be an inspired nugget of wisdom, of experience and of life itself. Resting midway is often more important than the path! What is all the hurly burly worth, if not a bit of spiritual pleasure can be had?

If American Jewry would think the way Gershon, the water carrier, did, fewer would fall victim to sudden heart attacks or car accidents.

I, for example, am in accord with Gershon. I sell my customers river water no more expensively than well water. They come to enjoy the pleasures and joys of Sabbath, and I have benefitted from enjoying their pleasure. I see fields and forests, rivers and waterways which lead me to the past, when everything was so sweet and comforting.

But far better for us to return to our new synagogue, where Binyomin had many tales to tell.

Binyomin was a jokester and enjoyed sharing his far-fetched tales between mincha and maariv (afternoon and evening prayers), when it was customary in the old synagogue to recite a chapter of the "Ein Yaakov."

"Children! hear the story of the two beggars from Smilovitch, 10 viorsts from Dukor," he began with great satisfaction to lay forth his verbal bricks as if he were setting out to construct a new oven.

"In Smilovitch," he continued, "a lame beggar who would wander across the homes and a half-blind female beggar would do pretty much the same. The two beggars became blood enemies. The lame beggar imagined that the blind one got the best gifts because she showed up first at shtetl festivities. For her part, the half-blind supposed the lame one was getting the better part of the deal because whenever guests arrived in town, he managed to line up first.

"As it happened the two argued and battled so long until a plague broke out in the shtetl and the community decided to marry the beggars to each other.

"If fortune is fated, it can come via a plague." In such a manner did Binyomin affix another shovelful of cement to his word bricks.

"What happened to them, Reb Binyomin?" we boys asked with growing impatience.

"The community prepared a royal-like wedding. The lame beggar received a new set of clothing and shoes and the half-blind beggar the entire trousseau of a bride, starting with a white bridal gown and ending with the requisite number of soft pillows and thick quilts."

Binyomin continued, "When the two, freshly bathed and spruced up in their royal-like wedding garments, stood under the canopy, one could veritably believe that a prince and a princess were being wed. The limping beggar looked like a young groom and the half-blind beggar under her bridal veil looked the very picture of a bride.

"All of the Smilovitch klezmers came to play at the wedding, and all the housewives baked a heap of sweets and tarts that would have sufficed for both Dukor and Smilovitch!

"If fortune is fated, it'll come via a plague if need be," and so did Binyomin add another word brick to his construction.

"Nu, nu, Reb Binyomin tell us more, where's the rest of the story?" we pleaded with him to no avail.

"Rev Tchala, the Rabbi of Smilovitch himself, officiated at the wedding and the entire shtetl swept into the big synagogue where the festive meal was held. All of the tables were bedecked, groaning with delicacies. The young beggar couple was in seventh heaven, seeing how big-hearted the community was.

"If beggars are fated to good fortune, it comes even via a plague," and thus again Binyomin affixed another word brick with a fresh trowel of mortar.

"Nu, please, Reb Binyomin tell us the end of the story, we're practically ready to say maariv (evening) prayers," we began to rush him, urging a quicker pace.

"Yes, children, you are in fact right. We have to ready ourselves for maariv. There's no point in dragging things out. The long and short of it is that the plague came to an end soon after the wedding and small children stopped dying."

"But what happened to the beggar couple?" we demanded of Reb Binyomin. "Tell us the happy ending."

"Yes, children, the beggar couple soon after the wedding sowed a big bundle and...

"... And may he have mercy and forgive their sins..." Binyomin suddenly shouted out in the darkened synagogue and all the Jews stood up for maariv.

Just so would Binyomin draw us with his stories, which always ended with a mystery.

18

THE TOWN'S INTELLECTUALS

D ukor outside is just now fragrant with the smells of Lag
B'Omer. Birds have returned from their warm southern
sojourns, and there's barely a house beneath whose eaves
a nest of avian couples cannot be found. Also, the storks return
from distant lands. But as soon as we noticed them across the skies
of Dukor we began screaming, "Birds, the nest is aflame. The nest
is aflame!"

I still don't understand what possessed us schoolboys to
frighten the storks with shouts of burning nests.

By the time Lag B'Omer rolled around, the mud paths had
dried out except for the big mud-scape on the so-called "Blotza
Street," also known as "Aunt Chaya's House."

Our river, the "Svisle," a grandchild of the Dnieper (the
Svisle empties into Berezina, which then drains into the Dnieper,)
was deep into spring, but one was forbidden to bathe there because
of "sfirah" [counting of days between Pesach and Shavuos, which
a sad period for Jews].

But even after Shavuos, Jews would avoid bathing in the river
so long as the "Svisle" (or Svislovitch) hadn't taken a life.

Our river, no matter its smallness and shallowness, would
drown a man each spring, which, as it happened, was always a
gentile because, as we naturally assumed, what can you expect if one
bathes even during the days of counting?

It happened once that a young man, a non-Jew from Village
St., had returned at night from the forest during the days of
counting (sfira) and had decided to take a dip in the deep part of
the river. As expected, he drowned. Several peasants took their
fishing boats to search for him. As night had already fallen and
nothing could be made out in the dark, a whole loaf of bread with

big yellow church candles wedged inside was set forth in the stream. Peasants who followed in its wake gazed intently into the illuminated waters.

How frightening was it to look on from the shoreline at the burning loaf with church candles lodged in its doughy part! The bread loaf appeared from afar like the head of a dead man, and the peasants in their boats with lowered faces struck us like mourners accompanying the dead man to his watery grave.

Not for nothing did my mother always say that every river in its nature is vindictive, all the more so during the days of counting (sfira).

Better that we return from the river to dry land so that I can acquaint you with Dukor's "Fifth Avenue," which was, in fact, the fifth and last street of our town.

The other four streets: the Smilovitcher St., the River Road, the Blotza St. and Synagogue St. didn't have a single tree to their name, but Fifth St., the so-called Chancellery St., was, it could be said, "the Nevsky Prospekt" of Dukor [Main Street in St. Petersburg].

This very street, bedecked in green already during Lag B'Omer, became on Sabbath evening the promenade of Dukor's intelligentsia, as well as its youth, who took the night air across "Fifth Avenue" all the way up to the forest encircling the bricked majesty of our noblemen.

(True, Dukor still had other big streets: Village St. and Kader St., which were canopied with trees and verdure, but these two streets don't figure in my Jewish calculations. Gentiles largely lived there. Day and night barking dogs scared away Jewish children).

In the small forest of "Algetshina" a variety of trees flourished, beginning with tall and thick oaks, as well as thin and drawn poplars. In the Beriozer streets soon after Pesach we would hollow out holes with sharp knives near the roots and by Lag B'Omer a sweet and clear fluid had gathered which was called "Bereiozovik." We schoolboys would run every Sabbath to "Algetshina" with straws to savor tasty "Bereiozovik." Afterwards we would spread out on a little hill and gaze at the Jewish intellectuals grandly promenading amid the trees and groves.

For example, Simcha Orem would suddenly appear, the biggest intellectual in our shtetl. He would promenade alone because his equal could not be found in Dukor.

He was the only man who sported a fancy French beard and his eyes were upturned to heaven. A miracle that he kept his mouth shut, otherwise a small bird would have easily landed there and made an unpleasant sound. How we schoolboys laughed at Simcha Orem! One schoolboy even recounted that he himself saw how Simcha Orem on a Shabbes early morning ran out of his home in bare underpants during a heavy rain to pry open a barrel.

But I held Simcha Orem in high esteem because of his youngest child, Berl, my friend. I would often visit his home, where it became crystally clear that Simcha was the greatest of our town's intellectuals.

He received a Russian newspaper from distant St. Petersburg called, "Bersheva Vedomosti," which he read through.

Simcha Orem's address was printed on top of the newspaper. He typically removed the address labels, brought them to synagogue where he boasted that he is known as far as St. Petersburg—the proof, if proof were needed, was that every day his address was printed anew, on a machine no less.

Besides this, Simcha Orem was a forester. Every fall he would hire a group of gentiles to chop down trees and haul them from the forest. Not all the gentiles stuck to the contract. Some got drunk, others fell ill. He insisted that these vagrants pay back the money he had given them. During the days of counting (sfira) he would receive many a summons from the court in Smilovitch to come and resolve his dealings with the peasants. These summonses smacked also of "imperial" power. The Russian eagle was printed on them, as well as the circular stamp of the Smilovitcher judge.

I asked Berl, Simcha Orem's youngest child, who had served as my vice-regal (at the time I was "chief" at Shmuel the Melamed's cheder) to get me these formal-looking summonses, all burnished with eagles and official stamps, of which I was in dire need for my own business. When important judgments between us schoolboys took place, I would cheekily call forth the opposing side by issuing Simcha Orem's summonses, refashioned to our purpose.

Understandably, Simcha Orem lost a lot of money as a result because he hardly knew exactly when he needed to travel to Smilovitch to adjudicate with his hired peasants.

Nevertheless, his six children were well-dressed, although if one looked closely they might betray a hint of poverty.

The only woman with whom Simcha Orem would agree to meet in "Algetshina" was Elke Aryeh Yitzhaks. Her husband, Aryeh Yitzhak, was also a forester and he returned to Dukor only for the big holidays—Pesach and Sukkus.

As far as I remember, Elke, wife of Aryeh Yitzhak, was the prettiest wife in Dukor (other than, understandably, my sister, Mirl, and my cousin Frada, who were still girls at the time).

Elke would read suspenseful novels and retell the stories to my sister and the Rabbi's daughter whom she befriended. Once Elke entered our home and informed my sister of the tragic character who had hanged himself in the novel she was then reading.

I nearly burst into tears from fright that someone in our town had taken his own life. I was ready to run and see the horrific sight, but my sister calmed me; after all, it was just a story in a book.

As Elke, wife of Aryeh Yitzhak, was well-read, Simcha Orem had much to discuss with her.

However, Masha the lunatic couldn't bear that Elke spent time with him, and would scream hysterically all over town that because of Elke young children were dying. I, however, knew it to be a lie. Elke had fine children of her own, and would never harm or put them in jeopardy.

So what if a maniac blathers away?

But once something did occur in Dukor straight out of Elke's novels. A boy in Smilovitcher St. did in fact hang himself in the attic of his father's house, and the whole town went wild.

As it appears, even in Dukor tragedies would happen, just as in novels.

In general, Smilovitcher St. was the longest and poorest in all of Dukor. Nearly all the Jewish artisans lived there, as well as other unfortunates with no trade at all. Also, the three Dardki students lived on this very street, which bustles with children, may no evil befall them.

One female teacher had so many children that the town jokers would ask, "Goodness, how does she have time to carry when she is always giving birth?"

However, the blessed arrival of a new birth never made a home too crowded. Poverty never pinches hard enough to block out the sun and joy, and that is its virtue!

Once Moshe-Aben, the tailor, got so tight in the head that he flipped out and shouted himself hoarse all across town, "For God's sake, Jews, the sky is falling."

From that time forth Moshe-Aben earned the nickname "Moshe-Aben the Skies Are Dropping," and we schoolboys would often run to Smilovitcher St. to see the heavens caving in.

19

I BECOME A BIRD

Soon after Lag B'Omer, my mother began to prepare for the wedding of my sole sister, Mirl, the eldest of the children.

My elder four brothers headed in various directions soon after Passover. Two of them, the very eldest, had taken on assignments with settlers in our region and the other two brothers (who later became S. Niger and B. Vladeck) went to Minsk to learn in the Tatar school.

My mother told all my four brothers that they definitely had to come for Shavuos because the Shabbes following will be the wedding of our only sister, may she be well.

I remained the only male in the house, who had to help mother and sister prepare for the wedding. One of the first and important tasks was refilling the quilts and pillows that had remained unaired. Mother did not have as many bedspreads as would ordinarily have been the case because each of my brothers took off with a quilt and a pillow.

But mother had stashed away on the roof a few heavy hereditary quilts on which my father had slept, and from this haul one could make five or six fine pillows.

Understandably, one had first to thoroughly air out the feathers of these rooftop quilts and only then turn them into plump pillowcases. Better to air them out indoors with closed doors and windows because the merest wind could send the feather stuffing flying every which way.

Mother carried two empty herring barrels into the bedroom and then we poured all the feathers in the quilts.

The barrels were set ever closer to windows where the pre-Shavuos sun shone strongly. My task was to mix every so often the upper and lower feathers. I soon began to sneeze from this work because from the barrels wafted a pungent air, as if from my Uncle Feitel, the Angel.

My sister said the odor arose because the quilts lay for years in the attic not far from the box of Pesach utensils. The quilts absorbed the fragrance of Pesach pepper and spices which mother hid between the wine glasses for the next Pesach.

But mother had another opinion. She knew quite well that all those hereditary quilts and pillows on which Jewish generations had slept had already absorbed the salty moistness of tears and other such humidities of feeling and pain. Is it any wonder that one sneezes, as one would from the spreading scent of freshly cut peppers?!

Although she didn't confess it to me, I could hear mother quietly murmur a prayer under her breath that all the pain and hurt that the feathers had absorbed from those who had slept on them should now absolve her daughter, Miriam bas Zev Wolf a"h, of any grief and make her bed soft and accommodating for her soon-to-be husband, Shmuel ben Yoel, who is known in Berezin as "Munia Genendes," at once uncle to my sister and in-law to my mother.

"God should give," mother whispered in her plea, "that my daughter and husband-to-be should multiply in wealth and respect on these hereditary quilts and pillows, and that their children should grow up to Torah, marriage and good deeds, Amen and Amen."

Mother didn't notice that no sooner had she entered the bedroom I immediately hid behind the clothes armoire. I hid because I feared that if she saw me she would faint from terror.

I looked more like a bird than a person as I was covered from head to toe in feathers. As mother herself would customarily rub my scrofulous body with a sticky ointment, my hands and my head remained stuck with thin feathers which tickled my nostrils.

Suddenly I sneezed behind the armoire and mother quickly understood I was hiding from her.

"My child, why are you hiding from me? Come out and help me shake out the pillows."

"I'm scared you will be frightened when you see me," I answered from behind the armoire.

"Why should I take fright?" mother asked in a slightly worried voice.

"Because I'm not a person, but a bird," I answered mother playfully from my hiding place.

Mother, having no time to play with me, led me out from behind the armoire.

"Woe is me! Just look at you!" mother shouted at the top of her voice.

My sister, the bride, heard mother's cry and came running into the bedroom; both took immediate charge in cleaning the pile of feathers clinging to me.

"If you put a cover over me, I might pass for a pillow," I said jokingly. But my mother and my sister were hardly amenable just then to such jokes.

Mother was consumed by the forthcoming wedding. She needed to order ten quarts of wine and ten quarts of mead from Hillel Kaylis, the only master of such matters in Dukor. She also had to order ten pounds of pike from the fishmonger and all sorts of meats from Yasha the Butcher. For the chuppah [wedding] dinner she still had to order several plump chickens from Village St., as well as enough eggs for the gefilte fish, for the potato pies; and, it being Shavuos, for butter cookies.

All this could be had for debt to pay up later, but the quarts of vodka could only be had with hard cash.

Sadly, mother didn't know how much vodka to order and, more essentially, for whom to purchase it.

Just then Reb Osher the teacher, father's best friend and himself a fervent Lubavitcher, stepped inside our home. Mother brightened at his presence because Osher, who was the best Talmud instructor in town, had taken charge over our father's orphans, and thus he had become a virtual member of the household.

"I tell you, Reb Osher, that God himself has sent you to us," mother said as she stood up from her chair and offered him a cushion to sit on.

"Sit, Reb Osher, sit!" she insisted.

Meanwhile, Reb Osher remarked that I'm sitting half unclothed on a bench, and my sister is plucking feathers from me.

"I see your youngest fell head first into a barrel of feathers," Reb Osher said jokingly.

"My dear Reb Osher, you know everything sticks to him! We were shaking the pillows for my daughter's trousseau when he fell into a full head of feathers," mother said.

"Don't take it to heart, Brocha, it's a sign that the young one, if God wills it, will manage to kick up feathers for our good Lord, as his older brothers have already done."

"If only I stood with him as I stand with my older children, a stone would fall from my heart," mother said, sighing.

"I don't know that you have anything to sigh about," Reb Osher said consolingly.

"See," Reb Osher continued, "you are giving your daughter in matrimony to one of your own, an uncle, who takes her to Berezin, all things said and done. And she still remains, one can say, in her own family. And I have further very good regards from your Shmuel. His rosh yeshiva in Minsk is astounded by him. Your [son] Shmuel is not only a master of diligence but also a star pupil. He is called the "Dukor prodigy" in the yeshiva. You should consider yourself lucky, Brocha, that you have such a son and you will surely take pride in your other sons, if God wills it. Also, your Boruch is said to be very capable and studious. As for the youngest, I tell you literally that you will take pride from him as well. He should only reach bar-mitzvah age, and then he'll be out of danger and live on his own merit. You can already order a pair of tefillin for him from Zusha the sexton. As soon as he dons the tefillin he'll become far healthier than ever. Tefillin, our sages remind us, cast off many maladies."

Just so did Reb Osher solace my mother, looking the entire time at his own fingers, as if they could deliver ever more words.

(Yes, I forgot to say that Reb Osher had the gift to entertain himself, keeping his fingers in motion the entire time, as if they were his sole listeners).

Suddenly, he stretched all his ten fingers in the direction of mother, as if each finger wanted to get its word in amidst a cacophony of sound.

"Actually, I came today because of Shmuel. They write in Minsk that I should speak with you, but I see that you are distracted so I'd better push it off for another occasion."

Mother replied, "Somehow you are speaking to me in riddles, in cloaked language, so I don't understand what you mean to say, Reb Osher. Did something happen to my Shmuel, God forbid."

"It concerns a financial matter of Shumel, nothing to worry about. You, Brocha, forgive me, speak nonsense." Reb Osher once again began to play with all his fingers in the air.

"Who has it in mind to speak about Shmuel at this very moment, when it's at the eve of the wedding?" mother responded to Reb Osher.

"As I said, we'll talk about it some other time, when you are not so distracted," Reb Osher nodded his agreement.

"You know why I am so consumed?" mother said. "I am distracted because of foolishness. When both the groom and the bride, thank heavens, are from the same side, I have to worry for both at the same time. For example, I don't know how much spirits and at what proof I should purchase for the wedding. Drink, after all, is a man's business; how should I know about such things?" all the while looking at Reb Osher as her sole salvation.

"A worse worry, Brocha, you should not have," he replied, a man who liked his drop.

Soon thereafter, Reb Osher made mother the following calculation: "For me and Zusha the sexton (shammes) you will get a quart of 97 proof because a teacher who works from semester to semester needs a drink of that proof, nothing else will do. In gematria (numerology), time, that is to say a semester, amounts to the number 97."

Reb Osher continued, warming to his point, "For the rest of the crowd who will come for schnapps and a piece of honey cake you need to get two quarts of 57% proof, derived from the word "mezonot" [food]. And as for the women who wish to take a swig, a quart of 42% proof will suffice. Thus with two rubles you'll keep all of Dukor merrily drinking away." Reb Osher said all this while spreading out all his fingers toward mother, as if each was ready to make a l'chaim (down a drink).

Elated by such calculations, mother suddenly remembered that she had in her armoire a quantity of 97% proof, which she once brought for my sister as a cure for a toothache. Mirl just washed out her mouth a few times and the rest was left in the bottle.

"Reb Osher, maybe you'll make a l'chaim?" she said.

He replied expansively, "A l'chaim can't be tossed away. Especially today when in a happy hour you are pouring the feathers into the quilts and pillows."

Mother handed him a full bottle of what appeared like schnapps and in a festive call, Reb Osher shouted to us three, "L'chaim, sister-in-law, l'chaim, bride, and l'chaim, plague!!"

"L'chaim to good life and peace!" we three responded in one voice.

I was so thrilled and brimming with joy that I could have leapt straight into the barrels of feathers.

20

A STORY ABOUT PISTACHIOS

A week before Shavuos mother sat me down to stir cinnamon. She deliberately sought out a sitting task for me so that I wouldn't stumble under her feet, all the more as it was Shavuos eve and she was consumed preparing for the wedding of her only daughter.

According to the Jewish calendar the wedding was scheduled to take place the Shabbes after Shavuos, but the groom had to arrive from Berezin a few days before the holiday.

We didn't await any other guests from Berezin because the groom's side was also the bride's, although it must be said he was a good deal older than my sister. After all, my sister's groom was also her uncle, the younger brother of my late father.

Understandably, Uncle Munia (so was the groom called) was much the senior of my sister, yet the two would not be estranged. After all, she would remain within the circle of the family under the same last name, Charney.

I kept trying to figure out the enmeshed family relationship which would connect us to Uncle Munia. Right after the wedding my uncle would become my brother-in-law and my sister would become my aunt! Their children to come would be my cousins and my nieces and nephews. My mother, who is now Uncle Munia's sister-in-law, would turn into his mother-in-law, and he to her at once a brother-in-law and a son-in-law.

My childish understanding could not wrap itself around these new sets of circumstances--how my uncle could be an in-law to both mother and me.

Somehow, wasn't Uncle Munia taking on too much? How in the world was I to address the groom who was now at once both uncle as well as brother-in-law to me, and my very own sister both sister and aunt to me? Even my own mother will now become more than a mother after the wedding comes to pass.

She will become the mother-in-law of my uncle—how in heaven's name do you call a woman who becomes the mother-in-law of her brother-in-law?

But, as said, mother didn't have any time before the wedding to answer all my silly questions—therefore she sat me down on a stool so that I could better grind cinnamon.

I must admit that this holiday task suited me very well.

It is curious to see how the long and hard sticks, which look like hollow pipes, are ground into dust. When one takes a bit of ground cinnamon on one's tongue, one already feels the divine taste of the Shavuos butter cookies.

But it wasn't only for the Shavuos butter cookies that mother was in need of cinnamon; but also chopped herring is tastier when coated with cinnamon, and noodle pudding benefits greatly from a dash of cinnamon as well—such that it smells of paradise itself!

Mother bought an entire half pound of cinnamon from Aunt Chaya's store. It was a big mountain of dried sticks which one had to break into small parts so they could fit into the stirring pot. Thus was I consumed several days in succession with the cinnamon business.

When Mother saw that I was free, without a stitch of work, she prepared a new kind of labor for me, preparing the burnt seeds.

Aunt Toybe, who was a mistress of food and drink, told mother that when one mixes sugar with burnt seeds one obtains the real taste of coffee (on Shavuos, after all, one is commanded to drink coffee).

Aunt Chaya, who had a full sack of pistachios in her shop, said that when one crunches burnt pistachios they take on the look of real coffee and one does not even need sugar.

However, matters were not so simple. A rumor emerged in town that pistachios only grow in a cemetery, and Jews were strictly forbidden to eat it.

And rumors, as we know all too well, spread; it was soon said that when a pistachio splits into two one sees on one half side a tiny Jew with a long beard, evidence that pistachios do grow in cemeteries and each is the reincarnation of a soul.

Understandably, once this rumor spread no one wanted to buy pistachios from Aunt Chaya. She claimed that if Jews were not permitted to eat pistachios the Jewish shopkeepers of Minsk would not carry them and, in any case, the city's spiritual leader would have forbidden it.

Once Aunt Chaya realized she could not get rid of the pistachios, she fell upon the idea of burning the shells and turning them into coffee beans. But she was scared to do this in her own home because Masha the Lunatic would see her mother frying the shells on a burning griddle and gaze at the parade of dead souls, and she would be driven off the deep end.

In that very chaotic pre-Shavuos period Aunt Chaya came over with a full dress pocket bulging with pistachios, and she proposed to my sister, the bride, to fry at least one shell to see what kind of coffee it would make.

My sister, never doing things by halves, poured the whole pile of peeled pistachios and began to fry them on hot coals. I went near the oven for a better view of how pistachios are thus transformed.

Suddenly I saw how the pistachios began to spring from the griddle and uttered "Holy, holy, holy" and split into two. I fell into a great panic and started to scream that the dead are springing from the griddle, much as in hell, heaven help us!

My sister took great fright upon seeing the pistachios' dance of death, and she poured the whole heap into the fire.

Only then did Aunt Chaya begin to believe that her pistachios were haunted. She promptly sent the whole sack back to the grocer in Minsk. A stone fell from my chest; I no longer would have to stir the fried dead souls. What a relief!

Also I'd be spared from stirring the burnt wheat, because a few days before Shavuos the groom arrived from Berezin, that is to say Uncle Munia, and among the bridal presents he brought with him were a few pounds of genuine coffee.

Uncle Munia understood that in Dukor we'd lack real coffee at Shavuos, which only noblemen drink. He thus brought along from his shop in Berezin all fine things difficult to obtain in Dukor.

Thus, for example, he also brought gewirtig, which is called saffron. When the saffron was put into the dough, the challahs turned yellow, like eggs. Saffron, it appears, looks like thin strands of very good Stamboul tobacco.

He also brought several hundred cigarettes of the real Stamboul variety. Just such a box of a hundred cigarettes he left on the Rebbe's table, so that all the Jews who would come to hear the Rebbe would also be able to smoke to their hearts' delight the Bereziner cigarettes [except on Sabbath, when smoking was forbidden].

Yes, I also forgot to relate that the groom traveled as far as to the Rabbi, who was his uncle and my grand-uncle. So it was that Rabbi Moshe Charney z"l was at once the chief in-law of both sides of the couple.

Together with my mother, the rebbetzin decided that on the first day of Shavuos the entire bride's side of the family would come as guests to the Rabbi, and on the second day of Shavuos the Rabbi's family would come to us.

Thus would bride and groom be able to meet on Shavuos, two days before the wedding.

The bride's side consisted of seven souls (mother and her six children) and the Rabbi's family of twelve (the Rabbi himself, his wife and their ten children). Together it came to nineteen people, with the groom making it twenty.

Alas, at that time my father, who would have been the twenty-first, was no longer among the living. I heard it said that Uncle Munia, who was to marry my sister, very closely resembled my father.

Understandably, I ran off to see the Rabbi, to look at the groom and thus to see with my own eyes how my father must have once looked.

Uncle Munia took great joy in his youngest nephew, who will, any minute now, become an in-law. He embraced me, even going so far as to kiss my forehead. He was twice my height. It is said that all grooms right before the wedding increase in height because they wear high hats.

Uncle Munia also wore the requisite hard high hat but his beard was trimmed. As it appears, my Uncle Munia was already then an enlightened man of the world. He even brought a Hebrew language newspaper in Berezin called "Hatzfirah" or "Hamelitz." ["Hamelitz" was the first Hebrew-language newspaper in the Russian Empire, founded in 1860.]

Even the Rabbi peeked into the paper but immediately pronounced that "there's nothing to be had."

"Jews don't need newspapers; it's all in the holy books," the Rabbi declared.

Uncle Munia stood up for his sacred "gazette" but I sided with the Rabbi, whom I loved very much.

I was in mind to return home and deliver the first greetings from the groom but Uncle Munia began to caress me and ask me about mother, my sister and brothers. I answered that everyone was, thank heaven, well and getting ready for the wedding.

"Better tell Uncle Munia the story of the pistachios," the Rabbi said suddenly.

I was surprised that the Rabbi knew so much about the pistachio affair, but as there are no secrets in a small town I told him the entire story, how the dead began to jump from the hot griddle, like the evil ones in hell, may we all be spared!

Uncle Munia burst out laughing. He said in Berezin the same tale had been told and now no one buys them anymore. Soon, thereafter, he opened one of his big sacks and pulled out one of his fine paper bags of genuine coffee.

One of the bags he placed on the table for the household's use and the second he gave me to give to mother as a present for Shavuos.

"Count Potocki himself [a Polish nobleman] drank this sort of coffee when he came to hunt in Berezin," Uncle Munia told the Rabbi.

I immediately returned home with the big present and from then forth the coffee demon took hold of me.

Every time I drink a cup of coffee (and that occurs at least 15 times daily) I imagine myself to be Count Potocki, who is off to the hunt through his fields and woods.

21

MY SISTER'S WEDDING

During the entire Shavuos week preceding my sister's upcoming wedding Dukor was turned upside down.

Already on Shavuos eve guests began arriving from the neighboring shtetls and villages, even though the wedding was scheduled only for the Sabbath after Shavuos.

Uncle Leizer and Aunt Sarah from Materova arrived on their horse and wagon. She was a direct sister of my late father and therefore she was a direct blood relative [sister] of Uncle Munia, the groom.

Both she and Uncle Leizer lived for many years in the village of Materova, ten viorsts from Dukor. She was smart and laconic. If, for example, one asked her what was happening in her village, she would respond with a dismissive smile, "What can take place in the village? One lies down with the goy and rises up with him."

Uncle Leizer, inversely, was shy and silent and looked like a Jewish farmer, although he was learned and wore a Sabbath-like gabardine. In the middle of summer he wore shiny galoshes atop his village boots.

When he was asked why did he have to wear galoshes, he answered modestly that when traveling to a joyous event in a town (Dukor he considered a town) one needed to dress differently than in the village itself.

Uncle Leizer, in fact, sweated heavily in Dukor but he got the best aliyahs, for which he paid handsomely.

Understandably, Uncle Leizer and Aunt Sarah didn't come empty-handed to the wedding. A full wagon of goodies accompanied them. A dozen live chickens and hens, a cradle of fresh eggs from under the hen, and overflowing baskets of vegetables. Sacks of potatoes and carrots were not lacking either. In addition, Aunt Sarah brought house furnishings for the young couple—silk and crocheted tablecloths and a swirl of handcloths which can be obtained at half price in the village.

And who just arrived on a count's horse and wagon if not Uncle Feivl and Aunt Rivtche, who owned a mill in Takarnia, ten viorsts from Dukor.

Aunt Rivtche was mother's youngest sister, who also laid claim to heritage of the Sheloh Hakodesh, and she remained a Hurvitch even after the wedding. Uncle Feivl's family was also a Hurvitch, but not from the side of the Sheloh.

Uncle Feivl and Aunt Rivtche also brought a full trunk of presents: a couple of sacks of "kruptshatke" flour and various sacks of grains.

I liked both Uncle Feivl and Aunt Rivtche a whole lot because they helped mother put a headstone on my father's gravesite.

A millstone had been split in two. Uncle Feivl dedicated half of the millstone for father's headstone. Perhaps it still stands in Dukor's cemetery with a bitter hole in the middle. The headstone reflected my father accurately. Like it, his life had been split in half (he died at the untimely age of 38).

Uncle Aryeh and Aunt Judashe just now arrived. She was the middle sister, the one between mother and Aunt Rivtche. And they came to Dukor in a barouche, just like big-city folk, because Pukhovitch is, after all, much larger than Dukor. And they didn't come, heaven forbid, empty handed. In their town they had a textile business that produced women's clothing and men's costumes. They didn't forget to bring some cloth for me, the youngest, and thus mother was able to sew a new suit for my bar-mitzvah (until my confirmation I wore the clothing and shoes of my older brother Boruch, for he outgrew them quickly).

All the wedding guests were quartered by Dukor relatives and good friends, while our home now stood bursting at the seams.

The wedding dinner took place in our house and I'm more than certain that on that wedding night Elijah the prophet doubled the size of our house so that all the forty-fifty guests could fit into

107

it. [Elijah the prophet performed miracles, see Book of Kings in the Old Testament.]

Predictably, mother had to borrow long synagogue tables and benches from the nearby shul. Electric lamps had to be borrowed from an old shop, which so brilliantly illuminated our house that at first I scarcely could recognize it.

Aside from all the close relatives from both sides, which in fact was the very same side, mother had also invited to the wedding feast Osher the teacher, who was my father's best friend, and Zusha the sexton, without whom no celebratory event in Dukor could truly get underway.

And wonder of wonders! My Uncle Feitel, the "Angel," also arrived. No one had expected him, although he was, as you may remember, the only living brother of my mother.

Uncle Feitel was centrally seated near the newlyweds and the Rabbi, but he kept his eyes firmly shut the entire time because he couldn't bear the strong light emanating from the electric lamps.

Also his wife, Aunt Chaya, came with their capable daughter, Frada, but the other daughter, Masha the Lunatic, was pitifully left home.

I was greatly miffed that Masha didn't come to my sister's wedding. True, Masha was insane but she still remained our cousin and we had to have great pity on her.

I knew that Masha would have spent the whole time cursing my sister. As no one wanted to marry Masha, I feared that one of her insane curses might actually stick.

I gazed with great sadness at my sole sister, who in a few days would depart our home forever.

My sister sat between her uncle-husband and the Rabbi. Her large, luminous eyes were set against the electric lamps ablaze with all the colors of a rainbow. As it appears, my sister had wept during the "badeken" ceremony (when the bride's face is covered by a veil). Her eyes were still moist, but this only added further charm to her face. It was in the light of the electric lamps that I realized just how beautiful she was, may no evil eye ever befall her. She also looked much younger than Uncle Munia, whom she had just wed. In his wedding best and top hat he looked like a pine set against a white birch (my sister wore a white wedding dress with a green garland in honor of Shavuos).

It occurred to me then to bequeath my inheritance of the Berezin house, where my uncle lived, to the young couple.

The Bereziner house was an inheritance from my late grandfather, Reb Yoel, my father's father. My father inherited a third of the house but with his death his inheritance transferred over to us, his five sons. So it was that my share amounted to a fifth of a third!

I had previously calculated that if one considers the house in its entirety—all the slates of the roof, the wood inside all the walls, the windows and doors, as well as the hinges, my inheritance, despite amounting to a mere fifth of a third, was still a considerable amount.

I asked mother if she agreed that I should bequeath my entire Bereziner inheritance to my sister so that Uncle Munia would not think he is taking a wife without a dowry.

Mother, it appeared, liked the idea and shared it with the rebbetzin, my great aunt. She immediately informed the Rabbi and he, in the midst of the wedding tumult, banged on the table and shouted to the women's section— "Silence! Quiet down! You should all know that Daniel bequeaths the young couple his share of the inheritance in Berezin. God should bless him with health and long life!"

"Amen!" the whole crowd shouted its approval in one voice and before I could hide behind my mother, Osher the teacher caught me by the hand and brought me to the bride and groom for them to thank me personally for my largesse.

Uncle Munia was the first who kissed me on my forehead and then Mirl, my sister, hugged and kissed me as well, as if she were bidding me adieu forever. My heart was so stirred at my sister's cries and kisses that the Rabbi winked at mother that we be separated, but as mother gazed at us she burst out crying.

A miracle: Osher, the teacher, who disliked emotional outbursts, suddenly broke the emotional spell with one of his gimmicks.

He smeared some paste on a piece of bread, mistaking it for honey, and burst out screaming:

"How bitter is the honey!"

Zusha, the sexton, who was pretty drunk by then, offered Osher a sweet glass of tea to wash away the paste, but he mixed up the glass of tea with that of a herring tail.

Reb Osher started yet again to shout. "Oy! How salty is the sugar" and from then on merriment took hold of the crowd.

Yet, in the midst of all the hoopla, Uncle Feitel, the "Angel," continued to keep himself aloof. He sat benumbed with eyes shut and in stunned silence.

He would have been lucky if he were led away to a small separate room, where the wedding unity ritual might have taken place.

In his chamber, suffused with a musty odor, which hadn't been aired out in twenty years, Uncle Feitel had penned "The Book Hapolze."

I am sure that Uncle Feitel must have described my sister's wedding, but as the manuscript was lost I took over his task, as it were, and have spent twenty years writing my own "Sefer Hapolze," in which honey tastes bitter and sugar salty.

22

I AM DRAWN TO BEREZIN

After my sister's wedding three of us remained in the house: mother, me and a hen.

The hen soon began to lay an egg; after all, a hen in such an enviable position is not to be slaughtered.

Uncle Leizer and Aunt Sarah had brought the hen from Materova, a village ten viorsts from Dukor.

Such a hen is not allowed out into the street for she can easily lose her way. When mother allowed her out of the hole under the oven the hen began promenading with very quiet and careful steps over the rooms of the house. Turning her head left and right, she took the measure of her new home.

The hen possessed an ugly habit. She left small silver-colored mounds in each of the rooms on account of her very healthy appetite. A hen, it appears, can eat endlessly, although she has a full stomach.

For example, I poured out a heap of seeds that she pecked at, slowly filling her gizzard, and it seemed that the amount was such as would suffice for an entire day. But when I poured out another heap, she fell upon it as if she were famished.

Nothing seemed to sate her. When she consumed all the feed and her stomach was filled to capacity, like a bursting sack of grain, she would then begin consuming a mound of crumpled bread as if she were still ravishingly hungry.

After these three heaping portions, the animal would wash it all down with a pot of water.

Have you ever seen how a hen drinks?

It's very funny to observe how she fills her beak with water, stretches her head high and lowers the water down her throat. She then shuts her eyelids as if she were thanking God for providing enough food and drink.

My sister did the same when she had to swallow the very large white tablets which she took to soothe her headaches. She would throw back her head and sip the water from the glass until the round tablets would slip down into her stomach.

Velvel the physician once said to my sister that her headaches could be attributed to her girlhood, but once she would marry she would rid herself of this discomfort.

Perhaps this was the reason my sister rushed to marry Uncle Munia from Berezin.

Each time our hen would consume her meal in her most curious way I had my sister in mind. I would imagine my sister waddling slowly and quietly about the rooms of Uncle Munia's house, as she got acquainted with her surroundings.

Also, it must be said that my sister stayed by herself in the house all day while Uncle Munia, her husband, stood in his shop from dawn to dusk just to earn his daily bread.

My sister's first letter from Berezin brimmed with sorrow. First, she informed us of the sad news that while Uncle Munia was in Dukor his store was burglarized, effectively cleaned out by Bereziner thieves.

It was so bad that he had to borrow a hundred rubles on interest to stock up his store anew.

And to make things even worse, my sister had still to rid herself of her Dukor headaches. And what's more, she pined for mother and me.

She came up with a plan that mother should move with me from Dukor to Berezin, where we would all be together.

Mother would then be able to open a ribbon shop, because there weren't many such stores in Berezin. I would finally get the right sort of medical treatment rendered by real doctors. Berezin boasted two good physicians and a big pharmacy with all kinds of salves and medications.

I found her plan much to my liking.

First of all, I longed for my sister, who had always treated me well. And secondly, I wanted to see the town my father was born in, and live in the ancestral home where he had once resided until he married my mother in Dukor. Thirdly, I wanted to be healed by a real doctor. The so-called hoary healing of the gypsies and the Tatars only made matters worse.

Even the schoolboys once scribbled a biblical verse in ink on my hand, "Witch shall not live! Live not witch. Be Gone!" [This may be based on the Book of Exodus, Chapter 22, verse 18.] This was to serve as an antidote against evil spirits. However, the magic ink had bitten so deeply into my scrofulous hand that my hand became entirely blistered. I suffered mightily but I now realize it was worth it because the anti-witch prayer drove out all the wicked ghosts. The proof: I am still alive, as you see, until this very day.

It irritated me that no one in Dukor took me seriously. Everyone regarded me as some kind of freak who might disappear at any time. Even my own teachers scarcely believed I would live to see the day of my bar-mitzvah.

I had a yen for learning. I had already mastered the tractate "Baytseh" and I enjoyed immersing myself in the great arguments between "Beit Shammai" and "Beit Hillel." I far preferred Beit Hillel because it was less strict than Beit Shammai. If Beit Hillel declared something permissible, Beit Shammai would immediately forbid it. Only in one instance did I take the side of Beit Shammai: the subject concerning an egg born on yom tov (holiday).

This took on a personal quality for me. Our hen had the habit of laying eggs even on holidays. As my health condition demanded that I have a freshly-laid egg every day I yearned for it, imagining drinking the egg before it had cooled off. But Beit Hillel declared that an egg laid on a holiday is forbidden and Beit Shammai, generally far stricter, had in this particular instance permitted it.

When mother saw that I was weighing on going to Berezin, she headed to take counsel with the Rabbi.

Mother called on Rabbi Moshe Charney z"l, my father's uncle, which I found a bit strange.

When he heard of my sister's plan to have us move to Berezin, he responded thus:

"Listen up, Brocha, if you're going to give up Dukor you'll have to go about it differently. You have worked hard enough so that your children can stand on their own feet. Daniel will be far better off health-wise when you have more time to spend with him.

You understand what I mean! Therefore, take your time in thinking the matter through. Don't run off pell-mell to Berezin, where I do not see any purpose for you."

I then had no idea what purpose the Rabbi was referring to. But I surmised from the sudden moistness of mother's eyes that some big new purpose must be afoot for mother and me.

When I later asked mother about this new "purpose" that the Rabbi referred to mother made as if she hadn't heard me speak and said nothing.

At night, mother took me into her bed, although the night was quite hot (generally mother would take me to her bed in winter when the house was cold).

Mother embraced me with her silken hands as if she feared someone would steal her precious bargain.

I fell asleep in my mother's arms, but my nose bled as a result of the great heat, which I only discovered in the morning when I noticed the red-smeared bed linen.

Just then the yellow gauze the Kiev professor had prescribed had run out. I said to mother: "See, if we lived in Berezin I'd be able in the wink of an eye to buy gauze in a pharmacy."

By the way, mother had sent through Leizer a package of food to my brothers, for Shmuel and Boruch, one of whom studied in the Minsk school and the other in Tatar school.

23

MATCHMAKING

Ever since my sister moved to Berezin after the wedding I became boss of our house.

I helped mother make the bed, sweep the house, dampening the floors first so as not to stir up too much dust. I fed the hen as soon as she started to crow and sat on the bed to protect her with a coverlet when she was ready to lay an egg.

I also assisted mother with kitchen work: sifting through the worm-eaten chickpeas and year-old barley. Even in the garden I would set out the wild grass in such a fashion that the beans would have something to entwine around all summer long.

Mother gave me a small bag of earth for use in my swift gardening work. The bag looked small and narrow, as if meant for a child; yet I managed to plant seeds that would come to outshine all the other garden plants, some of which grew quite tall and strong like trees.

Among the sesame seeds I planted Turkish wheat or corn stalks. When the beans darkened in color it was a sign that the Turkish wheat had ripened. (It was said that the Turkish sultan wore his style of beard because the Land of Israel then belonged to the Ottoman Empire).

I also planted poppy seed flowers, which grew tall and firm with heads resembling colorful butterflies, which, alas, did not keep long.

I was proud of my achievement, which earned the envy of my fellow students.

DUKOR

Given how consumed I was in summer with work around the house, the kitchen and the garden, I found little time for study. My teachers consoled mother that as I possessed a good head, in the end I would catch up with everybody.

I had by then already completed the Talmudic tractate "Baytseh." I practically knew all its five chapters by heart. After "Baytseh" the curriculum offered the three "Bovehs": Boveh Kameh, Boveh Metziah and Boveh Basra. In Hebrew they are known as the First Portal, the Middle Portal and the Final Portal. My friends informed me that these three tractates dealt with financial disputes, a topic of no interest to me.

I, however, was already enticed by the tractate "Marriage." The boys told me it was a joyous bit of Talmud. Even Osher the Teacher became strongly confused when the boys presented him with tough questions about husbands and wives. His rebbetzin screamed at him why he brings up connubial matters with boys who are not even bar-mitzvahed.

I was drawn to this tractate for many personal reasons.

First, I already knew that Osher had a match for my brother Shmuel, or "Mulya" as we called him amongst ourselves.

Mulya was then fifteen or sixteen and had already studied in the Minsk yeshiva, where he was known as the Dukor prodigy. Pomerantz, a very rich Jew and the first sexton of the Minsk shul, had cast an eye on my brother as a good potential son-in-law. Pomerantz invited my brother to eat at his home on the two most important days of the week — Friday and Saturday. My brother eagerly accepted this invitation because at the outset he didn't realize the rich man's intentions. The "bride" was then much younger than Mulya. Pomerantz went ahead and wrote a letter to Osher the Teacher requesting that he discuss this matter with my mother.

The following discussion ensued between my mother and Reb Osher:

"Listen up, Brocha," Reb Osher said to mother. "I want to tell you something but don't take it the wrong way."

"The wrong way? Whatever are you saying Reb Osher? God is with you," mother said soothingly.

Reb Osher, twisting his cigarette between his yellowed fingers, began. "I believe we should think seriously about the boys

116

... Your young daughter you have given in marriage; your eldest, Mendel and Zalke, have become already small breadwinners, but your middle son, I mean Shmuel ... I am telling you it's a real "shmaltz grub" (gold mine) ... Ha, Brocha, what do you think?"

When mother heard Reb Osher stumbling over his words, hiding behind clouds of cigarette smoke, she answered thus:

"Hear now, Reb Osher, you know I'm a simple woman and do not understand Talmudic twists and turns. Speak to me directly."

Reb Osher then spat out all the smoke in his mouth and told mother the entire story of the rich man Pomerantz who wants Mulya as a permanent food lodger, on condition that he later marry his daughter, who is said to be a beauty and already plays the piano.

"I'm telling you, Brocha, it's a gold mine! It'll be good for Shmuel and it'll be good for you." Reb Osher, as was his custom, began addressing his own fingers as if he already had snared the first "l'chaim" (drink) on account of the wedding to be.

Mother fell into deep thought. She searched for an answer that wouldn't, God forbid, insult Reb Osher.

After a while, she said, "You know, Reb Osher, the saying that it is better bitterness from God than sweetness from people."

She then continued, "I mean, Reb Osher, I cannot guess the future path of my children. God guided them until now and will, with His help, guide them further along."

Mother then pulled me closer to her as if to say that if she had someone to worry about, it was me, her youngest.

Only then did I understand that a rich Jew from Minsk wanted to purchase my brother from mother, and a sudden huge sadness befell me on account of Mulya, whom I love to this day.

This alone prodded me to begin studying the tractate "Kiddushin." I wanted to know if a father can marry off his daughter while she is yet a child, as our sages say, not yet a fully developed person. But I had an even more powerful reason for wanting to study "Kiddushin." I sought, as well, to discover whether a widow is allowed to marry for the second time and whether she must first get permission from her children or not.

This question disturbed me greatly because Masha the Lunatic blurted out the secret that a match was being sought for mother.

At first I consoled myself by dismissing it as the ravings of a lunatic. But when Masha told me all the particulars, I began to believe her. She explained that Uncle Feivl of Tokarnia, who had offered mother half a millstone as a grave maker for father, had already spoken to the Rabbi about someone for mother—a fine Jew, a forest merchant, a widower in search of a wife.

I then understood that Masha the Lunatic knew whereof she spoke. I remembered how the Rabbi winked that once my sister's marriage was done it was high time for mother to think seriously about "takhlis," namely herself.

Now it became clear to me why mother took me nightly into her bed and trembled over me, as if she feared someone could take me away from her.

When I began to lean on Masha to tell me where she had heard of this secret, the white of her eyes suddenly turned over and she shouted into my ear with a hot breath: "If you promise to marry me when you grow up, I'll tell you everything."

I then realized just how crazy Masha was and ran off home in tears.

When mother saw me in tears, she started to ask what had just happened.

I told her the truth, that Masha had frightened me.

"Woe is me, is there anything to a crazy woman's mumblings?" mother said, trying to calm me. She then told me the good news that she rented a room to Leah Meren, the bagel baker, and her daughter, Rivkele.

I was delighted with this piece of good tidings because Leah Mereh the bagel baker was a widow, and if mother is renting her a room, she can't be thinking of marrying herself.

Besides, mother agreed that Leah Meren should give us two fresh bagels every day for which, in turn, mother would give Rivkele a cup of cow's milk.

Rivkele, pale and thin, suffered from tuberculosis. Just like me, she needed more milk and eggs.

She, however, had two large luminous eyes, and she worked meticulously in weaving silken tefillin bags embroidered by lions and birds.

Leah Meren once told me that if I was nice to her Rivkele she would sew a tefillin bag for my bar-mitzvah (I was already more than eleven years old and an orphan is bar mitzvahed at twelve!).

Out of great happiness, I went into the garden to water the Turkish wheat. It hadn't rained for several days, and I was worried that my fine planting might wither.

Watering thus the wheat, I began thinking that because of Rivkele I needed to begin studying as soon as possible the tractate "Kiddushin." I had to know if a bar-mitzvah boy was allowed to be nice to a girl who is still a minor, as the wise men put it (Rivkele was my age, between eleven and twelve).

Suddenly I observed how a small beard sprouted from a planting of Turkish wheat. An irreverent thought lodged into my head that when the beard turned dark brown at summer's end I would plaster it on my face and tell Masha in a deep, thick voice: "Nu, Masha, I have a beard and mustache, I'm grown. Let's get married!"

I imagined how much crazier Masha would become upon hearing such talk and how all of Dukor would go topsy-turvy.

I didn't go through with this scheme. In the end, Masha is after all my own cousin. How pitiful to see that no one wanted to marry her, though she approached everyone wild-eyed: "Come, let's get married and steal away. Come, let's get married and be off."

What only a madwoman can think up!

24

FLIES

I suffered terribly in summer from a plague of flies, battening on to me as if I were a naked lump of sugar.

No matter what I did, they stuck to me like unwanted partners of my life and limbs.

Should I sit down to eat, the flies were the first to taste the dish. Even before I could make the blessing on a slice of bread and jam my plate swarmed with them. While at it, they also besieged my yolk and when I swatted them away, they had already left their visiting cards.

No sooner did mother hand me a glass of milk than a fly was bathing in it.

Were I to sit down to write a letter to my sister in Berezin or to my brothers in Minsk the flies would congregate on my ream of paper, turning effortlessly a "pasakh" (straight line) into a kometz (perpendicular line dividing a straight line). [These lines indicated how words were pronounced.] Unbidden, they festooned the page with their own markings.

True, Aunt Chaya had a kind of sticky paper in her store that once placed into a dish of water would drown flies. But can one drown a world of flies in a dish of water?

I would constantly walk around with a towel on my shoulder and drive them off every surface. But all this effort was for naught. They seeped in through any crack in the window.

Therefore, I would take great pleasure when a fly got caught in the glass of our kerosene lamp. You will remember that a glass lamp is broad on the bottom and narrow on the top. When a fly manages to crawl in, it's done for. There's no way out! The gaseous smell knocks it flat, and there it lies trapped in a glass prison. Only after maariv, or at dusk when the light is turned on, is the death sentence executed.

True, it wasn't all that nice for me to take joy at the whining of captured flies, but they so embittered my life that I entertained no pity for them. I must, however, declare at this opportunity that not all the flies in our home were angry and brazen. Thankfully a fair portion of these winged creatures would promenade back and forth on our window panes and simply take note of the outside world. These, I would say, were the community's poets.

Another cohort of flies enjoyed promenading with their heads bent and their feet raised. These I designated as the philosophers. To be sure, during my childhood I knew nothing about either poetry or philosophy, but I now understand the corresponding division of creative labor among flies.

The third category amongst them (and wouldn't you know it is the largest!) were proud and hungry. With murderous effrontery they tore food from one's mouth and danced merrily on one's nose tip and on the rim of an eyelid. For these I had no empathy and couldn't care less whether they found themselves trapped in a lamp glass or spider net.

The cry of a captured fly followed me for decades, until I heard it again in 1938 in a summer locale outside of Paris. I had become suddenly ill with pneumonia and had turned so weak that I didn't have the strength to drive the flies from my body.

My landlady hung some kind of small flypaper over my head, which looked like a yellow sticky cloth smeared on both sides. When a fly alights on either side of this cloth it meets its destiny— wailing all day until it expires with its last breath.

So it was that I once again heard the flies wailing near Paris and remembered the sounds that had tormented my childhood in Dukor.

Back in the shtetl I had written a song in which I expressed my deepest empathy for the fly's wail, one I appreciated all the more when I was driven into exile across the lands of Europe.

Here is the song:

"Various cries have I heard:
That of a child on the day of its bris,

That of a young widow at the gravesite of her husband,
That of a soldier lying in a hospital
With his feet blown away,
That of a cow which scents the spilled blood of her child,
That of a homeless dog that cries at the full moon;
But the strangest cry of all is that of a fly
For hours tearing itself free from a sticky cloth
Which seals its doom."

I know that this sentimental ditty has on the face of it no real connection to my childhood experience in Dukor. I deliberately weave it into this chapter to show the pedagogue and child psychologist that every childhood experience must sooner or later materialize in one form or another.

Surely, I couldn't have had the same sentiment during my childhood for a captured fly as I do now; nevertheless, thus has ever been the fate of the fly down millennia. And the knowledge that flies existed thousands of years ago I discovered via a story of Titus the Evil One [Roman Emperor who destroyed Jerusalem in the year 70 C.E. and died at age 41].

Titus the Evil One, if you recall, destroyed Jerusalem and burned the Holy Temple. God punished him by means of a fly, which entered his nose and then traveled to his brain, tormenting him to death.

I started to fear a similar fate. I already by then had cause to fear such divine revenge.

At fault was Yosef Velias, who had completed eight classes in a Minsk gymnasium and was known as a free thinker. He would visit his parents in summertime. I once met him in Algetshina, a forest near Dukor, smoking a cigarette on the Sabbath [when smoking was prohibited].

He took great fright, scared I would tell his parents of his great sin. He then violently forced me to smoke one of his "Sabbath" cigarettes.

He promised that come Sunday morning he would show that God did not exist and that, at least until the following day, I should take him at his word that everything stems from nature.

When I came the next day to obtain the promised proof of God's non-existence in the world, Yosef Velias took an empty beer bottle and placed a shelled hard egg on the narrow top of the bottle and asked me:

"Do you think that the egg can of itself slip through the narrow neck of the bottle and fall in one piece into it?"

"I think not," I answered with supreme confidence.

"I'll show you that in fact the egg can of its own accord slip through the bottle and land on the bottom, not, as you might think, a result of some holy utterance or citation but only arising from the power of this small piece of paper which I will first throw into the bottle."

Right in front of me Yosef lit a small piece of newspaper, let it drop into the bottle and quickly thereafter placed the boiled egg.

Wonder of wonders! The egg began to squeeze its way into the bottleneck, stretching in as it fell in one piece to the bottom.

"Aha! you see there's no God in the world!" Yosef exclaimed triumphantly. "It all arises out of nature! Rain and snow, lightning and thunder and all other things which you see and hear spring from nature. Now, Donya, you understand why I'm allowed to smoke on Shabbes? But don't you dare tell anyone!"

"I hear you," I answered confusedly and ran away, swallowing hard this big new secret, which had turned me into a renegade even before my bar-mitzvah.

When I met Yosef for the second time, I asked him quietly, "And who made nature itself?"

He had no answer. He just told me that I was too young to understand such grand subjects, but from his reply or lack of one I was struck by the realization that he himself was not sufficiently clear as to who had created nature.

Truth to tell, I still don't know until this very day who created all the wonders of nature!

Splitting the atom and flying across the sky had already been mastered, but to make an artificial egg from which a chicken could emerge has yet to be achieved.

But while I was still a boy, the trick of the egg in the bottle made an extraordinarily powerful impression on me. I kept on wondering about it secretly. Yet, when it began to thunder and there was lightning I became flustered and frightened and would utter the benediction "that his strength and power fills the whole world," as I wanted to be reconciled with the Master of the Universe.

As it appears, the Master of the Universe had long ago forgiven my youthful sins. He already had many opportunities to take revenge but instead he remained merciful.

I realized this clearly right after young Velias had turned me into a renegade. That very summer I took ill with blood diarrhea, i.e., a cholera or dysentery, an infectious disease arising from so many flies swarming the non-Jewish street. The non-Jewish boys overate green apples and pears and soon infected one another with this ugly affliction. As our house stood at the very head of Village St., I fell victim first.

Mother soon trotted out all the old-wives' cures and in quick succession I became again good and observant.

Among the various cures for a bloody diarrhea, the one that most appealed to me, was the "zmai" or "moerkop," as others called it. When one carried the amulet for two to three weeks continuously on one's neck, the bloody disease disappeared.

From the outside the "moerkop" looked like something cut from bone, but when one placed an ear to its open belly a strange internal hissing sound could be detected, as if several flies at once had got caught inside.

When I asked mother what hisses so, she answered that the sounds resembled those of the sea.

From that point on I would cover my head with the bedsheet.

This bad practice endured because each summer I would tremble on account of the flies.

Only here in America, where so-called "screens" have been introduced, have I finally freed myself from my childhood fly mania and I could begin breathing freely at night. America, indeed, should be blessed for having liberated me from my fly phobia, the torment of which was as long and interminable as the Jewish exile [from the Land of Israel].

25

THE FIRST KISS

In the month of Tammuz [during summer in Dukor] all of Dukor walked around with blackened mouths. It was, after all, the month of blackberries. For a mere two kopecks one could buy a full bowl of blackberries from a village lass. It must be said that those blackberries are never as tasty as those one picked off the vine oneself. True, but for that, however, one had to walk a whole day deep into the forest. But what joy to behold, as boys and girls in pairs marched off to gather fruit.

Furthermore, once in the forest one could gather mushrooms too. Our forest is famous for the yellow variety, which has thin stalks and broad tops, but with sides as thick as harmonicas.

No better dish exists than fried yellow mushrooms. However, in the forest one had to keep still for fear that if caught by the vengeful guard he would snatch the boys' caps and the girls' kerchiefs. Later he would make them pay for the return of their head coverings or somehow manage to bring him a quart of vodka.

According to existing law, one had to purchase a permit from the nobleman to gather as many berries as one wanted. But which crazy Jew would pay for something he could get practically for free from any village shiksa?

Mother would buy so many golden mushrooms and berries for the month of Tammuz that it sufficed for the whole winter. She would fry blackberries in the hope that it wouldn't be needed; for its juice was considered the last remedy for a weak stomach, may we be spared! She would, as well, fry raspberries in oil, in hopes—may it never be needed—that its juice would bring on a good sweat.

But, wait, wait! I'm not through with the blackberries, which nearly blackened my name across all Dukor.

This occurred on the 17 of Tammuz.

During this very long fast day, when even the religious articles can be said to fast too, mother used to go with me to Yeshaya the miller to fulfill an act of great kindness.

Yeshaya's water mill stood far behind the cemetery. A couple would drive us for practically no charge to the mill itself.

The visit to the mill owner was a big holiday for me, although on the 17 of Tammuz a Jew is not permitted to celebrate.

I believe that not all my readers will remember what happened to the Jewish people on the 17 of Tammuz. Therefore, I will convey concisely in the following lines what Osher the Teacher told us about this date.

On this longest and hottest day of the summer several misfortunes occurred, but at different periods of history. The first great calamity happened when Moses was at Mt. Sinai to accept the tablets. As he tarried too long on the mountaintop the Jews lost patience and fashioned a golden calf. When Moses finally descended with the tablets in hand and saw the sinful sight of Jews bowing to the golden calf, he broke the tablets out of great fright.

The second calamity occurred when the evil Nebuchadnezzar, the king of Babylonia, captured Jerusalem and three weeks later, on the Ninth day of month Av, destroyed the First Holy Temple.

In punishment, God had driven Nebuchadnezzar into the forest, where he assumed the look of an animal and chewed on grass.

The third calamity happened when the evil Antiochus, the king of Greco-Syria, conquered the land of Israel and forced the Hellenistic religion on the Jews, pity be on them. This was followed by the valiant effort on the part of the Hasmoneans, who drove out all idol worshippers.

The fourth calamity transpired when the evil Titus, the Roman Caesar, conquered Jerusalem on the 17 of Tammuz and three weeks later (again on the Ninth of month Av) destroyed the Second Holy Temple. God then punished Titus with the flea which entered his brain and finished him off.

All of the above enumerated calamities which struck the Jews occurred between the 17 of Tammuz and the 9 of Av. Therefore, the three weeks were instituted, during which all festivity and hair-cutting were forbidden.

Yet for me the 17 of Tammuz became the most joyous day of summer.

Mother and I set out for Yeshaya the mill owner with pancakes made of the finest flour, to be eaten with cold sour milk straight out of the ice-cellar. After this tasty morsel, which I remember as if it were yesterday, mother spent time with the mill owner's wife in her nice salon until the owner would rush in "to catch his heart," to eat something after the half-day fast.

His three daughters, each more beautiful than the next, went to pick blackberries and took me along. Mother was happy with this arrangement because with them there was no fear of the forest guard, but she warned me not to crawl into the bushes.

Peshe, the eldest of the three daughters, calmed mother, promising she would look out for me.

We wandered into the wild forest and I stayed very close to Peshe because she knew the lay of the land far better than her sisters. The younger two sisters, Puah and Feytche, stayed far behind, picking many forest flowers which they wove into beautiful wreaths.

Peshe and I continued further into the forest, but we saw no berries.

Suddenly Peshe turned to me and said, "I think, Donya, you are quite tired so let's sit on the oak bench."

I sat down and the surface was soft as a quilt.

Peshe then continued, "Donya, describe something about Dukor."

I replied that today, the 17 of Tammuz, was a very sad day in Dukor.

"What is the 17 day of Tammuz?" she asked.

I explained it all to her, everything that Osher, the teacher, had taught us.

"But that was so long ago," she interrupted.

"It was, indeed, long ago but Osher says that Jews are not allowed ever to forget what evil rulers did to them."

"And yet you went to pick berries instead of fasting on such a day," Peshe said, catching me by surprise.

"But I'm not yet bar-mitzvahed. I don't have to fast. But as soon as I start to learn the tractate of 'Kiddushin,' I will start to fast even on the 17 of Tammuz," I said proudly.

"What is Kiddushin?" she asked.

"Kiddushin is a part of the Talmud with instructions on how to marry," I answered gravely, as if I were already a Talmud student.

"Why do you need to know how to get married, if you are not yet bar-mitvahed?" Peshe asked, sneezing on cue.

"I don't need it for myself, but as they want to marry off my brother Shmuel I want to know if he is ready," I said, thus spilling the big family secret.

"Who wants to marry off Shmuel?" she asked with great curiosity.

"A rich Minsk Jew wants to purchase Shmuel from our mother and marry him off to his daughter, who already plays the fortepiano," I plundered on.

"How old is Shmuel?" Peshe interjected.

"Shmuel is my elder by four years—that's nearly sixteen!"

Suddenly Peshe burst out in peals of laughter that echoed through the forest. She kept rolling with such spasms of laughter that I stood off to the side, as you can imagine. But her cackling soon appeared in my face.

"Oh, Donya tells stories to be found in the romances I read. Ha! Ha! Ha! He! He! He!"

But suddenly Peshe asked me if I'm not afraid to be alone with a girl in the forest.

"Why should I be afraid?" I asked dumbly.

"I am already sixteen and I play the fortepiano," she said, laughing uproariously.

I could see that I would not be soon picking berries with Peshe. I pleaded with her to take me back to my mother at the mill.

"Aha! Then you're afraid to be with a girl in the forest," she declared, and before I could even start to reply, she grabbed my head between her soft hands and kissed my forehead.

The unexpected kiss burned me. I feared that a red spot would forever remain emblazoned on my forehead and all of Dukor would find out that a girl kissed me in the forest.

(Not for nothing had Osher, the teacher, warned us that in the three weeks between the 17 of Tammuz and the 9 of Av all the evil spirits crawl out of their hiding places, and that therefore great precaution must be taken.)

I began again to plead with Peshe to take me back to my mother.

Peshe took me by the hand and led me out the forest, but her hand trembled as if she had taken fright of someone.

At the rim of the forest we met up with Peshe's two younger sisters. They wore several bouquets of lovely forest flowers. Peshe placed one of the bouquets on my head and she said to her sisters, "He is still a child; he took fright in the forest."

I was thrilled that she placed the bouquet on me, which surely must cover the red kiss mark on my forehead!

I already then realized that a dybbuk lies in every girl, from whom I must hide not merely on the 17 of Tammuz.

26

A CHAPTER OF RUSSIAN GRAMMAR

Something had turned over in my mind ever since Peshe had kissed me on the forehead. I began to imagine that Titus' flea had made its way into my brain and was constantly muttering about Peshe.

I did not then know about such things as love.

In the tractate Kiddushin, which I then studied, there was talk about how a man can buy a wife, but nothing about love.

A blind power started pulling me to the mill as if with a magnet, to the very place Peshe sat on a soft chair in the large guest room and read a Russian book. As it would appear, one can discover a lot more in those Russian books than in our sacred texts!

I began to ask mother whether Zalman, the teacher from Humane, should give me a Russian grammar book.

Zalman the Brill (glasses) was a younger fellow on the cusp of military age. He wanted to take all the exams for the gymnasium. He decided to wear glasses as a way of indicating that he was nearsighted and no material for the Russian military.

But he sported eyeglasses not only because of fear of military induction. He needed them for his study. Those who wear glasses appear far more learned and intelligent than those who walked around without them. A teacher with eyeglasses earns 25 kopecks more a month than one without.

As a result, our shtetl soon nicknamed the Hu-maner teacher Zalman Eyeglasses, and thanks to him I learned all of Russian in one summer.

When I say all of Russian I, of course, exaggerate.

In those years, one studied Russian either from Kirpichnikov's Grammar Book or that of Blaustein's.

Gentile children used to study from the thin Kirpichnikov's grammar volume because Russian was their mother tongue and they already knew many of the rules of the language; but for Jewish children it was far better and worthier on the whole to study from Blaustein's quite thick edition.

Blaustein, after all, was a Jew, and he knew quite well that for Jewish children each rule had to be interpreted individually and enumerated specifically, and all the exceptions listed carefully.

Take for example the gender question. Kirpitchnikov, the Gentile, made it very simple. He says that if the genitive ends with a "ya," as in Konya, it is masculine, but if the genitive ends with "ee" it's feminine.

Blaustein wasn't lax when it came to setting a full table of Russian words with their proper masculine and feminine endings.

[skipping some fine points of Russian grammar]

Rivkele's mother, Leah Mere, the bagel baker, if you'll recall, became our neighbor soon after my elder sister got married.

She was a young widow, like my mother, with three children, two boys and a girl. Her older two boys, Avrohom-Meir and Yankl, were already "eating days" in Minsk. She was left with her youngest, Rivkele, who was my age.

Rivkele was very plain and thin. Mother said she suffered from tuberculosis. However, she had two big luminous eyes of blue and two braids.

I was miffed that her mother would wash Rivkele's hair with kerosene. All Sabbath long Rivkele smelled of the kerosene and I wasn't able to study Russian with her.

Oh yes, I forgot to tell you that I became Rivkele's Russian tutor because her mother couldn't afford the thirty kopecks a month to pay Zalmen Eyeglasses for Russian lessons.

DUKOR

Leah Mere, the bagel baker, had other intentions in having me teach her daughter Russian. She purposely made me her daughter's instructor so that I would grow accustomed to her.

Both widows, my mother and Leah Mere, had decided between themselves that when both their plague-ridden children would grow out of danger, they might perhaps, with luck, become a couple.

Rivkele once blurted out to me: "You know, Donya, mother said when we grow up, we'll get married."

Her remarks turned me red like a beet. My forehead began to burn just in the very place Peshe, the miller's daughter, had once kissed me. I took fright that Rivkele might just kiss me on my forehead because she too is beginning to talk this way.

As quickly as possible, I wanted to interrupt Rivkele and I commenced reciting Blaustein's grammar rules, according to my own playful system.

This approach helped me to memorize the rules as it helped Rivkele herself.

Tragically, she was not destined to grow up and marry me. She died soon after I was bar-mitzvahed. She survived long enough to knit a silken tefillin bag and had my name, Daniel, inscribed on it.

Her mother was disturbed that she had knit my full name, which ends with "el," the name of God, not permitted to be uttered unless preceded by a prayer.

It's possible that had Rivkele just knit "Donya" on the tefillin bag she might yet be alive this very day. Who can comprehend all of God's calculations as he governs his world?

I only know that to this very day I feel guilty for her premature death. I also continue to be bothered until today that on the Sabbath I couldn't play with her because the smell of her hair was too intense, a smell resembling that emitted from our Sabbath lamp, which would go on burning all night long during the Sabbath until the kerosene flamed out.

Rivkele's young life was extinguished like the Sabbath lamp.

27

ZUSHA THE SEXTON

Thank God funerals only happened very rarely in our shtetl. It may be that in Dukor, having no doctor to its name, no one knew when it was time to die.

It would happen at times that someone took very ill either at the nobleman's or at the priest's. A doctor would be summoned from as far as Minsk (five Russian miles, or about 23 US miles, from Dukor).

When Dukor got word that a doctor from Minsk was en route, many ills befell Jewish men and women in town, may we all be spared. One Jew would realize that he had serious heartburn, another remembered that he had high blood pressure, a third that he couldn't bear Jews anymore.

The women of Dukor made a beeline for the doctor. One suddenly suffered from spasms, another from stomach aches though she no longer could be pregnant, while a third couldn't get pregnant although recently married.

Young mothers carrying infants would insist on being seen by the doctor. One infant brought up the milk its mother had just offered; a second couldn't stop screaming day and night, and a third pitifully fell out of the crib and had water on the brain (a kind of English disease).

The Minsk doctor (self-evidently a Jew) would listen carefully with his wooden stethoscope and would knock everyone on the breastplate with two fingers. Afterward he would write out medical prescriptions, for which he received either a quarter or half a ruble.

The sick left very satisfied. In the end, they had gotten a bargain. If one had to travel to Minsk to visit the doctor it would have cost an arm and a leg.

The doctor himself left Dukor satisfied because he hadn't reckoned he would depart with all those quarters and half rubles. As soon as the doctor departed the shtetl all the sick men and women would immediately get well!

The prescriptions disappeared deep into cupboards, if only they wouldn't be needed. It is much more pleasant to sigh and to moan when one knows that deep, deep in the cupboard one can find a prescription of a famous doctor.

I heard a story that Moteh the butcher, who served as head of the Dukor community, was taking a hot bath in the steam room, and being thrashed with a thick broomstick by the bath attendant when he suddenly cried, "I am not feeling well!"

The bath attendant didn't take notice and continued to beat him with the broomstick and splash him with hot water.

Moteh the butcher broke out in a sigh, "Oy, I feel ill."

The bath attendant played dumb and continued to whip him with the well-thistled broom.

Moteh the butcher rolled off the top rung all the way to the bath floor.

Only then did the bath attendant pour cold water over him. When Moteh came to he began to scream at the bath attendant, "You idiot! If I say I don't feel well why do you continue to beat and pour hot water on me?"

The bath attendant responded defensively: "I'll tell you the truth Reb Moteh. When a Jew tells me he doesn't feel well at that moment I think, 'And who feels well? Do I feel well standing all of Friday on the top rung of the bathhouse steaming Jews? And which Jew finds himself well in these times?' If you Reb Moteh had said, God forbid, 'I'm sick' (mloshne) I would have immediately caught on that you were really not feeling well, and I would have immediately poured a cold draft of water over you before you slipped down."

All of the naked Jews agreed with the bath attendant. If one is about to faint, it is far better to say "mloshne" than "not well," which applies to everyone.

But, despite all the widespread non-wellness, a lot of Dukor Jews did indeed live to an advanced age. When their time came they passed away leaving all the prescriptions, which would surely come in handy for the children and grandchildren.

An unfilled prescription never spoils!

Zusha the sexton a"h (may peace be upon him), the town's scribe, had the most beautiful of deaths. All of Dukor prayed wrapped in his tefillin, had their mezuzahs affixed by him to their doorposts and read and recited from the many Torah scrolls he had inscribed during his very long life.

He was also the blood drawer at every Dukor circumcision, a post he was eminently suited for as his whiskers were burned off from too much snuff smelling.

And what a snuff smeller he was! Just before the arrival of the Sabbath he packed his nostrils to the brim with snuff to last him for the entire day of rest.

The remnants of his whiskers and even his beard no longer had a definite color and came to resemble flax, which is neither yellow, gray nor blue.

Though short of stature, he was broad-boned and agile. Whenever and wherever a toast was made, he could be found at the head of the line. A day would hardly pass where Zusha would not raise a glass.

Dukor Jews often had, as is customary, yahrzeits to observe. On each occasion the mourner would offer a bottle of schnapps with bagels. People in surrounding areas would also come to town to observe commemoration days. Understandably, Zusha was the first to raise a toast and the last to finish off the bottle.

Just so did Zusha the sexton pull in 82 years.

His best toast comrade was Osher, the teacher, who was the "khoyser" [assistant] of the elder Lubavitcher z"l (may his memory be for a blessing).

Once, when the two got good and drunk, Zusha suddenly said to Osher:

"Listen up, Osher. What do you think about getting a tipple? Do you think the Creator of the World cares, or for that matter your wife?"

I do not remember his reply.

I also do not know when Zusha became a widower. For as long as I remember him he was already a widower, and he would have to keep an eye on the women's section [of the synagogue].

When, at the age of 82 years, no longer serving the community, he asked for only three things to end his God-fearing life, namely: cake, schnapps and snuff tobacco.

Understandably, the Dukor community very respectfully met all his requests. One early morning Zusha's nephew, Herschele the Small, who himself was already north of forty, came running to the synagogue to announce to the Jews during their morning prayers that his uncle was on the threshold of death.

Immediately several shul Jews went to Zusha. They found him still alive and gladdened to see Jews had come to see him off for his final leave-taking. With his last breath he told his nephew that on one of the shelves lay a pair of ordered tefillin. He had him promise to make sure to pass them to those who had made the purchase, and that on another shelf lay a bottle of whiskey. Jews need to make a toast, he reminded them all. Hershele the Small filled the glasses to the brim. The Jews made first one toast, then a second, then a third until they emptied the bottle. Then Hershele the Small closed the shelves and left rapidly.

The other shul Jews placed their hands on each other's shoulders and began to spin around. Zusha's house was aglow with joy. Jews were singing and dancing. What a pleasure to die encircled by the Rabbi's melody. Zusha passed away joyously in the knowledge that Jews remain Jews even in the face of death.

When Hershele the Small a bit later placed a feather to his uncle's nose no movement could be detected, a sign that Zusha the Sexton had departed this realm.

"Blessed is the True Lord" everyone pronounced. Just so did Zusha take leave of this world in his 82nd year.

Obviously, the entire town attended the funeral. He was buried with full honors in the finest location in the cemetery.

Reb Zusha had arranged ahead of time that he not be placed too close to the women.

It appears that Zusha had a heavy heart when it came to the women of Dukor.

I was not fated to experience the funeral because I had by then left town.

I did, however, experience in Dukor a "funeral" for a living Jew.

A Jew suddenly took it into his head to leave for America. Fifty years ago America was indeed far-off.

Mother had told me that America was located on the far side of the world, where everything is topsy-turvy.

All of Dukor had great compassion for the Jew set to travel to the other side of the world!

The entire town went to see him off, as if he were already dead, of another world. All that was missing was Zusha with his alms box; after all it is written in the holy books that "Charity saves from death."

The traveling Jew's mother sobbed miserably. His wife also cried and his children followed suit loudly as well; even I shed tears, though he was not of my family.

We followed him all the way to the big bridge that crosses the town's river. Suddenly the driver realized he might not make it in time for the train in Rudensk. He then smote his horses and the wagon picked up speed, racing along on the sandy road, leaving behind a swirling cloud of dust.

We were all left on the road, as if we too had been whipped. Just so did a young healthy Jew disappear from Dukor leaving behind a wife and small children.

I often asked mother why Jews travel so far to America, the other side of the world, where everything is upside-down. She replied that nobody left for America for mere pleasure but rather out of pitiful need.

I was happy and indeed thanked God that my elder brothers did not know of the kind of need that drives a person to America.

28

I AM DRAWN TO MINSK

I became a bar-mitzvah on a Sabbath that fell between Yom Kippur and Sukkus.

Mother was gussied up in the same finery she had worn for my sister's wedding. For her it was no less an occasion!

She wore both her rings which she always kept secreted in one of her private drawers. One was her wedding ring, which she had taken off some twelve years earlier, when she became a widow; the other ring, also of real gold, looked like a sinuous snake with two green stones set in its head, like two serpentine eyes.

When mother put on both rings, she would forget entirely that she was a widow, and I would forget I was an orphan.

But at my bar-mitzvah everyone suddenly realized that my father was missing, the man who could pronounce the blessing "Boruch Sheh-potranee," a ritual which released him from the responsibility of carrying my sins on his account.

Despite having fulfilled the role and function of a father for twelve long years, mother was after all a woman, and when I was called up to recite my bar-mitzvah Torah portion she was not allowed to stand by my side on the dais the way my father could have. She sat with the women in the distaff section of the synagogue from whence she gazed at me with two large moist eyes, as if they were two projectors of light.

I felt the moist warmth of mother's gaze settling on my talit-wrapped back. I read my portion bravely, acquitting myself flawlessly and glided through my bar-mitzvah speech without any hitches during the festive feast that followed, much as if I were reciting the well-rehearsed Russian grammatical rules I had mastered via Blaustein's primer, which I still remember, although the biblical portion I recited has flown from memory. Perhaps because I knew from the outset I would have to recite my biblical portion but once in my life, whereas the gender declensions of Blaustein's primer would be remembered for all time.

I recall that as soon as I was bar-mitzvahed mother began treating me like a man. When I returned home from the synagogue on Friday evenings she would say, "Nu Daniel, say kiddush!" I was no longer "Donya."

I would recite the blessing over the two challah loaves, and she would piously reply "Amen," as if I were my father.

After my bar-mitzvah mother stopped taking me into her bed, which she had always done on cold winter nights. I felt disappointed, for there is nothing sweeter than falling asleep in the wintertime in the warm arms of my mother.

As mother began treating me like a man, I addressed her in the manner of an adult. I once told her, "Hear now, mameleh. I think you have to take me to Minsk to my elder brothers." All four of them resided then in the provincial capital.

The oldest, Mendel and Zalke, were breadwinners. True, one worked at the "cheap kitchen" on Rakover St. and the other at the "cheap teahouse."

My two other brothers, Shmuel and Boruch (the future Shmuel Niger and Boruch Vladeck), were still officially yeshiva students and "ate days," taking their meals at assigned Jewish homes, but in fact they were quietly studying trades and learning Russian.

My brother Boruch (or "Bonya," as we then familiarly called him) had already published a description of our shtetl, Dukor, in a Russian Minsk newspaper. He depicted its poverty and backwardness, which drew its meager sustenance from the surrounding poor White Russian peasantry.

Just at that time our beloved Rabbi, our elder great uncle, Rabbi Moshe Charney z"l, passed away. The leaders of the community searched for a mate for his eldest daughter, a man who could assume the rabbinic position and become the spiritual leader of Dukor and its environs.

They took umbrage at my brother Bonya because of his article. Which rabbi would want to become spiritual leader of a shtetl comprised of the down and out?!

I yearned to go to Minsk to warn my brother Bonya that he not dare show up in Dukor as long as a new rabbi had not yet been found. God help us, what could happen if he did; he very well might be slapped.

I was also drawn to Minsk because of Peshe, the miller's daughter, who had left to finish her studies. True, she was older than I was by four or five years, but she was the first girl that had ever kissed me on the forehead when I went off to pick blackberries in the forest.

Granted, it is a big sin to think of girls once one is bar-mitzvahed. It is written specifically in the Talmud that "thought is synonymous with deed." To think of something is already as if one had committed an act. But what could I do if Peshe's first kiss scalded my brain, just like Titus's fly had his, God protect us?

Of course, I never told mother why I read so many Russian books, where I sought to fathom the secret of love.

Not a word could be found in our holy books about romantic love, other than in the "Song of Songs," but that text is only a metaphor of the Jewish people, whereas in the Russian books Peshe had read things stood differently. Otherwise, why would she have kissed me on the forehead and then rolled in the grass, uttering "kha, kha, kha" and "khee, khee, khee." God have mercy on us.

Leave it to God to send along a musician who played on his instrument Russian songs to ravish the heart. Practically all were about love, unfortunate love, just like my very own. I picked up their tune and lyrics and was certain that Peshe, the miller's daughter, must be singing just such ditties somewhere in Minsk.

I believe that many of my dear readers still remember these heart-rending sad songs. I must admit that even now, whenever I hear one of them, my heart jumps as if Peshe were kissing me again.

At long last, mother took my huge yearning for Minsk seriously, although at first she couldn't understand what drove me to the big city, a place where she saw no purpose for me.

In her mind, if I were to stay in Minsk I would need to "eat days"—have my meals assigned to different households, like my older brothers. Then I would really go to ruin.

For thirteen long years mother cooked and guarded me as the apple of her eye. How could she suddenly let me go off, alone, into the big bad city?

True, all my four brothers resided there but the eldest two were already planning on leaving for America (the Russian military had summoned them for checkups) and the other two were betwixt and between. They spent half days learning in the yeshiva and the other half studying in the gymnasium.

Mother, however, had heard that in Minsk a doctor named Shapiro could literally save lives! He could cut and cauterize the sick parts of the body and the person was effectively born anew. By then I already had enough sick spots that needed eliminating!

Mother swept me off to Minsk.

We didn't travel with the wagon drivers, who took all night, but rather by rail. In Dukor it was customary that when taking someone ill to Minsk only the train would do, as it doesn't shake one's innards as does a plain-old wagon.

The train station at Rudensk lies ten viorsts from Dukor. To get there one hired a driver, who in two hours brought one to the train station. From Rudensk to Minsk is a mere two stops, which together take all of an hour.

But as I was already a bar-mitzvah fellow a quarter ticket would need to be purchased, at the cost of nine kopecks. The Jews of Rudensk convinced mother that instead of wasting nine kopecks I should travel under the bench.

As soon as Mother and I boarded the train she told me to quickly hide under the bench. She then spread her skirt as widely as she could and asked her neighbor to do the same; the two together looking like a fan opened to its greatest width.

My soul nearly gave out under the bench. It was awfully hot and dark down there, as in a chicken coop. I pulled at mother's skirt, pleading that she should save me. But mother insisted that I lay still because the conductor had not gone by yet.

I lay there gasping like a dying hen, listening to the whirring wheels under the wagons, which emitted such crazed sounds as could only be found in Blaustein's Russian grammar book.

Only when the train reached Minsk did mother pull me out from under, but by then I was entirely bloodied.

The great heat below caused a huge nosebleed. She then took me to the station pump and washed me all over, but the maddening, grinding sound of the turning wheels kept tormenting my brain.

29

A TINY HEAP OF EARTH

My first view of Minsk was not uplifting. While still at the station, I got my first ugly slap.

I was intensely eager to see the buffet in the station's first class. While still in Dukor we had heard that all the tables there were decked out in white cloth, even in the middle of the week. I couldn't even imagine that on a plain Wednesday tables would be covered in fine Sabbath cloth.

I just barely convinced mother she should give me a margin of freedom to take a quick glance at the buffet of the first class. She finally let me go because she felt guilty for having kept me under the train bench en route to Minsk.

But as soon as I entered the large, luminous dining hall of the first class, where aristocrats, priests and even a few neatly barbered Jews sat at bedecked tables, a tall, lavishly uniformed guard lunged at me as if he suddenly emerged from under the earth, grabbed hold of my collar and threw me out, as if I were, God help us, a pickpocket.

While mother stood waiting for me at a distance, she suddenly saw a tall Gentile clad in silver buttons dragging me by the collar. She assumed he was a gendarme, hauling me off to the police. She ran over and pleaded with him to let me go.

The tall guard spilled me into my mother's arms and warned her angrily that she must never again allow me to stick my Jewish nose where it was neither wanted nor permitted.

Mother made me promise that from then on I would have no more dealing with a Czarist regime composed of such evil men. I explained that I had, pure and simple, made a bitter mistake.

I had thought that it was only in Kiev that Jews had no habitation rights, only to discover that in Minsk they didn't even have habitation rights in the train station.

Mother declared that Jews are everywhere in exile and therefore needed to keep as wide a berth from Gentiles as possible!

Thus I discovered yet again, in the Minsk train station, that Jews are indeed everywhere exiled.

The first discovery was made in Kiev, where mother took me to a hugely prominent professor. We were not permitted to stay overnight because it was said Jews were attacked there.

Minsk struck me as a smaller city in comparison with Kiev, the metropolis where I had ridden on an electric tram. In Minsk, by contrast, we drove into town on a horse tramway.

It appeared comical that one horse dragged an entire wagon of people and their belongings. One could have thought that the horse possessed the steely strength of a train locomotive. But when the horse started puffing uphill, a second one, which waited in the middle of the street, was hitched as a helper.

Traveling thus along the Minsk tramway for the first time, I remembered Kusha, the wagon driver, who would load people and their belongings. But as soon as the road started to ascend he would pull off all the passengers because his horse didn't have the strength to drag the entire packed wagon uphill. He did the same when the road descended for fear that, God forbid, the horse might lose control and would go flinging downhill, flipping over with the wagon wheels spinning in the air.

When one angry passenger once piped up that people were paying Kusha for nothing because they walked more than they rode, he answered, "You think I bought my horse to ride him to bits? I purchased him so that he should show us the way. Without the horse, we would constantly lose our direction."

(Now I understand that Kusha's approach possessed a piece of experiential wisdom. Ever since horses were left idle humanity began to lose its way, certainly in the last fifty years).

One would absolutely not lose one's way on the Minsk tramway with the horses in the lead.

My last disappointment came when we finally reached the home of my Aunt Itke, my mother's eldest and richest sister.

Aunt Itke's husband, Uncle Yeshaya Grundfest, was a broker among the Minsk forest merchants. He took a cut from their business and, as it appears, earned handsomely. Their apartment was well furnished and their eldest children were settled in life. The younger two studied a trade but the very youngest, Rokhele, suffered from jaundice, remaining in Minsk as thin and pale as she had once been in Dukor.

I said to mother, "You see, when one takes ill in childhood one is sick for life. Even the best doctors in Minsk can do nothing for her."

I uttered this out of my very real fear of Dr. Shapiro, the physician mother insisted I see. He was reputed to be quick with a surgical scalpel.

I even once overheard a conversation between my mother and her older sister in which Aunt Itke, connected to the best Minsk doctors, said, "Your 'plague' can at least be helped by an operation, but mine is extinguishing like a candle; no operation is of use."

To which my mother responded quite suddenly, "Do you think an operation can help him?"

"Brocha," Aunt Itke replied with stern authority, "whoever Dr. Shapiro takes under his wing is once and for all cured."

When mother heard such decisive talk she wept inwardly under her breath so I shouldn't see her crying.

I stood with my back to both my mother and aunt and made as if I were not paying any attention, but rather playing with the Singer sewing machine, which I knew already from Dukor.

But as soon as I heard Aunt Itke's advice, hinting that my whole hand might have to come off, I became wild with fear and began to turn the Singer sewing machine's foot pedal at such speed that the rubber attached to the wheel jumped a very long time, and the wheel spun as if of its own accord.

Only in the evening did things take a very festive turn at Aunt Itke's. Uncle Yeshaya came to eat dinner, followed by his two unmarried daughters who were studying a trade in Minsk.

When all of us were already seated at the richly bedecked table all my four brothers appeared, once word got out that we had arrived in Minsk.

145

The eldest of my brothers—Mendel and Zalke—came from Rakover St., where they had positions in the cheap kitchen and tea house, which the Minsk rich kept in business.

The other two brothers—Shmuel and Boruch—came from as far as Kameroyka, where they had a very inexpensive room in which to sleep, while all day long they took classes in the heart of Minsk.

When my Uncle Yeshaya saw all my four brothers he became a different person altogether. He immediately rushed in to talk about Zionism, describing all the particulars occurring at the Zionist Congress then taking place in Basle. He read to them Herzl's talks that appeared in "Ha-Tsfira," as well as those of Dr. Nordau, Dr. Wolffsohn and the other learned men, whose names I heard for the first time in Minsk. [These men were leaders in the movement to establish a Jewish State in Palestine.]

My brothers nodded their heads as if in seeming agreement with uncle. But if one of them tried to insert a word or pose a question Uncle Yeshaya wouldn't allow him to speak because he himself wasn't quite finished talking about all that he had heard that day from the forest merchants in Minsk, as well as what he had read in "Ha-Tsfira."

Truth to tell, I then didn't understand a word of all that Uncle Yeshaya had hammered into my bewildered brothers' heads. What I did take note of was that he was the exact opposite of Uncle Feitel "the Angel."

Uncle Feitel was a recluse, a homebody, a quiet, holy man, while Uncle Yeshaya was a scattered talker, not religiously observant, although his beard was a lot bigger and a lot longer than Uncle Feitel's.

I attributed this to the fact that Uncle Yeshaya was my uncle through marriage. Had he not married Aunt Itke he would have remained a stranger to me.

But setting that aside, Uncle Yeshaya's hammering words, although largely foreign and incomprehensible, nevertheless continue to stick in my memory until today: especially "a drop - a heap of earth."

He explained the logic behind the new alms box arrayed near the old-fashioned pushke of Reb Meir bal Haness [Rabbi with miraculous powers]. The new one had a blue and white star of

David. Every coin dropped into the box went to purchase a heap of earth for Jews in Palestine.

"Children, you understand a drop, a pile of earth," he repeated with strong emotion. "This is our National Fund."

My older two brothers, Mendel and Zalke, who were earners, could no longer bear Uncle Yeshavye's tone of burning urgency and reluctantly tossed two coins into the blue-white alms box.

I was very glad that my elder brothers now possessed two heaps of earth in the Land of Israel and, as a consequence, I became a bit partner in this enterprise.

When the Jews, please God, will buy out the entire Land of Israel from the Turk (Ottoman Empire), I will then travel there and sit freely and openly in a first-class buffet without any hint of hindrance. When I remembered the paws of the gentile who shoved me out of the Minsk train station, I anticipatingly took satisfaction that in our new homeland no silver-buttoned guard would dare drive me out.

Before retiring to bed, mother gave me a coin and said, "I don't know yet about the remedies that Uncle Yeshaya's alms box promises, but those of R' Meir bal Haness must be acknowledged. Throw in this coin and God will have mercy on us."

I obeyed mother and went to sleep satisfied that R' Meir bal Haness was already on our side.

30

TISHA B'AV WAS THE HAPPIEST CHILDREN'S HOLIDAY

Tisha B'Av, far from being a sad occasion, was for me the most joyous children's holiday.

I found it curious to see all the Jews of Dukor removing their boots and sitting in their socks, listening in the synagogue to kinos, the mournful recitations uttered by the prayer leader [in memory of the destructions of both the first and the second Temples in Jerusalem].

Not all Dukor's Jews even had whole socks to their name. In one case it didn't cover his heel, in another it left his bare five toes sticking out unseemly. We cheder (school) boys would aim our pointed wood burrs at the beards of just those Jews who wore torn socks.

Taking a burr out of a long beard was sheer agony, like crossing the Red Sea. Only now do I realize the injuries we inflicted, the plain misdeeds we committed against the Jews with torn socks. They were, after all, the poorest of the shtetl, or the widowers who no longer had wives to darn their ripped socks for Tisha B'Av.

Mother herself would don very long socks with circles—a red one, followed by a blue or white one.

Right after the commemorative fast began the house burst with women. Mother recited all of Lamentations, as well as other fitting prayers, from her thick Chumash translation. The women's

148

hearts were torn by mother's heartfelt rendition of the destruction of Jerusalem. When she wept, the other women joined in.

I noticed that some women's naked toes also stuck out. I would have surely aimed some well-directed burrs at their hair.

Instead of weeping over the destruction of Jerusalem, the women could have at least sewn their worn socks for Tisha B'Av.

I was put out that while mother had to cry her eyes out, these women blew their noses into their slovenly underwear (handkerchiefs were then unknown in Dukor).

As the only "man" in the house, I would listen to the recital of the kinos but my chief pleasure was carving a small sword.

It was a custom among Jews during Tisha B'Av, when visiting family burial sites, to stick wooden swords in the graves of their fathers (why dead fathers need wooden swords escapes me until this very day).

My sword was the most beautiful one in Dukor because mother always had spare wood, which came in handy to dry cow's hide. In addition, mother possessed the sharpest knife in all of Dukor, with which she cut the toughest soles.

While mother was taken with talk of the destruction of Jerusalem, I would sharpen my sword in the light of the kerosene lamp in honor of my late father's grave.

On Tisha B'Av the entire shtetl set out for the cemetery. Not only did widows and orphans go, but even those who had not lost anyone. They went quite simply for the joy of the outdoors!

It was a nice, long walk. One first had to cross the length of River St. until reaching the "Svisle" as we called the Svislovitch River, and then to proceed toward the big bridge, which one hoped to pass in peace.

Tall trees, named "topolias," grew in the gentile cemetery. Black crows would circle the trees in winter and summer, screeching, "kra, kra, kra!"

The very same crows would from time to time alight on the spires of the two Dukor churches and screech with murderous cries, "kra, kra, kra!"

Far, far behind the gentile cemetery lay, with a thousand-fold separation in holiness, the Dukor Jewish burial place. No trees or even flowers grew there. It looked like a huge field with sharp-edged grass. The gray, low-slung stones lay strewn about like sheep.

My father's tombstone was the nicest; it had been carved from half a millstone. His was taller and newer than the others. A millstone is not soon covered with moss as the others were.

When I struck my wooden sword into my father's gravesite, I wondered whatever happened to my last Tisha B'Av sword.

According to my accounting five or six swords should have stuck out of my father's grave site, but on Tisha B'Av I didn't find a vestige of any.

Once I asked mother if she perhaps knew who took away the swords from father's grave. She answered that probably a heavenly angel flew off with them.

I would be very proud to know that my wooden swords made it as far as heaven, where they find themselves in my father's possession.

I would inscribe in paint my name "Daniel ben Ze'ev" so that the angel who gathers all the orphans' swords should not mistake one for the other.

But just on that very Tisha B'Av, when I had become a bar-mitzvah boy and when I had meant to carve thirteen notches in my sword so that my father now residing in heaven would know that from here on in he no longer need carry responsibility for my sins because I now have rightfully assumed it, God take pity; yes, on that very Tisha B'Av mother decided to take me to Dr. Shapiro in Minsk, forcing me to forgo with fear and trepidation the commemoration of the bar-mitzvah Tisha B'Av in Dukor, so vital to me and my late father.

Something in me persisted in thinking that the dead that lay buried in the Jewish cemetery, including my father among them, waited impatiently all year long for Tisha B'av, when grieving families appear at gravesites to pour out their hearts' pain.

Even a departed father wants to be visited at least once a year.

I began to press and to urge mother that we should make our way back home.

It was nearly the arrival of the Nine Days, a time when Aunt Itke only made warm dairy suppers because meat was strictly forbidden.

But I once noticed Aunt Itke preparing to grind meat into cutlets precisely during the Nine Days. I asked mother how this was possible. She then confided in me that Aunt Itke was secretly making cutlets, from pig meat no less, God help us! for her sickly youngest child, Rachel, who suffered from jaundice and who was expiring these last ten years like a guttering candle.

I became even more disenchanted with the city of Minsk. If the local doctors couldn't cure Aunt Itke's youngest, who suffered only from jaundice, the question arises how will they heal such a "plague" as me, who suffers from every sort of malady in the world.

In addition, I was scared silly that Aunt Itke, who always liked to compare me with her sickly Rachel, who was my age, could just as easily serve me the pork cutlets, regardless that I was already a bar-mitzvah boy and could not afford to sin even accidentally.

Mother was not in a hurry to return to Dukor because on that Tisha B'Av eve she had to close on a number of very important matters, which included whether or not she should meet with the Jew in Minsk, her designated match people whispered about.

Scatter-brained Uncle Yeshaya Grundfest was supposed to find out among forest merchants pertinent information about this designated Jew, himself a forest merchant, but on that very Tisha B'Av eve Uncle Yeshaya found himself completely consumed with news of the Zionist Congress taking place somewhere in Basel. He had his nose constantly in "Ha-Tzfira," which regularly published Congress reports.

It appears that the Zionist Congress had prevented him from meeting with those forest merchants who could have filled him in about the Jew who was being proposed as a match for mother.

Obviously, this big secret was kept from me, but my older brothers, who came at night to see us at the home of Aunt Ike, were in the know. They seemed always sad now, although none of them were any longer dependent on mother.

It disturbed me that my elder brothers were sad. As far as I can remember they were always joyful when they came home for Pesach or Sukkus. In fact, all the Dukor women blessed them. But in Minsk I could scarcely recognize them. They had become silent. At fault surely was Uncle Yeshaya, who never let anyone get a word in.

As soon as a brother of mine tried to get in a word edgewise about either the Land of Israel or Dr. Herzl, Uncle Yeshaya began to shout, "You're interrupting me! Let me finish!"

But just as Uncle Yeshaya never got around to finishing, so too will this chapter remain incomplete.

31

ON THE THRESHOLD OF
THE TWENTIETH CENTURY

Only in Minsk did I first realize that I have four big-hearted brothers.

The older two—Mendel and Zalke—were employed at the cheap kitchen in Minsk. They had told mother that if she left me with them in Minsk I would lack for nothing. I would be able to eat in the cheap kitchen and be healed by Minsk doctors.

The other two brothers—Shmuel and Boruch—told mother that if I remained in Minsk with them one (Shmuel) would go daily with me to the religious school to study a page of Talmud and the other (Boruch) would prove helpful as well.

I encouraged mother to leave me in Minsk with my brothers, as I had nothing to do in Dukor.

I didn't want to return to Dukor for this reason alone: I had promised friends that as soon as I returned to Dukor from Minsk I would explain to them in detail how a train moves of its own accord, but, in fact, found myself shamelessly empty-handed.

True, I had traveled to Minsk under the hood of a bench, but I had not achieved a full understanding of how a train actually operates. I only observed that the train had twelve wagons, the first of which was first class, the next two second class and the rest third class, if not worse. I also observed that the last wagon, the twelfth, was attached to the eleventh with heavy chains, and the eleventh to the tenth and so forth up to the locomotive. It's clear that as soon as the first wagon moved the others would follow suit.

But what initial power moves the locomotive, which then drags everything behind it, I couldn't say.

When I happened to ask one of my brothers if he knew how a train moves of its own accord he answered that it travels on the power of steam, and therefore the Russian word for locomotive is "paravos" (steam).

I then asked my brother that, if steam can drive an entire train, then why does not the bathhouse in Dukor, which is shrouded in so much hot vapor, move too. He answered that if the Dukor steam bath had wheels beneath it then it, too, might very well roll like a train.

But a bit later my brother added that steam by itself is insufficient. A spring pressing hard down on the wheels is what does the trick.

I found in those years the word "spring" (sprushinke) to be magical. After all, a watch works by the force of a spring, without any steam.

But in the year when I landed in Minsk (1901, at the start of the twentieth century) there were already greater wonders even than the steel train or the tramway.

One then already spoke of air balloons which could rise higher than the clouds. One had by then heard the American name Edison, who had introduced electricity everywhere, in phonographs, telephones, cinematographs, telegraphs, and the devil knows what else.

My elder brothers resolved to show me all the wonders of the twentieth century's arrival.

One Sunday, on a folk holiday, an event named "the twentieth century" took place in the garden of the Minsk governor. For ten kopecks per person all the great wonders of the world were on display.

I myself saw how quite a big air balloon, under which swung a basket with two live people, suddenly pulled away from the ground and rose so high as if to touch the stars in heaven. Fireworks exploded but no matter how high they flew they could not reach the air balloon.

My breath was stolen by the sight of the fireworks' red glare, how racing toward heaven they burst forth with such a loud bang and splattered into a thousand lights.

Soon thereafter on the open stage a half-naked female appeared covered from head to toe with springs and wires. She began then to sing in Russian this song:

"I am a telephone, I am a telephone,
An invention of Edison's
On every side I am a telephone
Invented by Edison."

Then the female turned every which way and showed the public to best effect all the springs and wires attached to her from head to toe.

Afterwards, a tall man appeared on stage in a black suit and black top hat. He claimed he was Edison. Next to him a horned box had been set up. The Edison figure sang a Russian ditty and soon thereafter the horn emitted the very same words which the half-naked female had uttered previously.

All the people in the governor's garden started shouting "Bravo, Edison!"

We then saw a screen on which suddenly voiceless images of people and animals appeared. Someone explained that this was a movie from America. Everyone wondered whether America possessed cats, dogs, and horses like ours.

When we finished with the "twentieth century," that is to say with the presentation, all of us five brothers went to Zakhariever St. to eat ice cream for mere kopecks.

Savoring slowly the multi-flavored ice cream I suddenly recognized Peshe, the miller's daughter, sitting with friends at one of the tables.

I felt my head growing intensely hot. I started to imagine that at any minute my head would be ripped from my shoulders much like an air balloon and fly skywards. Also, my heart beat wildly as if all of the wired Edison telephones worn by the half-naked lady were sounding at once.

It appears that I took great fright that Peshe, God forbid, might blurt out to my brothers the story of how she had kissed my head. Then I would burst like a rocket of a thousand lights that would not extinguish even when it struck the ground.

My brothers soon took note that I had suddenly become strongly confused. They quieted me down by saying that they would soon lead me back to mother, that is to say to the home of Aunt Itke, with whom we were staying.

My brothers were convinced that the "twentieth century" had confused me utterly.

One of them said to the others, "This has made too strong an impression all at once on the boy." Boruch, who himself teetered between boyhood and manhood, then told me, "Finish your ice-cream, and we'll head back to mother."

My ice-cream had by then melted into three streamlets—pink, green and yellow. The spoon had nothing left to keep it upright.

Suddenly I said loudly in front of my brothers, "You don't recognize Peshe, the miller's daughter?! There she sits at a table!"

My brothers took great joy upon seeing Peshe. They all approached her table, whereupon she said, "How lovely to see you and your guest. You have Donya with you!"

"Yes, mother brought him to visit the Minsk doctor, but he wants to stay with us permanently," they replied.

How proud I was that Peshe had mentioned my name and had even introduced me to her two friends.

We then left Zakhariever St. and headed toward Kreshtensker St., where Aunt Itke resided and where mother worriedly awaited my return.

When we approached the market where a high tower loomed, I noticed five lamps burning at its summit, which meant that a fire had broken out in the fifth district. (Yes, Minsk has five districts, much like New York has five boroughs).

I was then struck by the boyish idea that all the five Charney brothers resembled the five districts of Minsk, each burning to the uttermost.

My eldest brother, Mendel, was then aflame with the idea of going to America. The other, Zalke, was on fire to obtain a good trade. Shmuel, my third brother, was consumed with the idea of uniting Zionism with socialism. He even once spoke of this openly in the cheap Minsk kitchen. My fourth brother, Boruch, burned with the desire to better his Russian and become a writer. He had even written up our shtetl in the Russian paper "Minsk Listok."

And I, the youngest, the luckless shlimazel, was kindled by the secret flame of a first love, whose name was "Peshe."

When mother finally saw me aflame and confused from all the impressions and experiences that had just transpired in just one evening she touched my forehead, fearing I had a fever.

Aunt Itke calmed her and explained that I was frightened and confused by the operation I was to undergo the next day at Dr. Shapiro's.

Mother herself also seemed that evening, at least in my eyes, to be fire-kindled. She appeared red and aflame. That evening she couldn't seem to find a place to relax in the home of Aunt Itke. I believe mother was even more scared than I of my imminent operation.

Later I discovered that my elder brothers had purposely taken me that evening from Aunt Itke's home to the "Twentieth Century" so that mother could for the very first time meet with the Jew with whom she was to be matched.

You can imagine how happy mother was to see in front of her all her children and yet how guilty she was regarding me. On the very eve of my operation she had allowed herself to be talked into meeting with a Jew ready and willing to become a stepfather to all her six orphans.

32

MY SECOND OPERATION

If the first operation, on the eighth day of my life (circumcision), made me a Jew, the second, in the fourteenth year of my life, made me a person. True, the second didn't take place so openly and happily as the first.

The first, my circumcision, took place in our sukkah, where the finest Jews of Dukor had assembled in joy, whereas the second, the one done by the surgeon in Minsk, Dr. Shapiro, occurred in a side chamber of his large Minsk apartment, where he wouldn't allow anyone—even my mother—entry.

And what's more, Dr. Shapiro asked mother to leave his home for several hours. He found the presence of weeping mothers pacing in circles distracted him from operating calmly on their children.

Mother started to kiss me with weeping eyes, as if she was taking leave of me forever.

At first, I didn't mind that mother left me all alone in the hands of the "Jewish thief." I knew that Dr. Shapiro intended to help me, to do me good. I didn't even take fright when the physician, who addressed me in Yiddish, lay me down on a tall and narrow table which looked like a bench on wheels.

Soon thereafter he placed a kind of cotton mask over my face and asked me to count—one, two, three, four and so on, as if he wanted to see how far I could go.

I was initially angered to be treated like a child. I wanted to shine, to show off that I knew how to add, subtract, multiply and divide, but as soon as I reached the number thirteen, I could no longer count any further and became unconscious.

Dr. Shapiro had put me to sleep so that I should not feel the incisions he was about to make.

When I came to, I found mother and all my five brothers standing next to me. I had become the hero of the day.

Mother was in seventh heaven that Dr. Shapiro had managed not to cut off my entire hand as Aunt Itke had foretold; and I was in seventh heaven that everyone was now talking about me and wishing me only good.

Imagine my great luck when that very day even Peshe, the miller's daughter, came to Aunt Itke's home to find out how I was. In front of everyone she kissed me on the forehead, as if she were my bride or some such.

My older brother Shmuel, who was the same age as Peshe, suddenly reddened. I now realized that she had probably loved him secretly, but she didn't have enough courage to kiss him so instead she kissed me, the "plague," which pleased me to no end.

An impure thought popped into my head that if I remained sick, in a word, a "plague," forever, all the girls and women would find a way to kiss me, as this appeared to be their nature and custom.

Soon after the operation I felt like a general who had won a major battle. I convinced mother that during the return trip I not be placed under the bench as she had done on our trip from Dukor to Minsk, but rather she should spend the nine kopecks on a legitimate train ticket for me as was customary for adults.

My eldest brother, Mendel, who until today remains very good to me, although he has lived for more than forty years in Paterson, New Jersey, upon hearing me declare my travel wishes immediately took out ten kopecks and told me: "Here you have a ticket from Minsk to Dukor."

Out of great joy I burst into tears now that I could travel as an adult, and would be able to walk openly and freely from wagon to wagon, not fearing the conductor.

Mother had turned very sad seeing me suddenly crying, but Aunt Itke calmed her, explaining that a good cry would help expel the chloroform that Dr. Shapiro had used to put me to sleep.

Aunt Itke was right. After crying, I felt much lighter.

She then placed tasty morsels on the table, as if my bar-mitzvah were being re-enacted.

Suddenly, however, a tumult broke out in the house. Uncle Yeshaya blew in like a tempest, a man whose mouth spilled with the news of the whole wide world.

This time he brought us the sad tidings that Uncle Shmuel-Yoshe had suddenly died and had left an inheritance for mother— a golden ten-ruble coin.

In truth, until this very day I still don't know who Uncle Shmuel-Yoshe was. I only know that we had a legendary uncle or was it a great-uncle in Minsk, an old bachelor or maybe a widower who drank alone a full samovar of tea and then proceeded to thank and praise the Lord for having created man with such great wisdom, not excluding a full accounting of the biological equipment necessary for evacuation, as was stated quite literally in the prayer "Asher Yotzar."

Neither I nor my elder brothers had ever seen this "Uncle Shmuel-Yoshe." But when he suddenly died, a golden coin of ten rubles was found in his pocket with the express command that it be given to my mother, the widow.

When Uncle Yeshaya had very excitedly handed my mother the golden inheritance from Reb Shmuel-Yoshe a"h, she broke out into tears that this unknown uncle had thought of her before he passed and had given her this tribute.

Thus did mother and son weep together. However, mother's tears were worth the ten-ruble coin she received as an inheritance from Uncle Shmuel-Yoshe, and mine amounted to a mere ten kopecks which I received for the train ticket.

I thus got the impression that a mother's tears are worth a hundred times as much as a son's.

When mother brought me back by train from Minsk to Dukor, it was already the 15th day of Av.

I don't know how it is by you, but by us in Dukor the 15th day of Av is dedicated to matchmaking.

Osher the teacher, who was always the chief celebrant at happy occasions in Dukor, told us that the custom to finalize matches on the 15th of Av harks back to the ancient days in Jerusalem, where Jewish guys and girls would dress to the nines on the 15th of Av and be matched up. In fact, the bride-groom fair in Jerusalem had been instituted by the first king of the Jews, Saul, who hailed from the tribe of Benjamin.

(If you recall, the tribe of Benjamin sinned when several of its youths killed the chief wife of a foreign man. As a result, the other Jewish tribes in anger nearly slew the entire tribe of Benjamin, leaving no more than six hundred fellows who now were in a fix— they couldn't marry the daughters of any of the other Israelite tribes. But King Saul, who himself descended from the tribe of Benjamin, did away with this harsh decree and established the previously mentioned bride-groom fair, which by long tradition had come down to Dukor).

True, Dukor could never pull off such a festive carnival as had once taken place in Jerusalem; after all, the grooms and brides in Dukor on any given year could be counted on the fingers of one hand, but on the 15th of Av, my mother acquired the rosy look of an entire bride carnival.

She finally entrusted me with her great secret, which I knew already from before, that she had met in Minsk a Jew from the shtetl Zembin, near Borisov. Everyone, including my brothers, said that when she weds him it will be good for both of us, that is to say for me and for my mother.

Mother also informed me that this Jew was ready to support me even in Vilna, where there's a doctor with the kind of X-rays which I very badly needed, according to Dr. Shapiro.

She declared to all my brothers, and indeed to all of our Minsk relatives who had urged this match on her, that it all depended on me. If I agreed to it, she'd be on board. But if, God forbid, this could hurt me emotionally in any way, she was ready to stay with me until I would, if God wills it, be fully grown and find my destined one for good, long years.

I then answered my dear mother that if she found the match suitable, so did I. And if she wishes to see me grow up quickly, she should send me right after Sukkus to stay with my brothers in Minsk, where I would be able to study and to heal.

(Of course, I didn't confide in mother my big secret drawing me to Minsk—namely Peshe).

Mother at once penned a letter to my elder brothers, as well as to her older sister, Aunt Itke, that "Donya agrees," but added that she must first travel with me to Berezin to Mirl, her only daughter, who was soon, in a good hour, to give birth to her first child.

DUKOR

My sister, Mirl, wanted very much for mother and me to come to Berezin for her first childbirth. This was because she had taken pitiful fright on account of the story of another child-bearing woman who had turned the town upside down.

My sister, already in Dukor a gifted letter writer, went on to describe the entire story, which is worth retelling here.

33

A STORY OF A WIG PEG

When a mother travels to her daughter's first delivery, she ordinarily comes a few weeks ahead for a stay of some length, until the new mother can get, with luck, back on her feet.

But my sister didn't exactly know her due date. It was just then a leap year and Adar B messed up my sister's calendrical calculations. [In a Jewish leap year there is an added month, a second month of Adar.] She couldn't figure out if her due date would fall out during the High Holy Days or perhaps a week after Sukkus.

In order to hasten mother's arrival in Berezin my sister related in one of her letters the horrible story of a pregnant woman, about whom the whole shtetl said that her newborn boy would die before his circumcision on account of a wig peg.

As the awful story was once characteristic of many poor Jewish pregnancies of the time in our province, I consider it my duty to retell it exactly how my sister described it in her letter.

Many years ago, it was customary when a woman became pregnant that she would place under her bed a wig peg. After that, at every start of the month, she would place another peg and when nine wig pegs accumulated under the bed the woman knew already that she was due that very month.

It once happened on Polozhiner St., where all the Berezin poor lived crowdedly, that a woman had a child which she carried for not more than eight months, because under her bed only eight pegs were found.

The Talmud says that if a child is born in the eighth month it cannot survive. A seventh-month birth is fine and a ninth month is even better, the gold standard, but spare us an eighth-month birth, the baby is condemned to die.

All of Berezin ran to and fro on Polozhiner St. to see if the eighth-month old newborn still lived.

Every time a shtetl woman would arrive on the block she'd ask the mother the painful question:
- Does it still live?
- Do you still nurse it?
- Does it scream when it's hungry?
- Will there be a bris?

The new mother nearly went crazy from all the posed questions but still she felt guilty that her delivery arrived in the eighth month and, what's more, the infant still lived, as if to spite everyone on purpose!

When the day of circumcision arrived, the men of cloth and ritual agreed that the child needs to be circumcised because after all it is not a law decreed from Sinai that an eighth-month arrival must die! [The duty to circumcise stems from the Bible, which is a greater authority than the saying of the scholars in the Talmud that the baby must die.]

Dark confusion prevailed in the new mother's home. Should a circumcision or a funeral be readied?

The whole shtetl would have felt validated if the newborn had left this world. Rumor spread that it wasn't even human but, God forbid, a dybbuk.

The new mother tore at her hair, and on the day of the awful circumcision her terrible screams reverberated all along the street.

Only then did a poor neighbor, who could no longer endure the new mother's sorrow and woe, go to the Rabbi and confess that because of her the child was seemingly born at eight months when, in fact, like all normal Jewish children, it arrived on time, at the ninth month.

When the Rabbi asked the frightened woman how she knew that the child was born at the right time, she said that she had once gone to her neighbor to borrow a small pot but as it happened no one was at home. She noticed under the bed several wig pegs. She could not resist the temptation and swiped one of the pegs, put it under her apron and slipped out of the house. At that time a wig peg was a big fortune!

But now, when she found out what a single wooden peg had wrought, after all it was decreed that a child born at eight months must, God forbid, die, she felt it her duty to accept whatever harsh punishment would be meted out to her, if only the infant could live and be well and undergo the circumcision as Jewish children do according to the laws of Moses of Israel.

The Bereziner Rabbi, however, was a very smart decisor. He commanded that because the Jewish woman had confessed her robbery, all the Jews of Polozhiner St. should bequeath her one wig peg so she be blessed with a warm winter and thus not be compelled to steal them from under women's beds.

Thus did the awful story of an "eight-month" delivery end happily for both sides.

"Donya," mother said, "I fear that Mirl got entangled in this whole business."

Mother soon wrote to Mirl the whole truth. This Sukkus she would absolutely not be able to leave Dukor because this may be the very last time she will be able to celebrate the holiday together with all her five sons in the shtetl.

A proof, if one was needed, was that soon after Sukkus my elder brothers would take me to Minsk. Mother then would be left on her own, alone as a stone. She might then agree to the match with the Jew from Borisov's environs.

From Borisov to Berezin can be a hop, skip and a jump because of the steamboats, and she was planning to come to Berezin right after Sukkus. Mother said she only hopes that until then her daughter will not yet have gone into labor.

According to mother's calculations, my sister hadn't become pregnant in Adar A but rather in Adar B; therefore, her due date was a month later, in the month of Cheshvan. True, by then the steamboats no longer operated because the Berezina froze over. So she will come, if God wills it, with the Bereziner cart diver, who goes every week from Berezin to Minsk and back.

When mother finished writing the whole long letter to my sister a stone dropped from her heart. Only then did she take to all her customary month of Av chores.

In the month of Av, Dukor was swamped with ripened cherries, oversized cucumbers and hard wild blueberries. [This was summertime.] From the barrel of cherries, which costs less than a ruble, mother made jam which would last until the summer after next, as well as cherry liqueur.

Mother would pick the cherries that were to be made into preserves and fill a saucepan. She asked me to pick out those that still had some flesh on them, as it were. She would then put them into a very big white bottle. Once the unpitted cherries filled the bottle she added sugar flour up to the brim. Later, when the sugar had evaporated, enough space remained in the bottle to pour in a half quart of schnapps. Around Chanukah [in December] the cherry liqueur became so strong that I would become drunk on a mere cherry.

When mother finished preparing the preserves and the cherry liqueur she started in on the cucumbers.

She would soak in salt a full barrel of cucumbers. She would then jab several holes into the vegetables, so the salt-water could be efficiently absorbed.

In a matter of days the pickled cucumbers had already acquired a heavenly smell and taste. In a few weeks they would be ready to be served with sour cream, a lip-smacking morsel.

When mother finished with the cucumbers she would then start with the wild berries.

Before frying them one had to pick them over like chickpeas, very carefully because many were worm-ridden. This became my task, while mother peeled apples and scooped out their seeds. Wild berries fry better with slices of apple.

Mother would fry a load of wild berries, and in winter nothing tasted better than to smear them on a slice of bread or top them off with a fried slice of apple.

But in that famous month of Av, when I underwent my operation in Minsk and when she had first met her husband-to-be, I simply couldn't understand why mother was preparing so many tasty delights for winter when both of us stood on the threshold of new lives.

I was preparing to leave for Minsk and my brothers immediately after Sukkus, and mother was readying herself for my sister's labor pains. After that it seemed evident that mother would wed Reb Yisrael Isaac Klionsky of Zembin, which lies near Borisov. The question, therefore, arises: what was she doing frying so many pounds of cherries, berries and apples? Why was she salting so many cucumbers and preparing two bottles of cherry liqueur?

I couldn't resist and asked her this very question.

"Dearest mother, may you be blessed with health, I don't understand why you go to such lengths to prepare all these wonderful things when in a few months we will both depart Dukor forever."

"My dear son," she responded imperatively, "don't say, God forbid, that we are abandoning Dukor for always. Dukor will be with us wherever we end up."

For good measure she added, "And if I should connect with Klionsky from Zembin, do I then become, God forbid, a stranger? Won't you still come to me every holiday as always? Will you, God forbid, remain without a home, as should all the enemies of Zion? Will they not bless my children in Zembin as in Dukor? Don't say, Donya, that we will leave Dukor forever! Dukor will always follow us, no matter where we are. A Jew is not allowed to speak that way, my child."

Suddenly mother kissed me on the mouth and began to cry.

I weep now writing these lines——

What better proof can there be that Dukor follows wherever I go! Mother was exactly right.

34

TWO SISTERS SCHMOOZE

When mother fully realized that in a few months she would indeed have to leave Dukor for good, she turned awfully sad. When in such a state she'd go and pour out her bitter heart to her older sister, Aunt Toybe.

Aunt Toybe was my richest aunt in Dukor, a very learned woman. She knew all the stories and parables of the "Tsene Reneh" by heart and even read the paper, "Der Yud." She brimmed with sayings, phrases and adages for all occasions, the good and not-so-good.

When Aunt Toybe alone consumed a whole herring, she would cleverly declare that she had sent a "delegate" to her stomach to inquire what else it might want. (The word "delegate" she had acquired from reading "Der Yud," which printed reports about the Zionist Congress in Basel.)

When getting up from her midday nap Aunt Toybe would step up to the samovar and drink without stop tea flavored with cherry syrup. She would then begin to philosophize. She declared that everything derives from the stomach, by which she inferred that all Jewish troubles begin with appetite, that is to say, once boundaries are breached and everything is permitted.

To permit entails skipping mincha and maariv; reading profane books that pronounce apes to be the forebears of humans; and hastening the redemption of the people of Israel, as in the case of a certain Dr. Herzl sedulously trying to bribe the Turk! [The Ottoman Empire controlled the Land of Israel that Dr. Herzl wanted to turn into a Jewish state.]

"I tell you, Brocha, we are living in crazy times," Aunt Toybe consoled my mother. "I just read in 'Der Yud' that a young cobbler in Vilna shot the governor and was sentenced to hang. It doesn't stand to reason that a poor Jewish cobbler should set his hand against the governor himself! Brocha, you should be happy that your children are in Minsk and not in Vilna, God help us!"

"And what about you, yourself?" Aunt Toybe addressed my mother directly. "You should consider yourself lucky that you will not, God forbid, be dependent on your children in old age. You know children are compared to birds! As soon as their wings are grown they leave their nests. How does Scripture put it, 'Some I have nurtured and they have flown away.' But the Jew who is being matched with you, I hear, is a very fine and God-fearing man, a fiery Lubavitcher hasid who will esteem you like a gemstone. He will also be a good stepfather to your children. I hear he is some ten to twelve years your senior and you know the saying, 'Water never sours and widowers never turn old.'"

(To this day I still don't understand why Aunt Toybe thought of saying that a widower never gets old; perhaps because a widower doesn't have anyone to shorten his years.)

When mother heard these smart words of counsel and consolation from her elder sister, she showed Aunt Toybe a letter she had received from her "groom."

The groom, hailing from the shtetl Zembin near Borisov, stated in his letter that this very day in which he pens these lines marks the beginning of the month of Elul, when the blowing of the shofar begins, which reminds Jews the world over that the High Holy Days are fast approaching, fearsome days of atonement, prayer and charity. But as my mother had delayed her response to his offer that she move from Dukor to Zembin until after Sukkus, he decided on going to Lubavitch for the High Holy Days, where, if God wishes it, he will pray for a good year, which is to include my mother and all her children, may they all be well. And may God grant them long life so that in a goodly appointed hour we shall all be worthy of hearing the shofar blasts announcing the coming of the messiah, Amen!

At the close of the letter Reb Yisrael Isaac Klionsky (so my stepfather-to-be will henceforth be called) added a fine kabbalistic insight, that the letters of the month of Elul stand for, "I am for my friend and my friend is for me."

The kabbalists interpreted friend to mean the Creator of the Universe, because what other friend can one imagine other than God in the month of Elul? But Aunt Toybe had another take on the matter. She told mother that if the kabbalists had meant the Creator of the Universe they would have said so from the start, "I am to my God as God is to me." But because the sages decided to say, "I am to my friend as my friend is to me," they surely meant to say that during the month of Elul we all should become friendlier one to another—all the more so husbands to their wives and wives to their husbands!

I could barely contain myself from mixing into this quiet, heartfelt conversation between mother and Aunt Toybe. I wished to say to Aunt Toybe that "I am to my friend as my friend is to me" reminds me strongly of the "Lcha Dodi" prayer recited as a greeting to the Sabbath bride on Friday evening. I wished to emphasize that my stepfather is ready to greet mother in Zembin much like pious Jews welcome the Sabbath Queen on the eve of the holy rest day.

However, I made as if I hadn't heard a word or understood anything and just played with the chess pieces because I didn't want mother or Aunt Toybe to suspect I was listening in on their conversation.

I heard Aunt Toybe advise my mother that in her new home she shouldn't be too sweet or they would eat her up, or too bitter or they would spit her out.

Aunt Toybe meant to say that in the good hour when my mother weds the fine Jew from Zembin she should neither become too good to his children and grandchildren, for fear that she would become enslaved, nor should she be too stern with them for fear that they, her new stepchildren, God forbid, could foment anger and tension between the newlyweds.

Again, I strongly wanted to mix in and tell Aunt Toybe that my mother, may she be well and blessed, could neither be too sweet nor too bitter. My mother, after all, was hardened by circumstance: it's been thirteen years since she has been, as it were, playing chess by herself, not having a king bestriding the board of life, that is to say, a husband; and yet until this very day she hasn't made a false step. She brought up her own six children and even me, the schlimazel, she put on his feet and made a man out of him!

The words were on the tip of my tongue but I once again restrained myself because if mother heard such talk she would burst into tears of joy, hearing me finally speak like an adult.

True, it is possible that the very thought of comparing my mother's life to a chess game without a king had not come to me then. I can hardly imagine myself as a boy coming up with such a fanciful idea, but I also know that all these comparisons and equivalences that arise from my pen when describing my childhood years are not empty coincidences.

Just now I see that it was precisely in my shtetl, Dukor, that I absorbed during fourteen tough, contrarian years all the goodness and fineness bestowed by my mother and sister, all my brothers, cousins and all the other Jews who stood by me.

I also must add that I have inherited a good many maddening caprices from my uncles and aunts, yet I can say proudly that, owing to them, I may well have become a writer among Jews.

35

DUKOR GOES BY FOOT TO LUBAVITCH

In the period of Elul our shtetl would be overgrown with weeds. During the summer the Dukor sheep, cows and horses had chewed all the good grass, sparing only the weeds, which even the pigs wallowing in the streets would make sure to keep their snouts out of.

When I once asked mother why the earth gives forth such wild gnarly growths that even pigs avoid like the plague she answered that the fiery weeds remind us, especially in the month of Elul, of the iron rods which whip the evil ones in the world to come.

I started to ponder which evil persons in our shtetl would merit such punishment in the next world. I then went from house to house, and I must admit that I couldn't find even one in all Dukor to fit the bill.

In my eyes all the Jews of Dukor were righteous and religious, and even their wives were sufficiently God-fearing to serve as their husbands' footstools in paradise.

True, my cousin Masha the Lunatic would cast aspersions on such women, but what, after all, won't a crazy woman say?

All of Dukor consisted of fiery Lubavitch hasidim. Not only the town eminences but even the cart drivers and butchers, the tailors and cobblers, the villagers and all the poor were hard-bitten hasidim of this fold.

I had been told that in years past, when my father was still alive, scores of Dukor Jews would simply go by foot to Lubavitch for the High Holy Days.

True, from Dukor to Lubavitch is not a hop, skip and a jump and not all the walkers had enough energy to carry on their backs the herring and onions, the prepared delicacies and the bottle of schnapps which each hasid had dragged with him. In addition to which tallis and tefillin, a Sabbath gaberdine, the shirts and underwear all were absolutely necessary. Right after Rosh Chodesh Elul the footwalkers would collect among themselves enough money to buy a horse and wagon to ease their burden and make the journey to Lubavitch a whole lot easier. [The distance from Dukor to Lubavitch was about 294 km = 194 US miles.]

All the packages were heaved onto the wagon and the horse would then show the way to Lubavitch.

En route to Lubavitch the Dukor hasidim would travel through many Jewish settlements and small towns where they could stop and catch their breath with quite a nice "drink" (a l'chaim). In each Jewish settlement a few walkers would join in, heaping their own bundles onto the Dukor wagon. So it was that on the eve of the High Holy Days quorums of hasidim arrived in Lubavitch from the surrounding towns.

Osher the Teacher was the spiritual leader of these wayfarers, a man close to the Lubavitcher Rebbe and a dear friend of my late father.

But Shmuel-Sholem was the actual leader of the horse and wagon brigade, or, more precisely, "Shmuel-Sholem the limper," as we called him among ourselves.

Proof of his condition: Shmuel-Sholem had broken his foot when dragging out a sunken horse and wagon from the mud, but even in his wounded state he would vigorously take part in all the dances in Lubavitch.

"Hasidim must dance!" Shmuel-Sholem contended. Hasidic dances are a form of soul elevation; one tears free of the earth and approaches nearer to the Lord in Heaven.

This "limping" Shmuel-Sholem would dance on one foot with as much inspired enthusiasm as the other hasidim on two.

On Sabbath Shmuel-Sholem only spoke in biblical Hebrew. But as he didn't have much of a command of the language he spent all twenty-five hours of the holy day, from its initial blessings of the candles on Friday evening to the closing prayer of havdalah that divides the sacred from the profane, with sacredly sealed lips.

This very same Shmuel-Sholem once said my elder brothers would go down the road of conversion. He had seen them once on a holiday in shul wearing white paper collars (three kopecks a collar).

"I tell you, Jews, these white collars lead to the threshold of the church, God have mercy on us!" he said, boiling with rage.

He even tried to introduce a new custom in Dukor: how to split the sea while conducting the Pesach Seder. He placed a full pail of water in the middle of the house and, when he reached the point in the Haggadah when the Jews fled Egypt by crossing the split Red Sea, he would smack his limp foot into the pail, which turned upside down, and a sea of water would rush across the floor. He would then swim off to recite the other miracles of the exodus from Egypt, praising the Creator who had safely led him out of benighted exile.

Shmuel-Sholem's custom didn't catch on in Dukor because my father had once told him that if you could split the sea over a pail of water, you should recite over it "tashlich" as well.

This very same Shmuel-Sholem once told me that when my father's luck went south and his earning power diminished, he nevertheless contributed to the rental of the communal horse and wagon with which the Dukor Jews went by foot to Lubavitch in the month of Elul.

A proof of father's dedication was his willingness to sell our last goat so as to have enough to contribute to the communal pot.

I claimed the worth of that sold goat years later from a relative in Geneva. A sabra, she was a grandchild of the late Tzemach Tzedek [the third leader of the Chabad Lubavitch Hasidic movement]. Promenading with her once on the ever-snowed-in pathways near "Mont Blanc," the tallest mountain in western Europe, she suddenly asked me why I was so pale and thin.

I answered jokingly that her noted grandfather was at fault. Due to him, her venerable grandfather, my father sold our last goat and I was left without milk.

The very next morning I found a bottle of milk at my door with the inscription that from then on I would receive every morning a fresh bottle of milk which I should drink in the name of the Lord, as commanded by the granddaughter of a great man.

It's very well possible that on account of those "Lubavitch" milk bottles in Geneva I am alive today. This sentiment, born of the kindness of a member of the Schneerson family, drove me a few times in America to make a call at the headquarters of the now late Lubavitcher Rebbe on Eastern Parkway in Brooklyn.

Who can fully evaluate the extraordinary pull of those inherited drives by which we conduct our lives and our creativity?

36

DUKOR JEWS

Only now, as I am about to take leave of my shtetl, Dukor, I realize that I am still at the start, having left much unsaid. Until now I have barely described just one quorum of Dukor Jews, while the other minyanim (quorums) stand waiting their turn for me to include them in my family chronicle.

Certainly, each Jew of my town has kosherly earned his right to be remembered forever in my memoir.

In the end, all the hundred Jewish houses of Dukor were tied and bound together, as if they all belonged to one family. Among us there were no divisions between poor and rich, between pedigree and commonness, between scholar and artisan.

All were fiery Lubvaticher hasidim and, what's more, blazed with fervor.

Even the one and only misnagid (a Jew of anti-hasid bent) of our town, Sana the miller, I would say was a hidden lamed-vovnik (one of the 36 righteous men on whom the world stands).

He was not only one of the most learned men in town, but also a big charity giver. For years, at no charge, he led the congregation in prayer in the old synagogue, and the hasidim would kiss his fingers in gratitude. It is obviously high praise indeed when Lubvitcher hasidim put their trust in the only misnagid in town to be their prayer leader, even on the High Holy Days.

At the dais, Sana the miller would beseech the Creator of the Universe in the highest octaves; however, in private life he was a silent man. One hears it said that all lamed-vovniks are by nature silent.

For example, I can remember how Sana the miller would from time to time come into our house, greet us with a "Good Morning" and then sit down at the table in complete silence.

My mother knew already that because Sana the miller came to us straight from the mill, which is several viorsts from Dukor, he would not come empty-handed. She immediately placed a glass of tea with cherry syrup in front of him and asked him all manner of questions about his wife and children.

Sana's wife was also a person of pedigree, the daughter of the Rossover Rav a"h (may peace be upon him), a big and renowned Torah scholar. Not surprising, she had fine, gifted children, who now, I believe, all reside in America.

As soon as Sana the miller finished the glass of tea with syrup he would quietly say to my mother, "It is the eve of market day and I've brought you a gift." He would then drop a ringing twenty-five coin on the table.

Mother would be so deeply moved by this act of kindness that her eyes would moisten and she couldn't find words to properly thank him for his extraordinary benevolence.

By the way, my readers should know that this very same Sana the misnagid was also the beloved father of Peshe, the miller's daughter, who, you will recall, quite unexpectedly bequeathed me an "act of kindness" for which a soon-to-be-bar-mizvahed boy remains forever indebted.

Remembering the good deeds of Sana the miller and his family, I am angry to recall the unruly cheder boys who teased him about being a misnagid. But I am even more distressed that I, who remain indebted to my shtetl, Dukor, have still to describe nine-tenths of the inhabitants of my native town.

So, at the very least I will remember the souls of another quorum of Dukor Jews, who remain forever etched in my memory and who perhaps I may yet have occasion to describe at length in future depictions of my youth.

Here stands in front of me, as if alive, Velvel Izbortchik, who for decades remained the notary of our shtetl. I can still recall his official Russian rubber stamp with the name Wolf Idelchick, with which he signed all official papers and documents in Dukor.

All the official papers, as well as all other documents, were set in print by Hillel Blochman, whose curly lettering was unmistakable. He was the only Jew in Dukor whose name smacked of the substance he used. This was the same individual who addressed in cursive script the envelopes to America of the Dukor wives without ever charging them a penny.

Here stands the always distracted Hillel Kelyes, who in summertime would load wagons-full of cherries and in wintertime press raisins in the cellar so there'd be enough wine for Pesach in Dukor and its environs. He took on the look of a round barrel with iron hinges.

Hillel Kelyes had sent off his son to America, who soon returned, as he joked, because in the golden land across the sea the horses were so tall that ladders were needed to mount them.

Here, as well, stands Mendel the "Liamenshik," who introduced industries that sustained various Dukor families.

Add to this picture Moshe Aron, who had a house brimming with hats and caps but who himself wore a very tattered cap with a well-worn brim. He became a bloated bourgeois from eating too many potatoes.

Here, too, stands Velvel the healer, who possessed the largest fruit orchard in Dukor. In summer we cheder boys would pay him a kopeck every Friday for a shake of the tree. All the apples that fell to the ground as a result were considered ours. Although Velvel the healer's command of Hebrew was shaky, he, nevertheless, would greet his wife with a florid "Gut shabbes" upon his return from synagogue. She would report that all the trees in the orchard had bowed as one in answer "Gut shabbes, gut yor (year)!" [Good Sabbath, good year.]

Here, in front of my eyes, stands Yona the Kohen, the richest man in town, worth a fortune because he held the prize horses of Dukor. He walked around in linen undershirts and would wear the hat of a muzhik [a Russian peasant]. On the Sabbath and on holidays he donned the nicest clothing, which he had kept from his wedding, a man who nearly always received the first aliyah (call to the Torah). During the priestly blessing, his utterance of "May God bless and keep you" thundered above all other priestly voices in Dukor.

Here, before my very eyes, stands Lipa the tailor, who we called in our own midst Lipa Hamzun, with a squished nose and strong hands. He wandered about town empty handed because he had nothing to do at home. When Lipa the tailor once complained to old Rabbi Moshe Charney z"l (may his name be for a blessing), the wise man answered "Become a tailor."

To which he answered "But, Rabbi, I am a tailor."

To which the Rabbi responded "I mean you should really become a tailor, not just in name. Then you'll have a livelihood."

But Lipa was strongly drawn to become a kind of communal "hinge," and would become a sexton under the new rabbi in Dukor.

Here, too, is Israel the butcher, or Israel "Trapetzke," because he strongly swayed during prayers. He was the son-in-law of Moteh the butcher, of whom I have previously written. Despite the fact that he could slaughter the strongest ox, he remained a terrible coward; as soon as thunder and lightning began he would rush under the covers of a heavy quilt. But he became a big hero when he studied with us the tractate "kiddushin" (Marriage) and he explained all the different ways a wife can be obtained sacredly. But when it came to the third "way," he would send his wife out of the house because she would scream, "How can you teach such things to children?"

We would deliberately play dumb, although we knew all about the birds and the bees.

And here stands Fruma the Bereziner, who, as long as I can remember, was a widow. But before she became a widow she had only boys, who all died right after circumcision. After the birth of her last son, Moshe-Dovid, who came into this world soon after her husband passed away, it was decided not to have him circumcised, and, in fact, he did live. When this uncircumcised Moshe-Dovid started to attend cheder and ran with us to bathe in the river, we saw at once that he was not circumcised and began to call him such names as "Moshe-Dovid the Goy." His mother could not bear the way her only orphan child was treated, so she moved to Berezin, where this inconvenient detail remained unknown.

And if this Moshe-Dovid now also finds himself in America, I would be very thankful if he dropped me a line as to whether he allowed himself to be circumcised on his bar-mitzvah, as was agreed upon in Dukor, or if he remains to this very day, may we be spared, still uncircumcised.

All the above-mentioned Jews, as well as those I have talked about in previous chapters, follow me in all my wandering across the earth, and help me in all my daily struggles and dangers.

But, also, all the other not-mentioned Jews of Dukor, the cobblers and tailors, the butchers, the carpenters, the painters, the shop owners, the widows, the scholars, and the prayer leaders follow me amid all the pathways of my life. I live with their faith and breathe in their belief.

With the collective power of all of Dukor my mother raised her six children; and with the collective blessing of all Dukor she was able to raise me, such as I am, her youngest who later became the poet-singer and lamenter of his old, annihilated town.

I now ask all of my fellow Dukor Jews residing in the wide world to come serve as kindly intercessors, and beg the Master of the Universe that I finish my "Book of Chronicles," which my uncle, Feitel the Angel, sadly could not bring to conclusion.

37

A PESACH-LIKE SUKKUS

Did you ever eat meals off of Pesach [Passover] dishes? Have you ever united in one big holiday "the season of our liberation" with the "seasons of our joy of Sukkus?"

It was actually mother's inspired idea on the eve of Sukkus to take down the box of Pesach dishes from the attic and deliberately "leaven" them [make them non-kosher for Passover] in honor of our last Sukkus in Dukor. Mother knew that right after Sukkus our great leave taking of Dukor would be under way, which to her appeared as miraculous as the exodus from biblical Egypt.

She was not about to drag all her Pesach dishes and the entire household of goods all the way to Zembin, situated in back of Borisov, where the distinguished widower, a man of social standing and solid means, awaited her.

Her second wedding would take place in Dukor proper, and the Pesach dishes would come in handy for the special betrothal meal, which she would prepare for the last time in her old home.

When I saw the unpacked Pesach wine glasses and the Pesach wine containers, and the Pesach plates and soup dishes, I began to imagine that any minute a full delivery of matzhas would arrive so that we could do the seders in the sukkah. I was especially overjoyed when the Pesach box containing the seven clay utensils, all molded from one piece, were unpacked, resembling our own seven-headed family.

Mother made seven separate well-browned potato kugels, so that each of us would have his own portion. [With Mirl in Berezin, there were only six of them having dinner.] When no one was looking I quietly kissed the clay vessels, as if they were living siblings of mine who ordinarily I would see only once a year—for the Pesach seders. My head was buzzing in confusion. I myself no longer knew which world I was in: was it a Pesach- or a Sukkus-themed holiday?

Soon after Yom Kippur my elder brothers began to build a sukkah. Had they had enough building material, they would have set up a sukkah large enough to accommodate all the Jews of Dukor. We knew, after all, that this was the last Sukkus we would celebrate in our old home, and all Dukor would want to be with us.

My eldest two brothers, Mendel and Zalke, would certainly not return to Dukor, as they were now thinking of leaving for America. Mendel, the very eldest, would be the first to go because he luckily was exempted by the military draft board. My other brother Zalke would not have it so easy. He'd have to go to the draft board in four years hence; and should he leave for America before that, mother would be hit with a 300-ruble penalty—the law in Russia for Jewish draft dodgers. However, in view of the fact that mother would soon change her family name to that of Klionsky, the Russian authorities wouldn't know from whom to demand 300 rubles. Then my second eldest brother would leave with no headaches for America.

My two other brothers, Shmuel and Boruch, were still too young to think about America. But they were already consumed with the Land of Israel because Dr. Herzl of Vienna had by then set all Jews astir with buying out our ancestral homeland from the Turk [the Ottoman Empire].

I heard my middle two brothers, Shmuel and Boruch, relate that also in Minsk a certain Dr. Rosenbaum was preparing a gathering of all the Zionists in Russia, and would discuss purchasing the Land of Israel from the Turk. I considered myself lucky to be soon leaving for Minsk, where I would be able to hear more about the gathering to deliberate about the Land of Israel.

By the way, I remember that on Rakover St. in Minsk, just across from the cheap kitchen, where my eldest brother toiled, a tall Turk with a red cap and a black coat stood selling chestnuts for three kopecks apiece, as well as tasty bagels for a kopeck each. I quietly thought to myself that for the time being the Minsk Zionists would do well to buy the Turk's entire bakery and feed Jewish children tasty bagels to their hearts' content in the cheap kitchen!

But I didn't have enough time to think at length about such elevated matters. I had to be at mother's behest, for she always sensed something was missing in the kitchen. First it was a pound of raisins, then a quarter pound of cinnamon, or finally a glass of honey for baking dough.

She was constantly cooking, baking and frying, as if before a really massive wedding. I said that as far back as I could remember she had never baked or fried as much as now, on this eve of Sukkus. To which she replied that giving away her youngest is an even greater joy than giving away her one and only daughter. By this she meant giving me away to a wide, unknown world in which I would have to become an adult, just like my older brothers, may they be well.

On that eve of Sukkus, mother, for the first time in my life, clothed me from head to toe. There I stood in a new suit, a new winter coat with a fur collar, and fine leather shoes so that I not freeze in Minsk. Also included were shirts and underwear of the whitest cloth, as well as wool socks and handkerchiefs.

I felt a bit guilty about my brothers, whose clothing I would now no longer need, the kind they would outgrow so quickly, may no evil eye be cast.

But then the thought of what would be when I outgrew my new clothing before it wore out began to torment me. Who would make new and whole clothing then? Wouldn't my two eldest brothers be then in America and the other two would still be in need of help. They were still "eating days" in Minsk, although they were already occupied with other things.

I couldn't contain myself and asked mother, "Mamele, what will be in a year from now when I outgrow all my clothing?"

Mother, herself unable to bear it, burst into tears, declaring, "What do you think, my child, you will suddenly become an orphan, you will not come to me in Zembin every holiday? Zembin will be like a new home. I am doing all this for your benefit. You will be together with your brothers in Minsk. You will be able to heal there with the best doctors available. You will also be able to study in the best yeshivas. Your future stepfather, Klionsky, told me specifically that he will spare no expense on your behalf. Only get better and heal soon. He even sent a letter to Vilna, where it is said the best doctors in the world can be found. If Minsk will not work, we'll take you to Vilna. Klionsky's relative has an inn there, and you will feel as good as at home."

In just such a manner mother explained the situation in the half-darkened kitchen, mixing tears with cinnamon, tears with raisins and tears with honey.

I wanted to kiss her weeping eyes, but worried this could unleash a further torrent of tears.

I didn't want my older brothers to see mother crying, especially now that it was past Yom Kippur. Mother had already cried herself out during the fast day. But my brothers rarely stayed at home. They also felt that they would never see our shtetl, Dukor, again, whose field and forests drew them as children to play and act silly, like all the other boys.

I didn't join them in their merriment because, simply put, I felt ashamed: they were urbanites while I was still a small-town boy.

I knew that my brother Boruch was barely two year my elder, but he was nearly grown in comparison to me, a child hiding under his mother's apron. What's more, I didn't have anything to talk about with my older brothers, and vice versa.

They would joke around, sing, and look at mother, decked out in her best holiday finery, with great love. She beamed at them with such pride and pleasure that she looked veritably like a Sabbath bride, and even in chol-hamoed one might easily have addressed her as if she were Sabbath royalty.

The Pesach plates contributed ever more charm and festivity to the Sukkus meals.

When mother on the first Sukkus dinner handed out the well-known seven pots of kugel, each as if kneaded from one piece of dough, each lusciously drifting in oil with fried fat in the middle, I was strongly tempted to ask the four questions as if we were sitting at the Pesach seder. I quietly leaned over and asked mother, "Why is this night different from all other nights?"

Mother immediately repeated my questions for my elder brothers and soon the sukkah was hopping with joy and festivity.

But on the second holiday dinner in the sukkah mother no longer handed out the seven potato kugels in the seven, now-leavened clay pots.

When I began to demand that mother give us the tasty kugel, she confessed to me that while she was washing the seven clay pots they suddenly slipped from her fingers and cracked.

She, herself, was very distressed at this loss because she saw it as a parable of our seven-headed family, which was also slipping out of her hands and breaking apart into separate pieces. Mother consoled me with the biblical verse, "The plate has shattered and we have left..."

In fact, right after Sukkus all five of the Charney brothers took leave of Dukor. All of the shtetl followed our departing wagon, as if it were a funeral bier, God have mercy!

With tear-stained eyes, mother told my elder brothers that if I pined in Minsk to return home, they should forthwith send me back to Dukor. She would then travel with me to visit my sister, who was about to go into labor.

My brothers said nothing in response because they felt a cry tugging at their throats, which under no circumstances could be allowed to emerge from their lips.

On the way to the Rudensk train station we stopped at the cemetery, where my elder brothers took leave forever of father's grave site.

Good that mother did not witness this departure. She would have cried all over again.

Thus did the curtain ring down on my childhood in the old home.

But, in fact, your childhood years never quite end. As long as you live, they follow your footsteps in search of continuity and an end-purpose.

My mother believed that only in Minsk, with its great and renowned doctors and under the care and supervision of my elder brothers, would I find my proper betterment. May it be so, Master and Creator of the Universe!

38

WITH MY BROTHERS IN MINSK

From https://www.jewishgen.org/yizkor/minsk/min1_487.html [Yizkor Book Project].

[This chapter was translated by Judy Montel. The rest of the book was translated by Michael Skakun.]

My brother Boruch (eventually – Vladek) was two years older than I was, but at age sixteen he was a man in the full meaning of the word. Within a few years, as a condition of "eating days," he went over the Talmud curriculum at yeshivas and secretly prepared to be tested in the curriculum of the four grades of the Gymnasium [high school]. Those who passed the exams were allowed to be elementary school teachers or apprentices at pharmacy. To what did my brother aspire? I don't know. My second brother Shmuel (eventually S. Niger), who was two years older than Boruch, was already known in the yeshivas of Minsk as "The Ilui [Genius] of Dukor]", and a number of the wealthy men of Minsk had their eyes on him. However, Shmuel also studied Russian secretly and read books of the Haskala. My brothers Mendel and Zalke had positions in the cheap kitchen on Rakovi Street. This kitchen was the main residence of all five of the Charney brothers, each of whom had a special nature, though all of them were kneaded from the same dough.

My brothers helped one another as much as they could. The older ones made sure that I lived with them in the cheap kitchen.

My remaining two brothers, the yeshiva students, lived in a small dark room with an iron bed for the two of them; they looked after my spiritual sustenance.

My brother Shmuel took it upon himself to go with me to the "Totersher Shul" every day to study Jewish legends with me. Apparently, even then Shmuel considered Jewish legends more important than Jewish practice.

When my brother Boruch heard that Shmuel was introducing me to the world of legends, he proposed introducing me to the practical world, to teach me mathematics, grammar, geography, etc. And to ensure my existence, my brothers Shmuel and Boruch decided to give me their "days" at the places where they ate at the houses of the "Pans" of the city. These were good "days," that entitled the diner not only delicious meals, but even cash – "grivniye" or "gulden" (ten or fifteen kopecks) for small expenses, buying sweets or a book. And since their "days" were scattered all over Minsk I had the opportunity to get to know the city and its people. It is beyond my ken how my brothers were able to give up their "days" when they themselves were truly hungry. When I visited them once in their dark and narrow room I found the tail of a herring and rusks of dry bread, and dried figs. They used the figs to sweeten their tea. They put the figs into a kettle of boiling water and the water immediately became yellow, like tea, and even a bit sweet. When I told my brothers Mendel and Zalke about the want and poverty of Shmuel and Boruch they told me they themselves were to blame, they wanted to live a spiritual life, all of their resources were invested in the movement and they had nothing to spare.

My brother Shmuel was respected and accepted by the aristocracy of Minsk. When he took me to the well-known eye doctor, Kaminski, the latter received me in his splendid office with warmth and friendliness. The doctor ordered three cups of real tea, not fig tea, and additional abundant refreshments. They discussed political and other matters that I didn't understand for a long time.

One day Shmuel stood on the stool in the cheap kitchen and spoke for hours on end before the audience of Dr. Leon Pinsker, who was preparing the ground for a state in the land of Israel with his composition "Autoemancipation." However the state – said my brother Shmuel – must be built upon socialist principles, according to the "Kapital" of Karl Marx. The words "Kapital" and "Autoemancipation" were not clear to me then.

Meetings frequently took place in the cheap kitchen in which respected and established inhabitants of the city took part. The debates went on until the late hours of the evening. My brothers Boruch and Shmuel argued about the matter of the land of Israel, but Mendel and Zalke were preparing to travel to America.

PHOTOGRAPHS

The five Charney brothers. From left to right: Mendel, Daniel, Shmuel, Zalke, and Boruch, Minsk 1903.
From the Archives of the YIVO Institute for Jewish Research, New York

(From left) Daniel Charney with his brothers, Boruch Charney
Vladeck and Shmuel Charney Niger in Vilna, 1906
In *Barg Aroyf* by Daniel Charney, courtesy of Yiddish Book Center, Amherst
MA

The rented house in Dukor where Daniel and his siblings grew up
From *Barg Aroyf* by Daniel Charney, courtesy of the Yiddish Book Center,
Amherst MA

Brocha, mother of Daniel Charney and his siblings
Courtesy of Rosalind Charney Kaye

Tombstone of father of Charney siblings, Zev Wolf
From *Barg Aroyf* by Daniel Charney, courtesy of the Yiddish
Book Center, Amherst MA

Brocha, mother of Daniel Charney and his siblings, with her
sisters.
From left to right: Aunt Itke Grundfest, Aunt Yudashe Broyde,
Aunt Toybe Minkovitch, Aunt Rivtche Hurvitch, Brocha
From the Archives of the YIVO Institute for Jewish Research, New York

PHOTOGRAPHS

"Uncle Klionsky," stepfather of Daniel Charney and his siblings
Courtesy of Rosalind Charney Kaye

Daniel's sister, Mirl, at her husband's tombstone
From the Archives of the YIVO Institute for Jewish Research, New York

Daniel Charney
Courtesy of Suzanne Zoe Joskow

Daniel Charney
Courtesy of Miriam Charney

Daniel Charney (right) with his brother Shmuel Charney Niger, 1931
Courtesy of Miram Charney

(From left) Yiddish author Sholem Asch with Daniel Charney's
brothers Boruch Charney Vladeck and Shmuel Charney Niger in
the 1930's
From the Archives of the YIVO Institute for Jewish Research, New York

PHOTOGRAPHS

Daniel Charney's brother Boruch Charney Vladeck
Courtesy of Ezra Bialik

Daniel Charney's brother Zalke (Charles) Charney
Courtesy of David Charney

From left, Mendel Charney, Daniel Charney, and Shmuel
Charney Niger November 5, 1950
Courtesy of Rosalind Charney Kaye

39

IDEALISM AND PHILANTHROPY

B eats me if I know why Minsk Jewry has been crowned with such a swinish sobriquet. [The author does not say what the sobriquet was.]

According to my first Minsk impressions, its Jews were fine and genteel people. Even in the cheap kitchen on Rakover St., where the most indigent took their meals, I never encountered any rough or uncouth types.

True, even among the steady eaters at the cheap kitchen there were two classes of poor people — the three-kopeck and the five-kopeck eaters.

For three kopecks one would receive a pound of thick bread with a comparably thick krupnik (lentil soup); for five kopecks one would obtain a piece of meat in the krupnik. Obviously, the three-kopeckers secretly envied the five-kopeckers; but the envy did not elicit hate, as sometimes happens among women and children.

Quite often, two impoverished people would buy in partnership two meals, one for five kopecks and the second for three kopecks without meat, and then split the meat between them. In this manner both indigents had meat, for a total of four kopecks per soul.

In the cheap kitchen, one could, alas, spot pocket thieves and other colorful character types of the Minsk underworld, but very rarely would any of them brazenly slip a fork or spoon into his pocket which could then be sold for one or two kopecks. The cheap kitchen was after all their permanent "restaurant," where honesty and propriety had to be kept up.

The rich of Minsk, who underwrote the cheap kitchen, would arrive to view the Sabbath meal in session. At their head stood the big magnate, Goldberg, who had founded the kitchen. The well-heeled had come straight from Sabbath services at the Big Shul to see how the poor ate their Sabbath repast. Goldberg himself wore a black top hat and Mrs. Goldberg, dressed to the nines, stood bedecked with gems in her earrings and rings on both hands.

The rich ladies would in full view taste all the selections of the Sabbath table and would nod to their top-hatted husbands that all was good, indeed very good!

In nodding their rich heads, the women further enhanced the bejeweled splendor of their earrings, which sparkled with all the colors of the rainbow.

The rich men and women would leave very contentedly, acknowledging that in Minsk, thank God, there were enough impoverished people to purchase the well-off an honored place in the world to come. For their part, the poor were happy in the knowledge that the wealthiest members of society were concerned with their this-worldly welfare.

No antagonism or hate was felt between the sparkling "world-to-come-niks" and the ragged "this worldniks." It is apparently fated by God that the Goldbergs, the Soutines, the Kabakoffs, and the Pollacks should be wealthy and the eaters of the cheap kitchen should remain indigent.

A cheap teahouse stood side by side with the cheap kitchen. The administrator of the cheap kitchen was my own brother Mendel and the administrator of the cheap teahouse was my second, younger brother, Zalke. Zalke had to work longer hours than Mendel because the teahouse was open all day from 8 a.m. until 8 p.m., while the cheap kitchen opened only for lunch between the hours of twelve and two and for supper between six and eight.

I very much liked to sit in the teahouse and observe people arriving to drink their tea for all of one kopeck per portion, which consisted of quite a large white porcelain teapot containing around five glasses of tea and above it a small porcelain kettle in which my brother Zalke would pour a tiny spoonful of soda to make everything seep in better. Aside from these two teapots, the tea drinker would be furnished with a glass and three pieces of sugar.

At such a spacious tea ceremony one could sit for hours and talk amongst friends. The cheap teahouse was always crowded.

If someone had drunk the entire pot my brother would provide fresh boiled water for no extra charge.

I liked to sit with my brother Zalke near the "buffet" and talk about all and sundry. I once asked Zalke why my other two brothers, Shmuel and Boruch, didn't come to take tea here.

I knew that in other establishments instead of real tea leaden pots would be stuffed with dry figs, which served as a substitute for real tea and sugar, whereas in the cheap teahouse the clientele could for all of one kopeck obtain real sugar-sweetened tea. My brother Zalke explained that Shmuel and Boruch are big idealists and do not want to benefit from any philanthropy.

When I asked Zalke what is the difference between idealism and philanthropy, he explained that idealists don't want a world of rich and poor, all should, in fact, be equal. But the philanthropists do want the poor to remain impoverished forever and so afford them the privilege of conferring charity.

According to my boyish understanding, I perceived that it wasn't so hard to be an idealist if one possessed nothing. It is much harder for the "idealists" to be rich and give to the needy.

But truth to tell, until this very day I still don't know how to differentiate idealism from philanthropy. It seems to me that when an idealist sacrifices for his people or for his class, he becomes the biggest philanthropist! He bestows the maximum of what he possesses, indeed, goes so far as to sacrifice life and limb.

But it also seems true that the philanthropist who bestows his wealth for the needy of his people is already by definition a big idealist! (Take Baron Hirsch, Baron Rothschild, Baron Guinsburg, Jacob Schiff, Rosenwald, Warburg and many others!).

I might possibly have remained stuck with my limited boyish understanding. But because in my ensuing years I came to meet a lot of idealists who had become quite big allrightniks, as well as former members of the bourgeoisie who had become quite decent proletarians, I permit myself to continue doubting the great difference between idealists and philanthropists.

Here for example is my first Minsk doctor, who was both an idealist and a philanthropist. Although he was a Pole, his name was Malkevitch. As soon as he had read the letter which the eye doctor Kaminski wrote to him about me, Dr. Malkevitch said to me (in half Russian, half Polish):

"My child, you suffer from a very serious illness but thank God your disease is external, not internal. I'll try to heal you."

But before Dr. Malkevitch took to healing me, he began asking who I was, what I am and how come the eye doctor was involved when, in fact, my eyes are well!

So I told him the entire truth: I had four brothers in Minsk, two of whom work at the cheap kitchen and are planning on going to America; and the other two are big idealists, who want to purchase all of the Land of Israel from the Turks. Therefore, they have befriended the ophthalmologist Kaminski who is also a big idealist.

"And what are you?" the doctor asked me.

"I am nothing," I confessed. "I study the Talmud and eat days."

"You eat days?" Dr. Malkevitch suddenly asked in half-Polish, half-Russian. He apparently wanted to know how one goes about eating days.

I explained in half-Yiddish, half-Russian how poor yeshiva students who come from neighboring towns to Minsk to study Talmud are offered free meals, each day in a different home.

"And at night you don't eat? In winter the nights are longer than the days!" the doctor added. "Youth, Youth! You must eat more and better!" he insisted now in half-Polish, half-German. "Your primary cure consists of good food. When you will be sufficiently strong, you will be able to better bear the pain of the cure. Do you understand?"

"Yes, Doctor, I understand that the healthier I am the sicker I can be!" I thus translated the doctor's thought in my own idiom.

Dr. Malkevitch, it appears, very much liked that I understood his point delivered in three languages (Polish, Russian and German), and pinched my cheek, telling me to return the next day to receive the first phase of my treatment.

Upon departing, I placed a silver coin worth 25 kopecks on the table. Thus I figured if I have to come every day, save for Sunday, the physician will earn one and a half rubles every week.

When Dr. Malkevitch noticed the silver coin on the table, he burst out into such vigorous laughter that his black mustache stretched to its fullest length, as two hands of a watch marking a quarter to three.

"You are a foolish youth!!" he laughed in my face. "Take back the coin. Here, I'll give you one instead—make believe you are eating days by me as well. Understood?"

But before I could get my wits about me, the doctor slipped two quarter silver coins into my pocket and practically pushed me out of his office, underscoring that I arrive the next day on time.

This was my initial experience with my first non-Jewish doctor in Minsk.

Was Dr. Malkevitch an idealist or a philanthropist or simply a great guy?

40

EVERY CIRCLE HAS ITS QUADRANT

As it appears, it isn't so easy to grow up, to become an adult, when one has four older brothers for guidance. In fact, in Dukor, with mother at my side, I felt more pride and independence than with my four older brothers in Minsk.

In Dukor I not only helped mother in the household but even with business matters. Every month when mother would go to the fair in Dushitz I stayed put and became the single boss of her business. By then I'd already been able to sell to the cobblers all kinds of goods applicable to their leather trade, knowing exactly the prices of each item in question.

When mother would finally return late at night, hungry and frozen, she'd put down her heavy leather bag bursting with silver and copper coins and say to me, "Nu, Donyele, count and record how much is here!"

First off, I'd divide the coins according to their denomination: rubles to rubles, quarters to quarters, guilden to guilden, until I reached the copper pennies. Then I would calculate the worth of each denomination and record the amount on a piece of paper.

When all the numbers were written on the piece of paper it wasn't difficult to calculate the sum of the whole pile. All that was left was to add the worth of the IOUs, which mother kept in a separate compartment of her leather bag.

"Mother, you earned 33 rubles and 77 kopecks!" I shouted with glee into the kitchen, where she was boiling a glass of tea.

"Ach! it won't be enough to return the amount owed to Gemilas Hasadim," she answered from the kitchen.

"If the earnings are smaller than the amount owed to Gemilas Hasadim, why then do you schlep all the way to Dushitz and struggle all day?" I asked mother, as if I were already her partner in a business that obviously couldn't pay its way.

"My child, if I didn't travel to the fairs, how then would we live?" mother replied.

By then I already understood that even if one couldn't pay off Gemilas Hasadim, one still might have enough for subsistence. So it was at the age of twelve-thirteen, I became a real merchant.

How different I felt in Minsk under the strict supervision of my elder four brothers. Instead of becoming an adult in the big city, I became, under the tutelage of my brothers, ever smaller and more helpless than I had been in Dukor.

How true that it's no simple matter to grow up when four pairs of sibling eyes keep constant watch over you as a child, ever in need of love and sympathy.

Truth to tell, I secretly felt compassion for my older brothers, two of whom (Mendel and Zalke) barely eked out a living at the cheap kitchen in hopes of saving the first hundred rubles in order to leave for America. The other two brothers (Shmuel and Boruch) squeezed out slim wages in hopes of contributing to Dr. Herzl, who sought to buy out the Land of Israel from under the Turkish Sultan. Thus, they arduously collected kopecks for the Jewish National Fund alms box: a kopeck—a heap of earth.

Alas, for themselves they lacked the few kopecks to buy from the Minsk Turkish merchant a few tasty bagels to nibble.

Shmuel and Boruch were not simply Zionists: they were Labor Zionists. The difference between the Zionists and Labor Zionists was huge. The plain Zionists didn't care if a capitalist arrangement prevailed in the Land of Israel, as it did in most other countries in the world. As for the poor, they'd ultimately find what to eat, as had been arranged already in biblical times; but the Minsk Labor Zionists felt from the outset that the Land of Israel should be governed by socialist principles: differences between rich and poor should effectively be abolished. Therefore, they were ready to launch a political struggle even during the Czarist era.

"Zionism without political struggle is like a roll without salt!" Boruch once said at a meeting of the Minsk Labor Zionists held in the cheap kitchen. It took place at the time that preparations were afoot for the big Zionist gathering in Minsk. The leaders of the Minsk Labor Zionists were Aba Rubentshik, Berger, Lapidus and Chaika Cohen (Zhelubski), who wanted to prepare their own program for the forthcoming gathering.

My brother Shmuel presented a long speech at this meeting, but he spoke so profoundly that I couldn't quite make out his reasoning as to why Zionism must necessarily go hand in hand with socialism.

Truth to tell, I don't understand until this very day why Zionists needed to conduct a political struggle in countries they wished to flee. It's as if my mother went ahead and put a new roof on our rented house in Dukor before departing to her second husband in Zembin.

As it appears, I have remained a political simpleton until this very day, or perhaps I was passing as one in order to keep out of the high realm of politics.

I only know the "political struggle" of the Labor Zionists led to arrests which swept up even plain Zionists, one of whom, my own brother Boruch, ended up in the slammer when he wasn't even eighteen years old.

But this was a year later, when the Minsk gendarme Zubatov realized that his sweet talk to the Jewish workers and his false assurances even to the Labor Zionists would not convince them to give up their "political struggle."

Regarding the so-called "Zubatovchina" (Zubatov's crackdown), much commotion ensued, but as I didn't understand why Zionists who planned to emigrate to the Land of Israel needed to struggle against the Czar in Russia, I also didn't comprehend why Jews could ever put their trust in Czarist gendarmes.

Therefore, I had much more pleasure when I saw my brother Boruch secretly prepare to take four or six gymnasium classes.

When I arrived in Minsk, Boruch wasn't even seventeen years old but already knew so much of the worldly sciences. He already had mastered by heart national fables, geography and history and could do such difficult algebra equations in which such Latin letters as x, y, or z were used in place of customary numbers. So, for example, Boruch calculated that when multiplying x and y one arrives at z.

"This is more interesting than kabbalah!" Boruch once exclaimed to me with great satisfaction about such profound matters.

But even more, my brother Boruch liked to trace varying sorts of mathematical and astronomical figures and charts.

Here, for example, he drew a big circle, inside of which he sketched a quadrant, inside of which he drew another circle, which was a lot smaller than its predecessor, and in this last circle he drew yet another quadrant, and so on.

In this manner he folded a piece of a paper allowing him to draw five or six circles, each smaller than the next, and to sketch as many quadrants, each comparably smaller than the next.

In my eyes it didn't seem more than a fine game or toy to play with. But my brother explained that once he knew the diameter of the very first circle he would be able to calculate the diameter of all the other circles, as well as the measurements of each of the quadrants.

Boruch's declaration made my head wince, but smack in the middle of his explanation he suddenly asked me, "Does it hurt you?"

"What?" I asked confusedly.

"I mean the salve Dr. Malkevitch smears on your hand."

"Yes, it hurts very much," I conceded.

"Maybe you should stop smearing it then?" Boruch asked with great compassion.

"I don't know. The doctor says the salve will perhaps help cauterize the illness."

A bit later, after Boruch had calculated the size of his circle and quadrants, he again suddenly asked me, "It burns badly?"

"Like fire on the naked skin!" I answered.

"Then why do you keep quiet?"

"If I scream, will it change anything?" I replied.

"Dr. Malkevitch said when it burns strongly, we should take off the salve," Boruch responded while playing with his circles.

Instead of replying that I would not allow any of my brothers to remove the salve from my sick hand and thus see my big misfortune, I burst into tears like a small child and I immediately hid among mother's two big pillows, may she be well.

My brother was smart enough already to let me be for a while among mother's pillows (if my mother was unavailable, the pillows would do).

Boruch ran down to the cheap kitchen, probably to inform my elder brothers how much I suffered from this new cure.

A little later I heard in the room the very soft and quiet steps of my other brother Shmuel.

He looked at me with the same maternal (Tzena-Renah) eyes that mother possessed right after candle lighting.

From his look at me, I understood that we would not go to the Tatar school today to learn Haggadah, but rather we would all eat together in the cheap kitchen.

Swallowing my pain, I said to Shmuel in a chipper voice, "Look at what Boruch has sketched. He says that every circle has its quadrant and each quadrant has its circle! He says it's a piece of kabbalah! He also claims that when one multiples x and y one obtains z."

I went on in this manner so my brothers should not notice how Dr. Malkevitch's copper salve was driving me to sheer madness.

My brother Shmuel remained quiet as always. It appears he agreed with Boruch that when one multiples x and y one arrives at z.

Only now do I realize that both my brothers were right!

When I multiply, for example, Niger with Vladeck, I arrive at Daniel Charney!

In any case, I imagine it is so.

41

THE CITY LUNATIC

My weakness for lunatics stems from my childhood years. For this I can thank my cousin Masha the Lunatic, who was always very good to me.

She was very good to me because I always helped out her father, my uncle Feitel "the Angel," as he was called by the shtetl.

True, she would curse her father with such terms as "madman" or "unkosher limb" and what not. But she still feared him because he always talked with God, as is customary for an angel.

And as I often helped Feitel, I soon became for Masha a sort of second angel. Once, when she was especially vexed and disheveled, she pressed me against a wall when nobody was around and pleaded that I unconditionally marry her when I become an adult.

"What do you care, Donyele, if you marry me? Everyone says you won't live long. So what do you care if you go ahead and marry me?"

"If I won't live long, how will I then grow up?" I asked, trying to twist out from under her crazed body.

"Eat as many raisins and almonds as you can, then you will be grown as I am," she counseled.

I quickly realized that I was dealing, God have mercy, with a maddened Lilith, and out of great fright I promised Masha, in that heated moment, that I would unequivocally marry her as soon as I became an adult, if God wills it. (I was then pre-bar-mitzvah.)

From then on Masha filled my pockets with heaps of raisins and almonds so I should grow ever faster. But when I became bar-mitzvah I would enter Aunt Chaya's shop with my knees bent a bit so Masha wouldn't notice that I had become an adult.

I once asked Masha, "And what will you do if I die after the wedding?"

"Better to remain a young widow than to remain an old maid," she replied.

I realized that Masha was not all that crazy, as she was often characterized, and it hurt and pained me that nobody wanted to marry her.

In Minsk I silently missed both Feitel "the Angel" and Masha. It was lonely without them.

God arranged to send me a lunatic in Minsk as well. True, not a woman, but a man this time—the Minsk city lunatic named Morgenstern.

This Morgenstern fellow would quite often come into the cheap kitchen where, like all others of the poor, he'd eat his lunch and then while away hours in the cheap tea house, where he would very gladly share his ideas and stories.

I believe Morgenstern was more of a drunkard than a lunatic, but would deliberately act like a madman in order to more easily elicit a few coins from his listeners with which to purchase a new shot of schnapps.

"Do you know, my fellow Jews, how I became a drunkard?" he would suddenly ask a number of tea drinkers sitting nearby.

"It's quite simple! I once came to Monopolke to buy a pint of spirits for kiddush, whereupon I saw the bottles fighting amongst themselves, each wanting to fall first into Morgenstern's mouth; so I did, as Jacob our Father of yore did with the stones wrangling with each other as to which should serve as his pillow: I gathered the pints, turned them into a quart and drank them all." [Possibly referring to Genesis Chapter 28, verse 11.]

"When I drank the entire quart," he continued, "I obviously couldn't stand on my feet. I fell down in the gutter and thus lying fully prone I dreamt a sweet dream that I was on the brink of arriving in the Land of Israel because as it says point blank in the Bible, 'And they shall come to Zion in joy…' [cf. Isaiah, chapter 51, verse 11]. Let me tell you, my fellow Jews, it's just as the Scripture has it. The gutter flows into our River Svislovitch, which then empties into the Berezina River; the Berezina then sweeps into the

Dnieper which, descending into the mighty Black Sea, leads us at long last to the Land of Israel."

"Jews, isn't it so?" Morgenstern, wonderstruck, asked his listeners.

"You're right, Morgenstern. For you it's the most direct way to the Land of Israel," his listeners responded, giving him added courage.

"If so, my fellow Jews, then be so good and give me a little something for a quart of spirits because I cannot wait any longer to be in the Land of Israel!" he said, stretching out both hands to the poor tea drinkers. Nearly each then gave him a donation, some a mere groschen, others even as much as a kopeck!

I, too, would offer Morgenstern a kopeck because I greatly enjoyed his stories and ideas.

My brother who was the administrator of the cheap tea house told me then, "Now you see the difference between a Jewish and a Gentile drunkard: A goy who is good and drunk becomes a thief, breaks windows and puts up his dukes, while a Jew dreams of the Land of Israel and the world to come."

"And I am thinking just now about the difference between a male madman and a female lunatic," I responded to my brother. "When a woman goes nuts, she sniffs out sins in the shtetl and speaks about getting married; while the man goes off his rocker by translating verses from the prayer books and telling fine tales."

True, even Morgenstern would tell tall tales, especially when he would boast of his success with Lady Chatzkin, who dealt in Vistosky teas and would give him ten kopecks at a time every Friday.

"If you think, my fellow Jews, that I come to Lady Chatzkin because of the ten kopecks I get then you are seriously mistaken," Morgenstern explained. "She is the greatest beauty in town, and it is a pleasure to gaze at her! So I told her once that it would be better if she gave me a kopeck every day rather than a fistful once a week. To which Lady Chatzkin responded, 'How is that? If I gave you, Mr. Morgenstern, a kopeck each day you would lose out at the end of the week.' To which I said that 'I am ready, Lady Chatzkin, to lose a few kopecks every week, as long I can have the pleasure of greeting you every day with a 'Good morning!'""

Truth to tell, I myself became very eager to take a good look at this Lady Chatzkin with whom Morgenstern had become so smitten. When I once obtained the good fortune to come into her shop with an order from the cheap teahouse I realized Morgenstein was far from being a lunatic! She was indeed a stunning beauty and she smelled like a freshly minted tea box.

Until today, I still do not understand why Minsk decided to call Morgenstern the city lunatic.

"Were there not real crazies in Minsk?" I once asked my Uncle Yeshaya Grundfest, who knew all of Minsk by heart; after all, he was the broker of all the city shops. To which the much-scattered Uncle Yeshaya replied that the real lunatics sit in prison.

"Why in prison?" I asked.

"Because they want to overthrow the Czar!" he replied.

"Overthrowing the Czar is not madness," Aunt Itke, who read the "The Fraynt" on a daily basis and knew something about world politics, suddenly interjected.

"You don't know what you are talking about!" Uncle Yeshaya said, reddening.

"You should have seen how they look, the types who want to overthrow the Czar. If you had, you'd be whistling a different tune," he added for good measure.

Uncle Yeshaya then related how this very day he had been at the Vilna platform station (in Minsk there were two station platforms: Vilna and Brisk). He had seen a whole wagon of the arrested, now being driven all the way to Siberia. Each chained in irons, as if he, God help us, is a murderer. It happens, he explained, that these captives are Jewish boys, famished and forlorn, friends of Hirsh Lekert, who took aim at the Vilna governor.

"It's heartbreaking to look at them, but go help them when they are such lunatics! Trade youth, cobbler kids want to overthrow the Czar! Isn't that madness?" Uncle Yeshaya, looking straight at me through his befogged eye glasses, was waiting for my nod of agreement.

I didn't want to mix into the argument between my uncle and aunt because I was too young for such matters; but Aunt Itke really lanced into him.

"And plowing a whole stash of money in some wild scheme cooked up by a Zionist bank is not madness?!" she queried.

Uncle Yeshaya took this insult badly, became quickly infuriated and screamed at her that she was no better than a cow and in short there's no one to speak to.

I took strong exception to how my uncle insulted my aunt Itke, my mother's older sister, the nicest and smartest of all my aunts. I thought, you should forgive me, Uncle Yeshaya to be crazier than Morgenstern.

Morgenstern, at least, showed respect and love for a pretty lady, while my uncle shows no decency to my aunt, who in my eyes is a lot nicer and smarter than even Lady Chatzkin.

I was so stricken and tongue-tied that I suddenly burst into tears (in those days I cried easily because Dr. Malkevitch's salve ate into my skin, nearly driving me to madness).

Aunt Itke understood immediately why I was crying. She felt I was on her side. She embraced me as if I were her own child and kissed me on the forehead. I felt as if my very own mother were kissing me, and cried even more intensely.

Later, upon departing, I told Aunt Itke, "You think Morgenstern is not right? He claims the whole world is crazy but as you cannot run after a world full of people—they run after him."

42

I STUDY A PAGE OF TALMUD WITH MY POLISH DOCTOR

Years back, in 1903, people would promenade in Minsk. The city did not yet boast a Yiddish theater or movie house. As soon as one finished dinner, one took a postprandial walk.

Gubernatorska was the most popular promenade street in Minsk, as were various parts of Zahariover, which was very well lit. But not only Jewish youth liked to take a walk. Christian gymnasium students or young officers and their dates liked as well to promenade on Gubernatorska St.

It happened, as if by its own accord, that Jews walked on the right side of Zahariover St. at the top of the market, while on the left side, Christians strode a lot more calmly and quietly than on the Jewish side.

This can be attributed to the fact that the Christians walked in pairs, guys and gals quietly enjoying each other's company, while the Jewish youth hung out in crowds so no one would ever suspect that they had paired off as if they were already pretty much brides and grooms. Five or six girls at a time would stride forth followed by six fellows who talked to them at the top of their voices. Behind these fellows, a new line of girls would sally forth, followed right behind them by a new bevy of boys. In such manner did the entire Jewish side of the street fill up.

When a passerby had to cross Gubernatorska St. in the evening, he'd have to go along the cobblestone in the middle of the gutter because no space could be found on the sidewalk itself.

I, too, had to pass in the middle of the gutter nearly every evening, because had I taken the sidewalk my elbows would have been rubbed raw from the friction of waves of people.

This was my route every evening when I went to visit Dr. Malkevitch for my cure. (Why he saw me at night will be explained later).

Walking thus along the cobblestones between the two streams of people I could clearly distinguish how different Jews were from Christians. On the Jewish side of Gubernatorska St. everything was joyous and lively. Shouts, laughter, whatever you'd like, could be heard, while on the Christian sidewalk things assumed a very quiet tone, as if they were walking in a funeral procession. Just so did the Jews march back and forth on the narrow street, two different nations, each strange to each other, often disparagingly so.

At the office of my Polish Dr. Malkevitch, where I had nearly become a son of the house (ben-bayis), I soon surmised that such Minsk Christians of high society as officers did not much care for Jews.

Dr. Malkevitch himself was very nice and largely liberal but his patients were mostly of the epauletted sort. I never sat in the waiting room with the other patients because I couldn't stand their ugly talk about Jews. I, therefore, sat in the half-darkened corridor and read a Yiddish or Hebrew text.

When Dr. Malkevitch's servant saw that I was already sitting in the corridor, she asked me to spare her the task of opening the clinging front door. She instructed me that when a male comes in I should show him to the men's waiting room, and when a female appears I should show her to the ladies' waiting area.

At first I was taken aback that Dr. Malkevitch kept men and women apart. All other Minsk physicians, such as Dr. Shapira, the surgeon, or Dr. Kaminsky, the eye doctor, or even Dr. Luntz, who let his wealthy patients in through the main entrance and his poor patients through the back door, did not separate their clients in the waiting room. Dr. Malkevitch did so by gender.

Only later did I discover that my doctor was a sex specialist. One came to him to be cured of the "ugly disease," which people still find shameful. Owing to this, Dr. Malkevitch kept his male and female patients apart so as not to shame one in front of the other.

When I once asked my doctor why I never see any Jewish patients in his practice, he said Jews don't suffer from such diseases.

So that meant I was his only Jewish, and youngest patient.

I began to fear that I could get infected with an ugly disease. Some of the other patients took me for a porter because I sat in the corridor and opened the door. Upon leaving, they'd push a coin in my hand, but I felt disgusted to hold their tips, which I would immediately put down on the corridor table for the servant to fetch.

I once told Dr. Malkevitch the truth that some of his patients, both male and female, tip me because I always open the doors for them, but I fear their coins will infect me with their disease.

It was then that Dr. Malkevitch decided to see me in the evening after he had finished with all his patients, and thus could find more time for me. And he did indeed need a lot more time for me than for his other patients because he didn't merely attempt to cure me but spent time schmoozing with me about every side issue you can imagine.

So, for example, my Polish doctor wanted to know what it was I had learned in the Talmud. When I told him that by the age of twelve I had already studied the Talmud tractate of "Kiddushin" (Marriage) he was hugely astonished, and urged me to describe in great detail how Jews in fact marry.

Understandably, I had to use more Yiddish than Russian with the doctor, because how can you differentiate a "ketanah" (a girl of twelve and a day) and a "naroh" (a girl up till the age of twelve and a half) from a "bogeret" (a growing girl) and a "besulah" (a budding girl).

Lucky that Dr. Malkevitch possessed good German and thus grasped quickly the ways a Jewish man might consecrate a woman in matrimony, no matter her age, even if she still be quite young, barely a teenager.

Nevertheless, it remained very difficult to explain precisely the difference between a "ketana" and a "naroh." According to the Talmud, as mentioned, a girl can only be a "ketana" until the age twelve and one day; as soon as she reaches this point, she becomes a "naroh" until the age of twelve and a half. Subsequently, she probably becomes a "bogeret" or a "besulah." But as long as the girl is still a "ketanah" or a "naroh" she can be married off without her consent and then divorced also without her consent. It can happen, the Talmud derives after much argument, that a father can offer his half-grown daughter in matrimony and have her quickly divorced, as soon as he has second thoughts about the viability of the match. Then such a "ketana" or "naroh" becomes a real divorcee (grusha) and a priest (kohen) cannot marry her even though she remained a "besula." Just so can a married "ketanah" or "naroh" also become a widow, if sadly her husband dies.

"Miss Widow, Miss Widow! This is wondrous my dear boy!" Dr. Malkevitch nearly kissed me from great joy.

When I asked him how he could take such joy in so small a girl being already widowed, he told me that he was just now writing an article for a medical journal about the fine intricacies of Jewish family life, and my Talmud stories would come in handy.

He said that he was also writing an article about my illness, for the same medical journal. He added that I should consider myself lucky that I drag myself around with such an illness. True, the disease is dreadful, because no current cure exists, but I am lucky, he informed me, that I have the illness on my hand and not on my face, where in 99 out of 100 cases it appears, may God spare me.

Therefore, as I am the lucky exception, he wants to write about me in the medical journal published in far off Berlin.

He himself revealed his doubts as to his ability to cure me by the fiery salve alone, but declared he has an older friend in Vilna, a famous skin doctor, who has electrical implements with which to cauterize my illness. He would give me a letter of recommendation and the Vilna physician would cure me for no money.

I had to pass yet again across Gubernatorska St. but couldn't for the life of me recognize it. The whole Jewish sidewalk, which ordinarily overflowed with people, was starkly empty; while the non-Jewish side was, as ever, spilling over with promenading couples. I started to imagine that I had seen some of the officers, now walking so lovingly interlaced with their dates, at the office of Dr. Malkevitch.

By the time I arrived, fully exhausted, at the inexpensive kitchen and saw my brothers, I felt as if I had come from the world beyond.

They immediately pounded me with questions as to how had I managed to get here? To which I replied, "As always, with Gubernatorska St."

"You didn't see anything there?" my brothers inquired eagerly.

"I saw the Yiddish sidewalk was empty like a noodle board, but the Christian side brimmed with people."

"Don't go through Gubernatorska again!" my older brothers warned me. "Many Bundists were arrested there, far too many."

Suddenly everything became clear to me. It must mean that while on one side of Gubernatorska St. syphilis, decked out in epaulettes, promenades at leisure, on the other side the revolution born of the "Minsk mud" is violently cleared away (which Izzy Charik would sing about after the October Revolution).

When I told my brothers that I would soon have to leave them because Dr. Malkevitch was sending me to Vilna, their eyes moistened. As did mine!

43

A SMALL LETTER TO MOTHER

I f I've actually become a Yiddish writer, I have my mother to thank.

Already at the age of 14 I had to write her three long letters a week from Minsk, because in Zembin (near Borisov), where mother settled after her marriage to "Uncle Klionsky" (as we called our stepfather), the mail arrived only three times a week.

Uncle Klionsky picked up the mail himself. If he came back empty- handed, mother would be beside herself with worry, not knowing what to think (about her children).

Encouraging me to write a letter nearly every other day, Uncle Klionsky sent me seven kopeck stamps so as to prevent me from backsliding on the pretext that I didn't have enough pocket change for postage.

Mother herself wrote us once a week, at the end of Sabbath. She began every letter with the following salutation: "To my loyal and well-schooled children, Mendel, Zalke, Shmuel, Boruch and Daniel, may you live well together and individually and in good luck. Amen!" (In the body of the letter, mother called me Donya, not Daniel).

The content of each of the letters was nearly always the same. It appears mother missed me greatly in her new home. She wanted to know all the details of my life in Minsk. As for the oldest of her children she remained more or less calm, but she still regarded me as in need of constant warmth and love.

In every letter she reminded my elder brothers to constantly keep an eye on me. Minsk is a big city and I could, God forbid, get run over!

Mother asked me to write her the whole truth, not only about myself but also about my brothers, because they wrote little and infrequently.

Could I write the full truth about my brothers?!

Would she then understand if I wrote that one brother likes to make quadrants of circles and circles out of quadrants? And what would she make of our small Shmuel (he was shorter than Boruch, although he was older by two years) standing on a bench in the Minsk cheap kitchen and speaking steadily for hours in front of a large assembly about a Dr. Leon Pinsker, who in his book "Auto-Emancipation" (much earlier than Dr. Herzl) paved the way for a planned Jewish state in the Land of Israel, which Shmuel kept insisting must from the very outset be built on socialist foundations, according to Marx's "Das Kapital?"

Truth to tell, I then could barely understand the translation of such difficult words as "auto-emancipation," "Jewish state," or "capital." (That Jews had need of a "state" stood to reason but I couldn't fathom in the least how one makes "socialism" with "capital.")

Therefore I couldn't write mother the full truth about my elder brothers in Minsk, because the truth would have puzzled her even more than it did me.

Every other day I described to my mother my impressions of Minsk and my discussions with the interesting and curious Polish Dr. Malkevitch, who healed me without charging any money because I studied the Talmud with him.

I wrote the truth about Minsk which, in comparison with Kiev, a metropolis we had visited several years back, was a relatively small city. Instead of an electric tramway on which we traveled through Kiev's nicer avenues, Minsk's badly paved streets are home to a so-called plain tramway, but, in fact, nothing moves even an inch without horses. Such a set-up, I believe, would set my mother at ease. I simply couldn't be ridden over as she feared.

Nevertheless, Minsk possessed more of a Jewish air than Kiev. So, for example, it boasted a luminary of scholarship no less prominent than the Vilna Gaon a"h (may peace be upon him). When this scholarly eminence died his son-in-law took his place, but the latter was no match for his father-in-law. [The Vilna Gaon was a very influential scholar in the 1700s.]

But there is in Minsk a kind of holy Jew by the name of Reb Yaacov Meir, who is not lazy when it comes to rushing across the streets and informing the shop owners that the Sabbath is nearing.

When the Minsk shop owners heard that Reb Yaacov Meir called out the single word "brothers," they knew unmistakably that they must close shop very soon. Reb Yaacov Meir wore a hat with a broad brim covering his eyes so he should not be able to see the women who sit in the shops, and who he also addresses as "brothers" and not "sisters."

I took a strong liking to this Jew. His outfit of spread-out tails, which resembled wings, coupled with leggings which he folded into his long socks, made him resemble a bird. I imagined that as he ran across the streets of Minsk he could very well lift off and, much like Eliahu the Prophet, soar on high into heaven on the Sabbath.

Several Fridays in a row I ran after him in the Minsk streets and thought how different Reb Yaacov Meir is from my own holy Uncle Feitel, who doesn't budge in his place, although he is called "Angel" in Dukor.

I also informed mother that there were surely about forty to fifty synagogues and prayer centers in Minsk because each trade had its own shul! The tailors prayed separately from the cobblers, who similarly kept their distance from the carpenters. Even the Minsk water carriers possessed their own synagogue, which is named "The Seven-Water-Shul." Nearby, unsurprisingly, one can find a pump from which the carriers drew water.

I also wrote to mother that the cheap kitchen on Yureyver St., where my older brothers Mendel and Zalke are employed, is the frequented site of assemblies of the best people in the city, one in which vigorous exchanges about the Land of Israel could be heard. Understandably I didn't write mother that Boruch and Shmuel were intensely engaged with the Land of Israel debate, because that would have greatly agitated her. However, I did inform her that Mendel and Zalke were preparing to go to America, and added that the purchase of the Land of Israel seemed imminent, if only the Turkish sultan didn't drive too hard a bargain.

Thus did I pen a letter every other day to mother about something new in Minsk, thus keeping her calm about her children.

One time I went ahead and wrote her about the two sides of Gubernatorska St. where one could find nightly promenades of both the empty pocketed and the fully endowed.

Mother surmised that I probably suffered terribly from Dr. Malkevitch's cure. She came up with the idea that if I paid him he would heal me without subjecting me to so much pain. I assured her that, although a Pole, he treated me very well. He definitely wanted me to be well. He, therefore, decided to send me to Vilna where a noted skin doctor is to cure me with electricity—also for no money.

I wrote mother that my brothers were very unhappy with this arrangement because they wanted to have me near them, but since I might benefit from being in Vilna one of them is ready to take me all the way there.

Mother replied immediately that she herself would take me to Vilna because Uncle Klionsky has relatives in Vilna. In fact, they run their own inn. If God wills it she'll be coming with him to Minsk, and they'll work out a plan for my trip to Vilna.

I became very eager to get to know Uncle Klionsky better, a man so good to his stepchildren!

I began to count the days until Uncle Klionsky would safely arrive in Minsk, but I still had to continue writing a letter every other day to mother.

Thanks to these letters posted to mother, which I wrote for many years, I became, it would appear, a Yiddish writer

44

I WANT TO REMAIN A BOY

When I became more acquainted with the lives of my brothers in Minsk, I realized it wasn't worth my while to grow up. They had already become so-called "adults," and what did they have to show for it?

Two are decidedly unhappy with their positions in the cheap kitchen and are preparing to leave for distant America! The other two are dissatisfied with the way of the world and wish to rebuild it! In Czarist Russia such things could earn one a place in prison or exile in Siberia.

Is it then worth it to grow up?!

I couldn't become an artisan or a functionary; for that one needs two healthy hands, which I did not have. Nor could I become a bookkeeper or a teacher; for that I didn't have the time to study the way it was necessary.

And so the question arises what will I achieve by becoming an adult?

Unless to marry such a one as the crazy Masha, God keep me. And which clear-headed girl would want to wed such a schlimazl as me?

After fifteen years of my life I came to the realization that there's no point in my becoming an adult. As long as I live in one city together with my brothers I would always remain the youngest and thus the most pampered.

Aunt Itke's three daughters always kissed and caressed me, as if I were hardly even a boy.

Only later did I learn that my cousins kissed me because they were in love with the heroes of the fiction they read.

45

A TALE ABOUT VILNA

Minsk had two station platforms: one to Vilna, the other to Brisk.

The Vilna station was a huge enclosure with many lamps.

In the hall of the first class tables were covered, even in the middle of an ordinary Wednesday. The station was almost always full of Jews who spoke Yiddish because the Vilna train, owned by the Libova-Romner Railroad, went through such well-known cities of the Pale as Bobruisk, Homel, Minsk, Vilna and many others.

The Brisk station looked like a barn in comparison, a huge wooden structure lit by old-fashioned gas lamps. The passengers were largely non-Jews because this old station belonged to the Moscow-Brest Rail Line, which did not serve Jewish settlements. Only Jews en route to Borisov or Orsha took this line but not beyond Orsha, near Smolensk, where the Pale of Settlement ended; the stations leading to Moscow were entirely bereft of Jews.

I quietly felt regret that since mother married Uncle Klionsky of Zembin (near Borisov) she had transferred, one might say, from the big city to the village rail line. In a word, she had exchanged the Jewish Libova-Romner Railroad for that of the Gentile Moscow-Brest line.

Uncle Klionsky told us during the Purim feast in Minsk that the conductors of the Moscow-Brest line treated Jewish passengers far worse than those of the Libova-Romner track.

Thus, for example, once a Borisov Jew traveling to Minsk began to pray "shacharit" (morning prayers) in full religious garb, wrapped in a prayer shawl and tefillin, and started to shake vigorously in the direction of the train window.

He suddenly heard the conductor scream from behind, "Hey, Jew, this is not a synagogue. You have no business praying here!"

But the Jew was no fool; he turned around facing the conductor and said from under his prayer shawl (talit) "Do you then not know that the Czar has allowed us to pray here?"

"When did the Czar allow Jews to pray here?" the conductor stood flustered.

"When the train stops at a station I will go out with you on the platform and show you the decree allowing Jews to pray in the train wagons," the Jew answered with great assurance.

The conductor allowed the Jew to continue praying, but as soon as the train stopped at a station he came running to him to show him the decree that the Czar allows Jews to pray in train wagons.

The Jew descended with the conductor to the platform and proceeded to point to a sign that had four Russian letters which in his interpretation he took to be the Russian equivalent of "Jews are allowed to pray here (Molitz Bogu Zhida Dozvoleno)."

(The real translation of these four Russian letters, which are affixed to every train wagon, is, of course, "Moscow-Brest Rail Line.)"

Upon hearing the Jew's curious translation of the Russian letters the conductor fell into such hysterical laughter that the head of the station, who was ready to give the third clang, approached the conductor and the Jew to see what was going on. The conductor immediately told the station master of the Jew's idea that the letters stood for "Jews are allowed to pray here," whereupon the station master himself burst out into such a wild paroxysm of guffaws that the train was delayed several long minutes.

From that time on Jews in all the wagons of the Moscow-Brest Rail line are permitted to pray undisturbed because that conductor went ahead and conveyed this bit of outlandish lore to all his counterparts, until the fine idea cooked up by the Borisov Jew, a clever translation indeed, reached as far as the inner councils of Petersburg. Thus, did Uncle Klionsky finish his story with a flourish, which apparently is quite the anecdote.

By the way, this was the only joyous story that Uncle Klionsky shared in the company of his five stepsons, whom he met for the first time in Minsk. As it appears, he wanted to raise the importance of Borisov's Jews, who don't let themselves be pushed around.

Only then did I stop being bothered by mother's having moved to such a tiny shtetl, which can only be reached on the Moscow-Brest Rail Line.

But deep in my heart, I was very pleased that my route to Vilna runs through the big city platform, where even in the middle of a plain Wednesday cloth-bedecked tables were found in first class.

When Aunt Itke asked Uncle Klionsky why he doesn't accompany mother to Vilna, all the more so when he has relatives there, he replied that he didn't much care for the city.

"Vilna is a city of dry misnagdim (hasidic opponents) and, God help us, of maskilim (modernizers), too," he announced. He for one didn't care to look upon such a city, Uncle Klionsky declared in a huff.

One of my brothers (I no longer remember which) came to Vilna's defense and said to Uncle Klionsky, "How can that be, uncle?! Vilna is known far and wide as the 'Jerusalem of Lithuania,' which is world-renowned for its Vilna Shas (Talmud), which the Widow Rom and Brothers continue to republish! And what of the Vilna Gaon and Rav Yisroel Salanter, Strashun and Kalman Shulman, and the great Yiddish writer Isaac Meiir Dik and more and more, whose names just now escape me..."

Uncle Klionsky listened quite calmly to the protest of his stepson and answered thus: "If you would tell me that Vilna supports just one Lubavitch yeshiva I would, perhaps, agree with you that Vilna is, in fact, the 'Jerusalem of Lithuania,' as you say, but until today I have not heard that Lubavitch hasidim travel to Vilna to study Torah!"

"But here you're sending off your youngest stepson to Vilna! Is he not then a Lubavitcher hasid, may he be well?" Aunt Itke's child suddenly burst forth. (This is the same Malka Grundfest who had read many Russian novels. She'd often kiss me, calling me by the name of Russian fictional heroes with whom she fell in love).

I became strongly frightened that Malka, God forbid, might start kissing me in front of everyone, shouting, "Onegin, Nekhlentov, Don Juan!" and only the devil knows who else!

I immediately hid behind mother's chair as if looking for protection from my cousin, who I, in fact, liked very much.

My dear mother immediately understood how matters stood and took not only me under her wings but also her husband, Uncle Klionsky, who was deeply upset by the girl's remarks.

Mother said to Malka, "Are we then sending him to Vilna to learn? Would that I didn't have to send him there! My blood freezes when I think that I will leave him entirely alone in such a big, strange city."

"Children mine! What are you saying?" Mother continued dramatically. "Maybe we should not move him at all? Maybe he should remain with you in Minsk? Some say that his disease can heal by itself. What only doctors can think up! How many doctors have written him off, only for him to have survived more than one of them! Children mine! Why are you silent? Say something!" mother insisted, turning to my four brothers, who sat with heads lowered as if they, God forbid, were guilty of something.

My brothers, understandably, couldn't give mother any kind of advice or solace. They also were struck dumb by my imminent departure.

However, suddenly my brother Boruch, who was my elder by a mere two years, said to our mother: "Don't think that Donya is still a child! He understands many things better than us because he has suffered so. On the contrary, the further he will be from us the quicker he will become independent. If he can heal more quickly in Vilna than in Minsk then he must go to Vilna. After all, Vilna is not far from Minsk and if, God forbid, he doesn't feel at ease there, we will take him back to us. Didn't we say that, Donya?" Boruch addressed me directly.

"I have long said that without you I would more quickly become an adult, a grown-up!" I said, shooting out from behind mother's chair.

Suddenly everyone's mood became considerably lighter.

Everyone realized that I was not such a nebbish as they had imagined. It was decided that before I departed for Vilna all five

Charneys would be photographed together so that mother could see us all before her eyes for all time.

Also, mother for the first time in her life allowed herself to be photographed in a separate picture. None of us thought of having ourselves photographed with mother in one picture, which bothers me until this very day.

How lucky I would feel if only I stood in a picture with my mother!

46

BETWEEN MINSK AND VILNA

Only now do I realize that fathers and mothers are far bigger and better pedagogues than modern teachers, who have yet to find the right key to a child's soul.

Here, for example, mother sensed that I felt strongly downcast at leaving Minsk and all my four brothers, who had created for me the delicate illusion of a home.

Just as soon as we entered the train which was to take us from Minsk to Vilna mother handed me the two train tickets which Uncle Klionsky had bought for us and she said to me "Here, Donyele, hold the tickets. You'll be the one to show the conductor that you are already traveling on a full ticket!"

As it appears, mother remembered how she had guided me the first time to Minsk "under the bench" because she wanted to save the nine kopecks which a one-quarter ticket amounted to.

Now, however, mother was proud that she could pay a full ticket price to Vilna for her youngest. This was a sign that I had become, with luck, an adult, fully grown-up. And by handing me both tickets to show to the conductor she made me feel proud and elevated, as if I had in fact grown up.

Soon thereafter mother took out of her case the letter which Uncle Klionsky had written about me to his relatives in Vilna, who were designated to become my guardians, and she asked me to read it.

The letter was addressed to a Jew named Rav Nahum Pliskin, who had an inn at 1 Chopin St. From Uncle's letter, written in an exalted Hebrew, salted and peppered with Yiddish, I learned Nahum Pliskin to be a highly learned, book-loving, big-hearted and hugely welcoming (after all, he has his own inn) man. Uncle Klionsky described me as the youngest of his stepsons who stems from an elevated lineage going all the way back to the "Sheloh Hakodesh." My mother was by birth a Hurvitz and on my father's side I was steeped in high rabbinic pedigree. But aside from all these lineal connections, I have been, pitifully, struck by such an illness that only a renowned doctor in Vilna can fully heal. In view of this, my uncle asks his relative in Vilna to bestow his kindness on me and give and grant me a stay in his inn. In those periods when I will be free from medical intervention I should follow Torah study but not, heaven forbid, in the "misnaggdish" (anti-hasidic) yeshivas because I, his youngest stepson, am the son of a fiery Lubavitch hasid, who, may we be spared, was taken at a young age from the world, and on and on in this vein.

When I finished reading Uncle Klionsky's letter mother's eyes had turned moist with tears.

"See, Donyele, how he writes of you. He cherishes you!"

Mother quickly added that Uncle Klionsky instructed her to inform the Pliskins that I am to be fed well and to receive a soft, comfortable mattress. Uncle Klionsky said he would pay what is owed on a monthly basis.

"In addition, he gave me a gold imperial coin (15 rubles worth) so you should have enough spare change to mend a garment or a shoe if need be, and he even provided mailing stamps so that you could write us every other day."

Mother then continued, "Yes, my son, I've nearly forgotten the crux of the matter," as she held on to her leather case.

"I want to show you my ketuba (wedding certificate), which he gave me. Here it is. Read, my child, because you must know of it. Do read!"

I found out from reading Uncle Klionsky's ketuba that if he predeceased mother his inheritors must pay her 200 rubles and if, spare us, the opposite happens, then Uncle Klionsky will have to pay the 200 rubles to me, the youngest of the orphans.

"Why just me?" the clumsy question sprang from my mouth.

"Because you are the youngest and the weakest," mother began to explain to me.

"Precisely because I am the youngest and the weakest I could die before any of my older brothers. Wouldn't it be more proper to have put into the ketuba, at the very least, the names of Shmuel and Boruch! Mother, you know what the doctors say about me! And the pity is all the greater regarding Shmuel and Boruch than it is with me because everyone worries about me and no one about them!"

I suddenly found myself bargaining with mother about an inheritance which should happen only after 120 years [a common Jewish expression wishing one to live to age 120].

Mother perfectly understood my true objection but she refused to even consider the possibility that I could, spare us, die before her or Uncle Klionsky; and to better distract me, she, like a gifted teacher, began to tell me about my first niece in Berezin who had already made me an uncle.

This first niece of mine provoked fresh tumult in my head. This was the first child of my only sister, Mirele, who had married Uncle Munia (father's brother) of Berezin. So, for example, when I would come to visit two uncles would be in one house, Uncle Munia Charney and the other, yours truly, Donya Charney.

True, my uncle Munia is also my in-law because he is my sister's husband, and my sister is thus also my aunt because, after all, she is my uncle's wife. So, therefore, my niece is also my cousin. All of this genealogical transposition reminded me of my brother Boruch's algebra book, where one transposes an "x" for a "y" to arrive at "z."

This strange equation led me to burst into laughter. Mother was eager to know what suddenly had led to such an explosion of mirth. I replied that I was overjoyed to have already become an uncle!

Mother understood that this alone was not the real reason for my laughter, but in order to keep up the illusion of my adulthood she suddenly said, "You, too, if God decrees it, will also become a father!"

"Me, a father? How is that possible, Mother, a blessing on your head?"

"It's quite simple, my child! You are already, banish every evil, a youth of fifteen. In several years you'll turn eighteen. You have nothing to fear from the draft. So, at eighteen you will, with luck, marry and become the head of a household of your own!'"

"What are you saying, dear Mother! Which girl would want to marry me? I am, after all, deformed."

"Donya, don't talk nonsense!" Mother veritably screamed at me. "A man is never malformed or misbegotten. You think I didn't see how Aunt Itke's girls clung to you, like fleas to honey? All liked you a whole lot! And I'll tell you a secret. Uncle Klionsky in Zembin already has two granddaughters, the older of whom is about your age, and he even has spoken to her that when, if God wills it, you complete your cure in Vilna, he will make a match between the two of you."

Listening to mother explain the new linkage contemplated between me and my stepfather's granddaughter, I once more burst out in laughter and mother once again insisted that I tell her why I was laughing so strangely. "This is the second time your laughter is so inexplicable. Tell me, child, why do you laugh thus?"

I told her the truth: that I'm laughing because of Boruch's exercises which he derives from a book in which Latin letters are used instead of numbers.

I suddenly explained the matter to mother in Yiddish. "It stands to reason, for example, that five times eight is forty, but if one should multiply the Hebrew letter 'hay' (which amounts to five) by 'chet,' (which amounts to eight), one also arrives at forty. However, I find that comical, although the multiplication amounts to the same."

"Why then does Boruch make such strange calculations?" mother wanted to know.

"He wants to pass exams for six classes of gymnasium, if not more, to become an instructor," I answered with pride at my brother's high ambitions.

"And what is Shmuel up to?" mother wanted to know.

"Also, Shmuel is secretly learning secular subjects but what he wants to be, I do not know."

"And I thought that Shmuel and Boruch will become great rabbis of broad renown!" mother said with much disappointment.

"Don't worry yourself, dear mother, the world will yet reverberate with their names, great renown is to be theirs. You'll see! A new era is emerging! There is talk of emancipating the Land of Israel. Not all Jews can wait until the arrival of the Messiah! And there's much talk, dear mother, of freeing the entire world from slavery and of abolishing wealth and poverty. Shmuel and Boruch are fervently enmeshed in all this. Hundreds of people come to the cheap kitchen to hear their speeches, which are known across all of Minsk."

"I'll tell you the truth," mother interrupted me. "I don't understand a thing you are saying. How do Shmuel and Boruch come to such things? And what do Mendel and Zalke have to say about all this?"

"Precisely on account of this, Mendel and Zalke have decided to leave for America, because if Shmuel and Boruch succeed in their goals — all Jews should go to the Land of Israel and all differences between rich and poor be abolished — then the cheap kitchen will shut down and Mendel and Zalke will lose their positions," I explained.

Mother, once again, interrupted me, saying that I was not addressing the matter at hand. According to me, it appears Mendel and Zalke will have to travel as far as America because of the delusions of Shmuel and Boruch!

I myself realized that I had scrambled my thoughts, but it wasn't my fault. I wanted to come across as a grown-up and to inform her of all the momentous things spoken at such length in the cheap kitchen.

What a miracle when the conductor announced we were about to reach Vilna!

Speaking thus to mother, I hadn't observed that the train had crossed the long passage from Minsk to Vilna. We quickly packed our bags. I felt angry that I had spilled so much about my elder brothers in Minsk.

Mother turned very sad upon hearing all this, and I even more for having shared it.

47

A FULL CELLAR WITH SUMMER FRECKLES

My first impressions of Vilna were hardly uplifting. Already while at the station I realized that Jewish poverty in Vilna was worse than that in Minsk.

Porters scuffled for our baggage. Each wanted to earn a few kopecks. Who knew how long they would have struggled and sworn bitter curses at each other had not a very red-haired girl appeared and asked us if we were the Klionskys.

"Yes, we are the Klionskys," mother replied quickly.

"And I am one of the Pliskins!" the red-head presented herself. "We received a telegram from Minsk that you were to arrive with this train."

(Uncle Klionsky had sent a telegram to the inn requesting that we be met at the station. Wasn't that really nice of stepfather?)

The porters dropped us altogether because they knew Pliskin's inn was very close by and thus there was nothing left to fight over!

Then the red-haired girl chose a porter that always serviced the inn, and we went by foot to 1 Chopin St, which was really two minutes from the station.

It was already 8:00 p.m. The short station street, which led directly to Chopin St., was well-lit. I soon noticed on both sides of the street a bevy of heavily-rouged girls or women who constantly winked at the men leaving the station for the city.

I acted dumbly and asked our escort who these heavily-rouged women were. The red-haired girl of our inn flushed a deeper crimson and all her summer freckles danced across her white cheeks, like frightened flies.

Instead of answering my indiscreet question the red-faced girl said with pride, "Here is our house!"

It was a stout five-storied pile on the corner of two streets, but the entry was on Chopin St.

(I knew by then that Chopin was a composer who had written a famous funeral march played at all big funerals, but if he has an entire street in Vilna named after him why then is Chopin so sad?)

The porter carrying our baggage, who went ahead first, suddenly halted. We watched as he descended quite a stretch into the earth.

The red-haired girl warned "Be careful. The steps today are a bit slippery."

I glimpsed the wooden shield which hung at the entrance, or more accurately, at the dizzying drop into the cellar. It read, in Russian script, "Pliskina Inn."

I took mother by the hand and began slowly to descend with her into the basement. I counted twelve steps strewn with ash and pieces of coal. (It was soon after Purim and the Vilna winter had not yet given way.)

Behind the glass door, which led straight into the inn, another three steps suddenly materialized, which none of the guests expected. Therefore, one never entered the inn as a proper human being but rather fell in like a drunkard.

A miracle it was that the entire Pliskin family awaited us at the bottom of the three steps. Mother fell directly into the arms of the landlady, whose hair and face also were reddish in color; and I fell into arms of a brunette (since I live I've had much more luck with brunettes than with blondes).

As soon as we descended into the cellar the landlady sat us down at the big table, which occupied a good half of the inn room.

At the head of the table sat the owner himself and flanking him on the sides the five Pliskin children: two brunette girls, two red-heads with many summer freckles, even though it was still winter, and a boy aged 10 — the youngest.

Mother handed Mr. Pliskin the letter written about me by Uncle Klionsky (her husband).

The inn owner, it appears, was very near-sighted. He read Uncle Klionsky's letter more with his nose than with his eyes. I watched him following each Hebrew line of the letter with his nose, but as the missive was written in half-circled script, as was customary among religious Jews, so too did Pliskin's nose make half circles as it descended the page in order not to lose his way.

When Pliskin finally finished Uncle Klionsky's letter, he lifted his tired eyes and nose and said with great amazement, "Oy vey! You are of such great pedigree, stemming from the Sheloh Hakodesh — no mean origin!"

"His (meaning Uncle Klionsky's) first wife was also of a high station, but not of such noble pedigree as yours," Pliskin said directly to mother.

(Mother dropped her eyes, as if she felt guilty: the first wife's pedigree was not that elevated).

"She [meaning Uncle Klionsky's first wife], my cousin, may you be blessed with long years, was also from Plisa but sadly she was not blessed to have naches from either children or grandchildren. May she be a good intercessor for us all!" the owner added, sighing heavily.

But then his wife, who already had offered us all a pot full of tea, shouted at her husband, the inn owner, for bringing up the first wife of my stepfather, who had long departed this world.

"Nahum, stop talking foolishness. For now, thank God, we are still in this world and we need to eat supper. Children, get dinner on the table," Mrs. Pliskin ordered her four daughters about.

Three rose immediately from the table to help their mother, but the fourth, even redder than the one who had picked us up at the station and who appeared to be my age, didn't budge. She sat right opposite me and kept looking straight at me with her sparkling summer freckles. Even the black pupils of her eyes appeared like two illuminated red lamps, and I was more than certain that this girl could see in the dark, like a cat.

A bit later, I learned that this girl felt ashamed to rise because as soon as she'd leave the table I would immediately see that she, pitifully, limps.

Mother and I left to wash our hands in the kitchen, and while I was waiting my turn for the towel the silly question began to torment me: What connection would I have to the Pliskins had my stepfather's first wife still lived?

Had his first wife not died, I thought, I would never be related to him or connected to the Pliskins, and I'd never travel to such an inn, in a cellar no less, nine feet deep in the earth.

True, the cellar seems quite cheerful. The four girls constantly looked at me with much love, as if I had actually become a close relative of theirs.

The eldest, in whose arms I had miraculously fallen into at the bottom of the stairs leading to the inn, seemed so weary and sleepy, as if it would take a coin to get her to start breathing, like the Cleopatra of the Minsk Panopticum.

You see, the second, the redhead who picked us up at the station, was full of life, readying the table in a jiffy, filling a basket brimming with bagels, such strange ones, the kind only Vilna bakes. Did you ever see a bagel with no hole? On the contrary, ordinarily the larger the hole, the more expensive it is. Thus, for example, the Turk in Minsk charged a whole kopeck for one bagel because a Turkish bagel has a very big hole, while the average bagel of the Jewish Minsk bakers went two for a kopeck because their holes were so much smaller. But Vilna bagels had no holes at all. You couldn't even pull a thin thread through them!

Even my mother was confused by the sight of so strange a bagel, which was not a real bagel, at least to us. She asked the landlady by what name these baked goods were called.

"Do you not see, Mrs. Klionsky, that these are fresh bagels, just now arrived from the bakery?" the red landlady answered, her cheeks aglow with summer freckles.

This reply cut me to the quick. It was the first time I heard mother addressed as Mrs. Klionsky.

Mother just then seemed so distant to me, as if she, heaven forbid, was a stepmother. Mother immediately sensed my forlornness. She cut the bagel into two, spread it with butter, and handed it to me. "Here, Donyele, eat in health!"

Mother poured so much love and tenderness into these few words that no "Mrs. Klionsky" could ever have equaled.

I bit into the buttered bagel with relish and only then did it dawn on me why the Vilners are called "noshers." Only such big noshers could have thought up the idea that even the hole of the bagel could be filled with dough, so that nothing goes to waste.

The Pliskins, the owners of the inn, comparably left no corner of their cellar inn unused. They placed a bed and a night table wherever they could, and called it a bedroom. It was enough to hide the bed behind a few Spanish screens and the guest already had a "room" of his own.

The seven-member Pliskin family had to eke out a living from such an inn!

When I asked the redhead who had brought us from the train station where Geogrieveski Prospekt was, where mother and I would head tomorrow for my first appointment with Dr. Sviederski, she answered truthfully that she had never been there because almost all of its inhabitants were Christians, but she knew how to get there. One had to take the train to travel the length of Zavalna St. and then quite in the distance was Geogrievski Prospekt.

Mother decided that, in view of the length of our coming journey, we would need to go to sleep that much earlier.

"But where are we to sleep?" Mother most delicately inquired of Mrs. Pliskin.

"What are you saying, Mrs. Klionsky? A separate room awaits you. You will slumber like nobility!"

This effectively meant the bedroom of the very owners themselves, which consisted of two small beds, one next to the other, a wooden table and a nail to hang our clothes.

Thus did I practically sleep in one bed with "Mrs. Klionsky," who sighed heavily all night. I, too, sighed unmistakably all night. All the summer freckles of the landlady and her two redheaded daughters danced in my dreams, and I thought I'd go crazy!

Have you ever heard that summer freckles bite each other?

48

VILNA URCHINS

Initially mother had intended to stay with me in Vilna the entire week until I became accustomed to my new home. But when we both fully realized what the cellar inn of Uncle Klionsky's relatives entailed, we became heavy-hearted.

Mother was even ready to take umbrage with her husband for sending us into such a hole, but how could he have known the looks of the abode of his first wife's kin as he had himself never been to Vilna?

I too, as it were, took Uncle Klionsky under my protection, and spoke up for him. I actually talked mother into leaving for home and hearth in Zembin.

"I, alas, have had to come to Vilna to get healed so I must stay, but why should you, dear mother, be miserable a whole week for no good reason?" Thus did I attempt to convince her with logic and reason, but a mother's heart knows no logic.

"No!" she pronounced, "I will not leave Vilna until I will see that you have some kind of home."

We then simply decided to ask the Pliskins how they intended to house me.

As it turns out they already expected this question, because the red landlady laid out on the table the entire plan for me.

"Today we are purchasing folded bedding to be placed far from the window so that your son need not be disturbed by a cold wind blowing in," the owners replied in unison to mother's query.

"Why folded?" Mother interrupted. "I'm scared he might slip off."

"The skin doesn't stick to a fold," the landlady uttered with the confidence of a resounding truth.

"He'll eat together with us all, like our very own child, and if he will wish in the middle of the day to snack on a bagel and tea or anything at all he will always receive it by us! He should only not be bashful!" the red-haired lady said, looking at me with her reddened unslept eyes, and I immediately assented to not ever being bashful.

"And what will it cost?" mother was keen to know.

"I'll tell you the truth, Mrs. Klionsky, even if we charged three rubles a week for your son, we wouldn't in the end even earn three groshen," the landlady seemed to concede. "Thank God, we eat a piece of meat every day and on the Sabbath fish, as is customary in all proper homes," the landlady began boasting about the fine arrangement that awaited me.

"And my husband informs me," she soon added, "that if your son will teach our daughter to write and count, we will then charge you no more than ten rubles a month."

"With which girl?" I blurted out.

The landlady immediately said that she meant her daughter who, pitifully, has a sick foot. "As she was born with a sick foot, you should be spared, she couldn't attend school as often as need be, and so she has fallen behind in writing Russian and doing arithmetic," she explained.

"She is by me, no evil eye be cast, a thoughtful and tireless helper, but she has difficulty calculating the costs for customers. Therefore, it would be very helpful if your son would spend an hour every day with her and thus the total cost of his stay would drop by two rubles a month," the landlady further elaborated.

"What do you think, Mrs. Klionsky, isn't that a square deal? They are, after all, the same age!" the landlady winked at my mother with secret intent.

I don't know if mother picked up Mrs. Pliskin's secret intent, but I immediately caught on for how I was to spend time with her daughter who had fallen behind in her studies.

Already, yesterday evening, I saw the pitiful girl devouring me with her eyes as she sat bound to the table!

True, I had never seen in all my life such big, humid eyes in a girl, but it is said that a girl with a blemish starts thinking of boys much earlier than healthy girls do.

Even more, a boy with a physical deformity also begins to think of girls before a healthy fellow does. It's perhaps because a sick boy is more pampered and cosseted by his mother, elder sister and other relatives, and thus is made to be more feminine and sentimental.

Be that as it may, I immediately grasped that the landlady of the inn wants me for a son-in-law, but I took fright that I could catch summer freckles from my soon-to-be red-haired student.

I immediately replied to the landlady that we first have to see the doctor and to learn what his plans are.

"Maybe he'll send me back to Minsk!" I offered by way of suggestion.

Mother and I went by foot to Georgrievski Prospekt, where Dr. Svidersky resided. We deliberately went by foot so mother could see a bit of Vilna and would have something to recount of the so-called "Jerusalem of Lithuania."

The way was quite simple. We had to turn right on Chopin St. to get to Major Stefan Road which would take us all the way to Zalvaner, which then would lead us practically to Geogrievsky Prospekt.

As it happened it was a nice day, although at night it had rained. It was the first post-Purim rain, which comes to flush away winter.

When we exited the cellar inn our eyes brightened. We saw a huge swathe of sky and people, many of whom were rushing, probably to the station.

Earlier that day, when I sat at the breakfast table, I only saw feet through the cellar windows: big heavy wooden-shod male feet and fine ladies' feet thin as a hairpin, as well as children's feet in tall boots like flowers in a vase. At times it proved hard to determine which feet belonged to whom.

Outside, I realized that nearly all the feet dancing in front of the cellar window belonged to Jews. I took great pride that Vilna, may no evil eye be cast, boasts so many Jews.

But, alas, the streets of Vilna didn't welcome us in friendship or Jewishly in spirit.

No sooner did we approach the Grand Stefanovskaya, we were splashed with mud which lay stuck beneath each board of the gutter. Vilna's citizens knew how to maneuver their streets, but such new arrivals as mother and I had no idea that after a rain a huge mud fountain lies behind each wooden board, which soon covers you from head to toe.

As mother had dressed for the doctor's visit in her Sabbath best and I had on polished shoes and galoshes, we entered a courtyard to shed as much of the mud as we could. Whereupon we were encircled by a number of boys who each tried to help us crawl out of the mud. One brought us a broom, another a bowl of water. But mother quickly realized that none of it would be any real help and that we had to return to the inn for a change of clothing.

When the Pliskin family saw us return so quickly they encumbered us with many questions as to what had happened to us.

When they did find out, Mrs. Pliskin began to curse herself for not having warned us to take heed of the gutter, whose boards aren't nailed tight.

In a while, mother emerged from the darkened room where she had changed but she looked altogether differently, as if she had been fundamentally altered in her very being. I could scarcely recognize her — pale, frightened, and wet eyed.

"Mamelah, what's the matter?" I ran over to her side.

"They cut out my pocket where I kept the fifteen rubles (the golden imperial coin)," she sighed of her new misfortune.

Only once before in my life did I see my mother in such a worried state: several years back in Dukor when they stole all the leather in our shop.

I immediately began to console her. "Remember, mother, how they stole us blind in Dukor and yet, thank God, you brought us up in full dignity, so why do you take the loss of the golden imperial coin so much to heart?!"

The Pliskins also solaced mother that the world had not gone under and that Uncle Klionsky maintained good credit with them.

Mrs. Pliskin started again to curse herself for not having warned us of Vilna's urchins in a timely fashion. Just you try playing with this bunch of characters! Proof that the very same boys who seemingly helped us wash away the mud had also cut out mother's pocket.

I confess to my readers that I might not have included this episode of the Vilna urchins in my family chronicle had not the following turn of events come later to full fruition.

Some thirty years later, it can be said, I got back the golden imperial coin.

It was 1936 when I came to Vilna with the good-hearted intention of becoming a city inhabitant. The pedagogical circle of the special society dedicated to the education of "defective and criminal street children" had decided to proclaim me as honorary president of the "Vilna street urchins."

I readily took up the position largely because heading the society were several well-known pedagogues such as Roza Simchovitch, Vita Levina, and Tiltcha Tiktin, who amazed me by their dedication and self-sacrifice to the abandoned Jewish children. Once again I saw in my mind's eye the Vilna urchins, but in a wholly different light!

In our school, these wayward youth studied how to be proper citizens. When their fathers, professional thieves and robbers, who having spent more years in prison than in freedom would visit our special school day devoted to the children's holiday to snatch a bit of "nachas (pride) from progeny," I'd recognize in them those tough pocket thieves who, some 30 years ago, robbed mother blind.

Such was my recompense!

That is why I say that nothing is ever lost in time and eternity. Every childhood experience sooner or later achieves its rightful realization!

Also, mother was soon solaced when she witnessed the heartfelt reception I received at Dr. Sviederski of Georgrievski Prospekt.

No sooner had he read the letter written by Dr. Malkevitch of Minsk, Dr. Sviederski embraced me as a father would his own sick child. He solaced mother, saying he would heal me into adulthood with his electrical lamps.

Dr. Sviederski also had sharp eyes and a long, gray beard. He also possessed the same height and broad shoulders of Uncle Klionsky. He lacked only one thing: He spoke Russian instead of Yiddish.

Several days later mother returned to her new, quiet home in Zembin, and I remained all alone in Vilna amid a sea of lice and freckles.

But as a result of this arrangement, including the aforementioned worthless bedding, I developed an even stronger nostalgia for my small shtetl, Dukor, and the sheer power of this longing drove me to write this very book.

EPILOGUE

The Nazis brought the Holocaust to Belarus, including the Minsk region. It is estimated that they murdered roughly 800,000 Belarus Jews (or about 90% of the Jewish population of Belarus) during the Holocaust.

https://www.facinghistory.org/resource-library/resistance-during-holocaust/holocaust-belarus

Fortunately, the following members of the Charney family were safe in the United States:

All five Charney brothers reached safety in the United States. Mendel and Zalke (Charles) came to the United States in about 1904. Shmuel and Boruch (Baruch) engaged in revolutionary activities and the Czarist regime imprisoned them. Their stepfather, Yisrael Isaac Klionsky, paid bribes to get Shmuel out of jail after he had been tortured. Boruch came to the United States in about 1908. Shmuel turned his attention to literary activities and came to the United States in 1919. Mendel lived in Paterson, NJ while his brothers lived in New York City.

Daniel Charney also engaged in revolutionary activities and he moved from place to place. He was involved in helping Shmuel and Boruch get out of jail. He wrote for publications in Europe. He came to the United States in 1925 but failed his medical inspection at Ellis Island and was sent back to Europe. He lived in many cities in Europe, including Vilna. He and his wife, Chaya (Anna) Kissin, had good years together in Berlin and Paris, befriending other intellectuals and artists. They succeeded in entering the United States in 1941. Daniel wrote other memoirs, including one about the period ending in 1914 (*Barg Aroyf*, or *Uphill*), and another about the decade 1914-1924. He also wrote poetry, and he wrote for *Der Tog* and *The Forward*. He lived in Brooklyn, NY but by 1950 he was living in sanatoriums in Liberty, NY and then near Boston. Fans sent him coffee, brandy and cigarettes, all of which were prohibited in the sanatoriums. But while he had those treats his room became the social hub for the sanatorium staff. He also had dozens of wind-up toys in his room for his amusement and for any children who visited him. He died in July 1959, when he was 70 years old.

Daniel Charney did not have children of his own but he adopted Chaya's two daughters, one of whom, Mignon Charney Chasen, came to the United States before him. She and her husband, William Chasen, had two daughters, Barbara and Laura. William Chasen knew Yiddish and he loved visiting Daniel in the sanatorium and listening to Daniel tell his stories. The other daughter Daniel adpoted, Lily Charney Kravchinsky, survived World War II, the Stalin era and antisemitism in Russia, and came to the United States in 1995 with her daughter, Tamara.

Daniel never found a cure for his scrofula condition despite many treatments. As an adult he did not want people to see or touch his right hand. When he was in company he put it in his pocket or wore a glove.

Daniel's father, Zev Wolf, had two brothers in Berezin. One brother, Shmuel, married Daniel's sister, Mirl, and he died in about 1928. The other brother of Daniel's father was Aryeh Lev (Leib). Four of his children came to the United States. Three sons came in the 1890s and were living in Paterson, NJ when Mendel arrived and settled there. A daughter of Leib moved to Paterson, NJ a few years later.

Daniel's father had a sister, Sarah, who married Leizer Cantor. They came to the United States with their two daughters by about 1910, living in New York City and then Connecticut.

Three daughters of Rav Moshe Charney came to the United States. Rav Charney was the brother of Yoel Charney, Daniel's grandfather, and an uncle of Daniel's father. After Rav Charney died in about 1900, Nissen Telushkin came to Dukor to become the rabbi. He married Rav Charney's oldest daughter, Fruma Sarah, and he continued to be the rabbi until he left with his wife, daughter, and son, reaching the United States in about 1925. There was a community of Jews from the Dukor area living in Brooklyn, NY and Rabbi Telushkin became their rabbi, serving until the 1960s at the Bnei Yitzchak synagogue. Two other daughters of Rav Charney, Nene (Gnendel) and Chasha, also came to the United States.

Daniel Charney with (from left) his wife, Chaya (Anna) Kissin, and their daughters Mignon (Minna) and Lily in about 1924
Courtesy of Suzanne Zoe Joskow

GLOSSARY

A"h	Alav/Aleha hashalom, may he/she(deceased) have peace
Akdomos	A poem sung on the holiday of Shavuos (Shavuot)
Akraitshik	The foam that forms on top of boiled milk
Aliyah	Coming to bless the holy Jewish scroll during prayers
Asher Yotzar	A prayer to God for creating the human body as it is
Balabusta	A good homemaker
Bar Mitzvah	A boy is 13 years old and is required to obey the Jewish laws
Beit Hillel/Shamai	Two schools of Jewish scholars, at times having had opposing views on Jewish law
Boveh	A section of the Talmud, a source of Jewish law
Bris	Circumcision of a baby boy
Brocha	A blessing (bracha)
Bund	A secular Jewish socialist organization
Chabadnik	A follower of the Chabad hasidic tradition
Challah	A type of bread eaten on Sabbath and holidays
Cheka	The Bolshevik Secret Police
Cholent	Slow-baked vegetables, perhaps with meat, for a Sabbath meal
Chol Hamoed	The middle days of Pesach (Passover) and Sukkus (Sukkot), when work and travel are permitted, unlike the first and last days
Commandments	The laws set out in the Pentateuch, numbering 613
Compote	Fruit cooked in a sugar syrup
Chumash	The Pentateuch, the five books of Moses

Dreyfus Affair	A French officer named Alfred Dreyfus, a Jew, was convicted of espionage in 1894 although he was innocent
Dybbuk	A human spirit that wanders restlessly until it finds a haven in the body of a living person
Earlocks	Sidecurls that hasidic men grow in front of each ear
Ein Yaacov	Compilation of stories, parables and biblical interpretations from the Talmud, a source of Jewish law
Erev	Evening, when used in conjunction with Sabbath or a holiday it means the evening when Sabbath or the holiday begins
Esrog	Yellow citron fruit used for ritual on Sukkus (Sukkot), looks like a lemon
Essen Teg	Eating day. Jews in a town invited poor Jews who were studying in Jewish religious schools for a meal once or twice a week.
Four Questions	These are part of the Pesach (Passover) ritual, asking how Passover night differs from other nights. The youngest person who is capable asks the questions and the adults answer.
Galitzianer	A Jew from former Galicia, now part of Ukraine
Gefilte fish	A fish ball made of ground deboned fish and eaten on holidays
Gmilas Hasadim	Charitable organization lending money to poor Jews in need
Goyim	Non-Jews
Haggadah	The book containing the ritual for the Pesach (Passover) evening observance
Hasid	An adherent to devotional and spiritual Jewish worship
Hasidus	Hasidic teachings of a mystical Jewish movement

Haskala	The Jewish Enlightenment movement to teach Jews secular subjects in addition to Jewish matters
Havdalah	A prayer to mark the end of Shabbes (Shabbat) on Saturday evening
High Holy Days	The Jewish New Year and Yom Kippur
Holy tongue	Hebrew
Kabbalah	Jewish tradition of mystical interpretation of the Bible
Kaddish	A prayer recited many times a day and also recited for a dead person
Kishka	A dish made with stuffed intestine
Kohen	A Jewish priest, with a special role in the prayers blessing the congregants
Korben Mincha	A prayer book for women in Yiddish
Kosher	Conforming to all the Jewish dietary laws
Kriyas shma	A prayer recited several times a day
Kugel	A baked pudding, served as a side dish
Landsmanshaft	A society of Jewish immigrants from the same place
Lag B'Omer	A Spring holiday on the 33rd day of the count from Pesach (Passover) to Shavuos (Shavuot)
L'chaim	To life, said before having a drink
Lcha dodi	A prayer recited on Friday evening as Shabbes (Sabbath) begins
Lchu Neranina	A prayer recited on Friday evening as Shabbes (Sabbath) begins
Likras Kala	A part of the Lcha dodi prayer
Litvak	A Jew from Belarus or Eastern Poland
Lopatkes	Shoulder blades
Lubavitch	A part of the Chabad movement of hasidic Judaism
Lulav	A palm branch used for rituals on the Sukkus (Sukkot) holiday
Maariv	Evening prayers
Maot Chitim	A charity raising money for poor Jews to give them funds necessary for celebrating Pesach (Passover)

Marzipan	Confection of crushed almonds or almond paste, sugar and egg whites
Matzah	Thin, crisp unleavened bread, which Jews traditionally eat during Pesach (Passover), when eating leavened bread is prohibited
Matzah farfel	Matzah broken into small pieces
Melamed	Teacher
Mentch	A person of integrity
Mezuzah	An enclosed parchment of religious texts affixed to a doorpost as a sign of faith
Mikveh	Place where people have a ritual bath for purification
Mincha	Afternoon prayers
Nachas	Pride
Nebbish	A timid and unsuccessful person
Nebekh	An unfortunate person
Neilah	The final set of prayers on Yom Kippur
Niggun	A hasidic melody
Nine days	The first nine days of the month of Av are days of mourning for the destruction of the two Jewish temples (centuries apart), and one may not eat meat except on Shabbes (the Sabbath).
Nosh	A snack or light meal
Omer	Count of 50 days from the second day of Pesach (Passover) until Shavuos (Shavuot)
Oneg Shabbes	The joy of the Sabbath
Pale	The Pale of Settlement was the area of the Russian Empire where Jews were allowed to live.
Palestine	The name of the geographic area that includes the State of Israel
Pesach	Jewish holiday (Passover) marking the exodus of the Jews from Egypt
Pig meat	Jewish law prohibits the eating of pig meat.
Pliage	Plague (in local idiom)
Purim	A holiday to celebrate that the Jews escaped death at the hands of Haman in the Persian Empire

Pushke	A metal box into which one puts coins for charity and other Jewish causes
Rav/Reb	Rabbi, religious leader of the community, but the term is sometimes used just as a sign of respect for a man
Rebbetzin	Wife of a rabbi
Rosh Chodesh	The first day of every month in the Jewish calendar
Rosh yeshiva	Head of a yeshiva, a school to study Jewish texts
Russian mile	A Russian mile was about 4.64 US miles, or seven viorsts (7.468 kilometers).
Sabra	A person born in Israel
Schlep	Pull
Schnapps	A strong alcoholic drink
Scrofula	A condition in which the bacteria that cause tuberculosis cause symptoms outside the lungs
Seder	The Pesach (Passover) evening meal, including prayers and songs
Shabbes	The Sabbath (Shabat), from Friday evening until after dark on Saturday night. Working, cooking and smoking are prohibited during Shabbes.
Shabbes lighting	The ritual of lighting candles on Friday evening in honor of the Sabbath
Shavuos	The holiday in the Spring (Shavuot) celebrating God's giving Moses the Ten Commandments
Shlimazel	An unlucky or inept person
Shor Ha-bor	Hasidic allegory about a leviathan and a bull attacking one another
Shtetl	Small Jewish settlement in Eastern Europe
Shiksa	A non-Jewish girl or woman
Shiva	Seven days or mourning after a death
Shul	Synagogue, Jewish house of communal prayer
Star of David	A six-cornered star, a symbol of the Jewish people
Sukkah	A temporary hut that Jews build to eat in during the festival of Sukkus (Sukkot)
Sukkus	A holiday shortly after Yom Kippur when Jews sit in a sukkah

Takhlit	Purpose
Talit	A prayer shawl sometimes worn during prayers in synagogue
Tarhana	A dried food based on a fermented mixture of grain and yogurt or fermented milk
Tashlich	The ritual during the Jewish New Year of casting one's sins into the sea
Tefillin	Black leather boxes containing Hebrew parchment scrolls worn by adult men during morning prayers except Shabat and holidays
Torah	The Pentateuch, the five books of Moses
Tractate	A portion of the Talmud, a source of Jewish law
Tzemackh-Tzedek	Third Rebbe of the Chabad Lubavitch hasidic movement
Tzena Rena	Yiddish translation of portions of the Old Testament, prepared for women
Tzimmes	A stew of sweetened vegetables, sometimes with fruit and possibly meat
UJA	United Jewish Appeal, a charitable organization to help poor Jews
Viorst	1.0668 kilometers, or one seventh of a Russian mile
Yahrzeit	The anniversary of a person's death, when a family member says Kaddish in memory of the dead person
Yizkor	Prayer for a dead person, recited by a family member
Yom Kippur	The holiest day of the year, when Jews fast all day and pray for forgiveness of their sins
Zionism	The movement to establish a Jewish state in Israel
Zionist Congress	Meeting of Jews from different countries to discuss establishing a Jewish State in Israel
Z"L	May his/her memory be blessed
Zohar	A book of Jewish mysticism

NAME INDEX

A

Aron, 178
Asch, 196

B

bal Haness, 146, 147
Bal Haness, 9
Belmont, 1
Berezhankers, 72
Bergelson, 4
Berger, 206
Blaustein, 131, 132, 139, 141
Bleicher, 1
Blochman, 177
Brothers, vii, viii, ix, 226
Broyde, 192
Byron, 1

C

Cantor, 246
Charik, 218
Charney, ii, iii, ix, 4, 44, 53,
    68, 69, 71, 80, 82, 85, 100,
    103, 113, 139, 156, 179,
    185, 186, 189, 190, 191,
    192, 193, 194, 195, 196,
    197, 198, 208, 231, 245,
    246, 247
Chasen, 246
Chatzkin, 211, 212, 213
Cohen, 206

D

Dik, 226
Dimonstein, 2, 3, 4, 5

E

Edison, 154, 155
Esenin, 1

G

Goldberg, 200
Goldbergs, 200
Grundfest, 145, 151, 192,
    212, 226
Guinsburg, 201

H

Herzl, 146, 152, 168, 182,
    205, 220
Hirsch, 8, 9, 201
Horowitz, 69
Hurvitch, 107, 192
Hurvitz, ix, 50, 230

I

Idelchick, 177
Izbortchik, 177

J

Joskow, 194, 247

K

Kabakoffs, 200
Kaminski, 187, 202
Kaminsky, 215
Karabvetcher, 9
Kaye, iii, 191, 193, 198
Kaylis, 96
Kelyes, 178
Khashin, 4
King Saul, 161
Kirpichnikov, 131
Kissin, 245, 247
Klatzkin, 4
Klionsky, 167, 169, 182, 183,
    193, 219, 222, 224, 225,
    226, 227, 229, 230, 231,
    232, 234, 236, 237, 238,
    239, 240, 242, 243, 245
Kravchinsky, 246
Krudompay, 75

L

Lapidus, 206
Lekert, 212
Lenin, 2
Levin, 14
Levina, 243
Lubavitcher, 66, 96, 135,
    173, 175, 176, 226
Luntz, 215

M

Malkevitch, 202, 203, 207,
    208, 213, 215, 216, 217,
    218, 220, 222, 243
Marx, 188, 220

Meir, 9, 79, 131, 146, 147,
    221
Mere, 131, 132
Meren, 118, 119
Minkovitch, 192
Montel, ix, 186
Morgenstern, 23, 24, 210,
    211, 212, 213

N

Napoleon, 22
Niger, ix, 13, 50, 69, 72, 94,
    139, 186, 190, 196, 198,
    208
Nordau, 146

O

Orem, 91, 92

P

Pinsker, 187, 220
Pliskin, 230, 235, 236, 238,
    240, 242
Pollacks, 200
Pomerantz, 116, 117
Potocki, 104, 105

R

Rabbi Osher, 37
Rayzen, 2
Rom, 226
Rosen, 68
Rosenbaum, 182
Rosenwald, 201
Rothschild, 201
Rubentshik, 206

S

Salanter, 226
Schiff, 201
Schneerson, 175
Shapira, 215
Shapiro, 141, 145, 150, 157, 158, 159, 161
Shimanovski, 84
Shklovsky, 14, 22
Shulman, 226
Simchovitch, 243
Skakun, ix, 186
Soutines, 200
Stalin, 3, 246
Strashun, 226
Svidersky, 241
Sviederski, 238, 243

T

Telushkin, 68, 246
Tiktin, 243
Tzedek, 83, 174, 253

V

Velias, 122, 123, 124
Vladeck, ix, 13, 34, 50, 69, 72, 94, 139, 190, 196, 197, 208
Vladek, 186

W

Warburg, 201
Wolffsohn, 146

Y

Yitzhaks, 56, 57, 58, 92

Z

Zelig, 57, 58
Zeligs, 57
Zhelubski, 206
Zoriger, 64

www.ingramcontent.com/pod-product-compliance
Lightning Source LLC
Chambersburg PA
CBHW060331100426
42812CB00003B/949